LIGHT FLASHES
IN THE
TUNNEL

by

JIM SHARER BENTLEY

The Pelican King of East Bay

LIGHT FLASHES
IN THE
TUNNEL

Copyright © Jim Sharer Bentley

All rights reserved. No portion of this publication may be reproduced, stored in a retrieval system, or transmitted by any means—electronic, mechanical, photocopying, recording, or any other—except for brief quotations in printed reviews, without the prior written permission of the publisher.

Editors: Earl Tillinghast and Regina Cornell
Cover Design: Lucas Art & Design

Indigo River Publishing
3 West Garden Street Ste. 352
Pensacola, FL 32502
www.indigoriverpublishing.com

Ordering Information:

Quantity sales: Special discounts are available on quantity purchases by corporations, associations, and others. For details, contact the publisher at the address above. Orders by U.S. trade bookstores and wholesalers: Please contact the publisher at the address above.

Printed in the United States of America

Library of Congress Control Number: 2017964347
ISBN: 978-1-948080-08-8

First Edition

With Indigo River Publishing, you can always expect great books, strong voices, and meaningful messages. Most importantly, you'll always find…words worth reading.

DEDICATION

This is dedicated to the one(s) I love, so say I and the Mamas and Papas in their song of the same name. I can't improve upon that message, and the thought of a dedication conjures up CMA and Oscar speeches that drone on forever while viewers nod off or retreat to their refrigerator. Of course, the list of thank you's is always destined to be long because a lot of people help us along the way. Same for me, but at my current core are the following angels:

My brother is my well.

His kids are the touchstone.

My kids and Ambo are my support group.

My daughters- and-sons-in-law, with my grandkids and Matt, are my pleasure.

Aunt Teresa, Uncle Skip, the Gerretys and Jim Fromm are my friends.

My mother, sister, Aunt GeeGee, Uncle Frederick Francis, Aunt Hazel Morrison, and many other teachers have been my inspiration.

The Escambia School Food Services ladies are my true loves.

Kirk is always on my mind.

SECOND DEDICATION

To my two young publishers at Indigo River, Adam Tillinghast and Dan Vega (names listed in alphabetical order as my OCD dictates), not just entrepreneurs, but philanthropists as well, who willingly, even eagerly, took up the challenge of breathing life into an old man's drivel and dreams. Good luck, boys!

Table of Contents

I - Tracer Shots to the Psyche   1
Light Flashes in the Tunnel   1
The Amateurs   1
It's So Important to Be Important   3
When the Mighty are Weak and the Weak Are Mighty   4
We Spend Our Life Summarizing   4
It's the Boring Stuff That is the Staff of Life   5
Familiarity Breeds Confidence   5
Comfort Zone   6
Of Kingdoms and Chariots   7
Breaking Away   7
Dawdling and Gawking   8
Chilling Out   9
Glib   9
The Gift of Gab   10
What's in a Name?   11
Nicknames   12
Impatience   13
Fellowship Begets a Pelican King   14
Smug   15
Naked Women   15
I've Got an Ace in my Hole   16
Words that Sound Their Meaning   17
You Feckless Bastard   17
That Dog Don't Know Sic 'em   18
Writing Something Pithy   18
Common Man   19
A Load of Hooey   19
I see What You're Saying   20
Rock-Paper-Scissors   23
Life is Like a Game of Solitaire   23
Our Vehicle is Our Tomb   24
Truck Stops are America's Wellsprings   24
It Ain't Nothing But a Thing   25
Wanna Look Thin? Wanna Be Loved?   25
Great Danes are Wussy Pussies   26
The Anorexic Anemone   26

Finding Yourself	27
So Close and Yet So Far	28
The Great Yawning Abyss of Time	28
Time in the Sun	28
You Don't Always Have to Color Inside the Lines	29
Time Ninnies	29
Holy Smokes! I'm on Fire!	29
Never Smoke a Cigar on an Empty Stomach	30
NO TRESPASSING! Violators Will Be Prosecuted to the Full Extent of the Law	30
Veritas	31
Pants on Fire	32
Virtual Reality	33
The Lamp of Joy	33

II - Worshipping at the Throne — 37

Universal Truth	37
You Reap What You Sow	37
The Pure of Heart Get Extra Points Upstairs	38
May the Good Lord Bless and Keep You	39
Peace Be with You	39
She's Spiritual, But Not Religious	40
The Maiden of Dishonor	41
Raison D'être	42
Blue Funk	43
Honk If You Think Jesus Is Proud of You	44
Why I Go to Church	44
Plunk Your Magic Twanger, Froggy	46

III - Birth Rite — 47

The Slaughterhouse	47
Reverend Mothers	48
Black Sabbath	48
Impetigo	49
It Takes a Village	50
The Purple Wristband	52
Out of the House of Many Windows	54
Siblings	55
Siblings Know Who You Are at the Core	55
Family Taxi Service	56
Party Line	57

Black Sambo	59
Don't Overdo a Compliment	60
Sense of Propriety	61
Dispensing "The Word"	62

IV - The Three R's — 65
Melting Pot	65
Fifties Cool	65
At the Corner of Paradise and Purgatory	67
Polishing Your Balls	68
Quaffing a Brew with Me Mates	70

V - Bearing Arms — 71
Military Service	71
Low-Water Bridge	71
April Fool	76
Welcome Home	80
Here Come Da King	81

VI - Looking for Love in All the Wrong Places — 85
The Perfect Man, The Perfect Woman	85
Love at First Sight Is a Cruel Hoax	85
Two Minuses Don't Always Make a Plus	86
You're OK, But I'm Perfect	86
Eye Candy	86
True Beauty	86
Girls That Are Friends, Not Girlfriends	88
Women	89
Enough Is Enough!	90
Women Always Take the High Road	91
Grace Kelly Loved Me First	92
Free Love Is an Oxymoron	93
Western Dating	93
The Dichotomy of Love	94
Love Is Not Always About Making Love	95

VII - Chasing the Dollar — 97
Success Is Not a One-Answer Quiz	97
Damaged Goods	97
Let Someone Else Share Your Pride	98

Black Velvet Gloves	98
Two Cents Worth	99
Yammering and Clamoring	100
The Macro-Micro Combo	101
Home Is Where the Heart Is	102
Small Towns	102
The Small Town Is Our Womb	103
Bagelheads	103
The Dirty Whore Social Club	104
Key Lime High	104

VIII - Spawning Ground   107

True Love is Fifty-Fifty	107
Throwing Down the Anchor	107
Why Stay-At-Home Parents Are Predisposed to Alcoholism	108
Period. The End.	109
Captain of the Turd Patrol	111
Anything for Pumpkin	111
Why the Turtle Is My Friend	112
Bridging the Communication Gap	113
When It Is More Blessed to Receive Than Give	115

IX - The Fallout from a Natural Disaster   117

The Magic of Wood	117
The Temporalosity of Our Existence	117
Ivan the Terrible	118
The Anchor Is Within You	121
The Next Best Thing	122
Knickknacks	123
Charity Begins at Home	124
Coming Through the Rye	124
Standing Ovation	126
American Home Base	127

X - Irreconcilable Differences   129

Marriage and Divorce	129
The Last Happy Couple	129

XI - Roamin' in the Gloamin'   135

Foot Traffic	135

Walking for Sanity	135
Let Us Go Then While We May	136
Everything Else Is Just Routine: A Tribute to the Appalachian Trail	136
Skip Church. God Is on the Appalachian Trail.	138
Judged by the Company We Keep	141
That's a Lot of Words to Describe a Stick	145
Outside the Zone	145
The Teddy Bear's Picnic	146
Bear Bait	147
Birds That Stick Their Heads in the Sand	149
A Classroom in the Woods	150
Connections	152

XII - The Wake of Love — 153

Everybody Works, Nobody Shirks	153
Moving Patton's Third Army	154
Reading the Fine Print	155
Sticks and Stones	155
Chortling	155
Owee Technology	156
Three Children's Tales	156
Babies Ain't No Pushover	157
One Big Smacker for One Fine Baby	158
Wrangling the Tee-Tot	160
Worn to a Thin Frazzle	161
The Backside of the Fussy Clock	162
Hunting the Venerable Wormie	162
The Little Engine Who Couldn't	163
Boogers, Poop, Monsters, and Spiders	164
Everybody Has a Hiding Place	164
Kids Live in the Moment	165
Separation Anxiety	166
The Walking Scab	166
Ready or Not, You're a Grandparent	167
A Rhapsody in Dynamic Tension; Otherwise Known as Sibling Rivalry	167
Grumpy Old Man for Hire	170
Children for Sale	172
The Ogre in the Basement	172
Ma Bear's Mad Dash Cleanup	173
Monsters and Mayhem	174

Communing with Your Demons	175
I'm Sweet on You	176
A Perfect Day in Paradise	176
Wanderlust	177
Packing for the Trip	178
Love Can Be Smothering	180
He Scared the Death Out of Me	180
I'm Not a Big Fan of Healthy Food	182
Bakugan and Falafel	182
Slug Bug—No Tag Back!	183
A Reading and a Rendering	184
A Cell Phone for Tootie	186
A Kick-Back Day	187
Twinkle	187
Plan B	190
Believability	191
Revisiting Stinky-Clinky	192
The Conundrum of Giving and Sharing	195
The Raccoon Tree	197
I'll Leave You to Your Own Devices	199

XIII - Adventures in the Mind — 201

Winning the Lottery	201
Geocaching the Sierra Madre	201
The Incredible Lightness of Being	202
I Gotta Be Free	203
Hawkers, Hucksters, and Flea Merchants	203
There Are Signs Everywhere	205
Alone, But Not Lonely	207
Gourmet Food from a Box	207
Muddling Through	208
Cornballs and Dreamers	209
Reverie	209
Dreamers Need Some Reality to Survive	209
OCD and Voyeurism Are Among My Better Traits	210
The Little Sabine Meat Market	211
A Man of Means by No Means	212
Too Much Information	212
The Murphy Bed	213
Occupying Your Space	213
Don't Rain on My Parade	214

XIV - Communion During the Passage — 219

Gratitude	219
A Tree Falling in the Forest	219
Nuances	219
Friends Welcome Anytime, Family by Appointment Only	220
Good Things Do Happen to Good People	221
Contributing to the Delinquency of a Major	223
Forever Amber	225
The Sister Woman	228
Insatiable Appetite	230
The Camp Director	231
The American Heartland	238
The Dirt Devils of Windy Ridge	238

XV - Keeping Your Addictions and Doctors in Balance — 241

When the Body Is No Longer a Temple	241
Get Fat Slowly, Lose It Fast	242
Weighing In	242
Don't Go Down the Cookie Aisle	243
Don't Supersize It, Romanticize It	245
Just Add Water	246
Where's the American Spirit of Adventure	246
It's the Little Things That Count	247

XVI - Distilling the Spirit — 249

The Vibrant, Active, Over-Fifty-Five Adult Lifestyle	249
Perfect Weather Bliss	252
The Last Train to Clarksville	253
Exhausting Your Options	255
Life Is Also a Spectator Sport	255
Rituals	255
Hygiene	256
Giddy	256
Old Age	257
Relaxing Is What I Do Best	257
When You Can't Chew the Leather, Change the Cat Box	258
Fading Away	259
Drooling and Dribbling	259
Riding the Ragged Edge	260
The Age of Disgruntlement	260

Fear	261
Exhilaration of the Soul	262
A Little More Juice	262
Blabber-Mouthed Women and Domino Men	263
Do Not Disturb: Renaissance in Progress	264
Sacking In	264
Fantasy the Best Reality	265
Time Lapses, Not Mind Lapses	266
A Piss in the Wind	266
The Pillbox Time Clock	266
The Check Is in the Mail	267
The Rules of Self-Engagement for Ancients	268

XVII - It's Curtains when the Fat Man Croaks 271

Riding the Flat Line into Eternity	271
A Hug Before Dying	271
That's the Long and Short of It	272
The Last Gulp of Life	273
Grim Poem on a Tombstone	274
Miss Me But Let Me Go	274
Final Words	275
Parting Advice	276
The Time to Call It Quits	278

XVIII - Appendix 281

ACKNOWLEDGMENTS

Beyond my dedication, I am compelled to singularly mention the following people who have lifted me to accomplishments beyond my natural ability:

Of course, first, last and always, I must acknowledge the love of my Creator, whose inspiration and promise of salvation gave me sustenance for this text. All glory and honor and praise be unto the Holy Triumvirate: the Father, the Son, and the Holy Spirit. Amen!

My brother, Frederick William Bentley, AKA Freddums, who has persistently—yet lovingly—pushed me to reach further, do better, accomplish more: "Do it now, do it for me, do it for Mom."

Dr. Norris D. Hoyt—known as Nagasaki by his students outside his presence—my predominant English Literature teacher at St. George's School, who seldom gave me above average grades and who usually circled large sections of my papers with a red pen and the inscription "BS"; but on my last paper for him, gave me a 95 (no paper's perfect) with the note, "This is a graduation gift, undeserved but you will grow into it. Keep writing. NH." Thank you, good doctor. This book's my only shot, but I'm not sure you'd give it an unqualified 95 because, you know, there's still a lot of BS here.

My eldest child and son, Sean Christopher, and his wife, Robin Machelle, who took me into their home and care for three years after Hurricane Ivan, encouraging my continued writing by setting me up on their computer and giving me the extended time to type up and print both my Light Flashes in the Tunnel and my

AT Journal. Many of these flashes have emanated from our shared family dynamic. Simple thanks and I love you's are not enough!

My youngest child and son, Paul William, and my ex-sister-in-law and now dear friend, Aunt Teresa Banfell, who badgered me without mercy to get off my tired old ass and put pen to paper. Thanks and I love you's are enough for them; damn their unrelenting hides!

My literary mentor and publisher's father, Earl Tillinghast, the Wise Old Intellectual Owl, who I've never met but pleasantly nudged me along through the maze and mysteries of the publishing world. Whew! You're unbelievable. How did you do it?

The women in my life, past and present. Starting with my mother, aunts, and female cousins, my life has been a continuous parade of delightful female acquaintances and their gifts. It is a fact that I, as most men, have been shaped by the women in my life. If I can feel accomplished in any way, it is a tribute to the majesty of these women who molded me. Thank you!

"...now I am more than happy that I can at least write. And if I haven't any talent for writing books or newspaper articles, well, then I can always write for myself...I must have something...that I can devote myself to! I want to go on living even after my death! And therefore I am grateful to God for giving me this gift, this possibility of developing myself and of writing, of expressing all that is in me.
I can shake off everything if I write, my sorrows disappear, my courage is reborn...for I can recapture everything when I write, my thoughts, my ideals and my fantasies."

Anne Frank: The Diary of a Young Girl

I. TRACER SHOTS TO THE PSYCHE

Light Flashes in the Tunnel

It seems that most of us, as ordinary passengers down life's tunnel, are only occasionally impacted with extraordinary thoughts of genius, bursts of inspiration, just simple observations. We are wanders by day and night—dreamers; schemers; mental nomads mostly engrossed in a search for food, shelter, and friendship, our highest aspiration. We bump along to the cadence and rhythm of life. While not always seeing the light at the tunnel's end, we do experience random flashes of insight and wisdom while en route. These flashes make up a curious patchwork collection of captivating scenes and occurrences about our lives that shape our attitudes and take up residence in our memory. That's what this journal is to me—random experiences and revelations that were highlighted during my passage through the tunnel.

The Amateurs

My twenty-eight year-old son Paul phoned during my colonoscopy prep day to implore me, his sixty-eight year-old nontechnical father, to get a computer.

"Dad, you need to write a book! Today, computers can do just about anything from researching subjects to editing text. They'll set your margins, double space, embolden letters for easy reading, create paragraphs, and check for correct spelling."

"That's nice," I responded. "Can computers also think up something to say that's relevant, humorous, and hasn't been written before and then compose it into sentences and paragraphs while I'm doing my laundry? Besides, where am I going to set up a computer in a 10-ft.x 25-ft studio apartment—make that cell—already crowded with the few things I *do* need, like a Murphy bed, sofa, closet, refrigerator, stove, sink, toilet, and shower?"

"Get a laptop," Paul said in quick retort. "I take mine with me everywhere. You can sit in Panera Bread and compose on a keyboard while drinking coffee and eating a bagel."

"Paul, I can't see myself in Panera Bread at one of those high tables amidst a sea of kids all banging furiously on their keyboards while I'm frantically hunting and pecking on mine."

"Fine," Paul said, sighing. "If you can't deal with a laptop, get an old-fashioned pad of paper and pencil and start writing; fiction or nonfiction, stories or poems. I'll give you a week to come up with a subject. Then I'm checking your progress, but you've got to write *something* besides your grocery list."

The following day, after getting into Aunt Teresa Banfell's car, my designated driver to the Endoscopy Center, she turned up the volume on *The Secret* tape and said over it, "Jimbo, you need to write something. You need to visualize it, write it, and publish it. You have a way with words. I know you don't believe you are funny or have any unusual writing ability, but it's not what you say as much as how you say it. We all enjoy your cards. In fact,

Amber and I have saved every one of them. Write something and know that if Paul told you the same thing yesterday, it's not coincidence, but a message for you to act on. Nothing in life is a coincidence."

So, the day after my fourth colonoscopy, there I sat—well, leaned actually—not only empty-bowelled, but empty-headed, with lined pad and ballpoint pen in hand—a fat, old, low-tech man starting with the most appropriate subject I could think of: the encouragement of two bighearted people who love me. And that's the beginning and the end, the yin and the yang, the essence of life, the unconditional sharing of ourselves with other creatures—love.

On the other hand, could these two bighearted people that I love be telling me what I want to hear, be massaging my considerable vanity, stoking my fire, coloring in my dream—everyone's dream— to be the published author of some notable work and widely-acclaimed for it? Frankly, after only the most cursory review of a few notable authors, I'm back to the realization that I'm not funny and do not have marketable writing skills. But what about that vanity? Maybe a little visualization wouldn't hurt.

It's So Important to Be Important

Everybody needs to be assured that their life has importance, that they have unique traits not found in others, that they make all the difference to someone else or to some cause for reputation. We all smile wryly at our strengths, at being the best in some capacity, whether we get a standing ovation from many; a mere pat on the back from a few; or even just a solitary look of envy from one. Self-confidence is an aphrodisiac for the soul.

When the Mighty are Weak and the Weak Are Mighty

We are taught and learn from early childhood that everyone is a worthy, necessary thread in the fabric of global humanity. We are pieces in a galactic puzzle that requires our individual contribution to complete the universal truth. The weakest link theory doesn't apply because we are all weak and all strong, each composed of a different mix of unique plus and minus traits. Great athletes may not be able to play a musical instrument. A great composer may never have played football. Some of us are miserly and selfish. Others are generous and philanthropic. Our uniqueness assures that we contain a seed that transports us in directions not experienced by anyone else. Of course, we can develop further common traits through exposure, education, and practice, but there will always be within us that defining profile from our passage through life's tunnel.

We Spend Our Life Summarizing

The end-of-life story is that our life passes before us as we pass into eternity. Of course it does, not in a single flash, but in successive flashes along the way—like this squib about flashes, like the many squibs in this diary, this book. Living, for humans, is a continuous mental summary. You can't move forward in math or science without building upon the past. Certainly our history is a summation of past accomplishments. Prayer is summary, listing that for which we are thankful and begging forgiveness for remembered misdeeds over and over. This is right, that is wrong. This is good, that is bad. Life is summary. I've got to do these three things today, take along with me the grocery list on the refrigerator, recover past education and employments for an application, learn the rules for refereeing soccer, announce at a kid's baseball game, remember the ten most important points for the test, sell cars, manage a restaurant, arrest an errant citizen, and operate a Moon rover. It's all about summary as we sort through the baggage of our lives, ever reviewing the past, cleaning out our garages, to prepare for the future when we jump into the Great Wide Open with nothing but a carry-on bag.

It's the Boring Stuff That is the Staff of Life

My grandson Boomer asked his mother if the first grade gardening project, the plot the students were about to prepare for tulips at the neighboring Green Tree Elementary School, would be boring. His mother wisely said, "Not the first couple of shovelfuls," which she hoped would stoke his enthusiasm and at least get him going. But the plain fact is that any meaningful gardening project requires hundreds or thousands of shovelfuls; and, after the first few, it's deadly boring. The same is true for the pulse of our daily regimen. Over and over, our ritualistic habits—shaving, dressing, eating, and driving to work—are the no-brain music of our souls; and we learn to like it that way.

Familiarity Breeds Confidence

Considering the ritualistic habits we develop to exact some control of our destiny and sanity, nothing gives greater self-assurance than the familiar path behind us. We regiment each ritual of daily life to decrease stress and sustain longevity: appointments, meals, exercise, hygiene, medication, projects, sleep, social life, shopping, travel, visits, and work. We schedule the time, we define the amounts and type, we commit personal resources, we decide apparel and contribution, we suggest the place, we hone our talents, we research options, and we fill in the blanks ahead of us. It is natural to fear a continuum of reacting to the unplanned and unexpected, so as much as possible, we project ourselves into the future to shape it before we get there. In doing so, we must push the familiar ahead of us to ensure arrival into our comfort zone. Hence, familiar times to arise and execute morning ablutions, to take our pills, to meet our family and friends for brewskis, to read something redeeming, to employ our exercise regimen, to finish our homework or term paper, to complete our shopping list, and to attend church services for the salvation of our soul. And when we hit those familiar marks that we've projected into the future, our whole being is awash with the tranquility of the ages. We are restored, confident, exuberant, and expectant of the coming future.

Comfort Zone

The term "comfort zone" is a whole course in psychology in and of itself. It describes the mental balancing mechanism that prevents us from going over the edge. The zone differs with each person and within each person as we dabble and grow in the experience of life. Staying sane requires that we not go further or faster than the zone can adapt. That's why people jump off buildings and vets have post-traumatic stress disorder. Nourish your spirit along with your body.

Of Kingdoms and Chariots

Your kingdom is more than a house. It is the comfort zone of your life and all humankind that extends beyond it. Your chariot is your wheels—your Harley, your truck—your transportation throughout the kingdom. The Bible reveals, "The Kingdom of God is at hand," which soapbox fundamentalists interpret to mean the end of the world or the human race. Dates are projected for Armageddon (e.g., Y2K), and we are challenged to rid ourselves of all evil before the Day of Judgment. Of course, the Kingdom of God is at hand. He is already in every one of us!

The sweeping image of catastrophic destruction wrought in explosions of fire and brimstone is, less dramatically, replaced by our individual mini-catastrophes and trauma. My own comfort zone, at sixty-six years of age, was rocked by Hurricane Ivan, with the resulting loss of my house and all of my personal possessions. It was then I truly learned that my kingdom extends beyond my portals to the domiciles of family and friends and to the hearts of all along the way. Comfort is described by love, wherever it resides, and salvation goes to those who extend their love to God through the humanity we touch. The chariot is our transport between the human islands of our life, and goodwill is our deliverance from sin and the bridge to a Heaven beyond earthly things.

Breaking Away

As previously mentioned, each of us must nurture our comfort zone and project familiar benchmarks into the future to sustain mental balance. However, it must be said that the occasional emergency, though disrupting, does jolt us out of a sometimes boring and hellish sameness. It often requires reassessment and adjustment in our outlook. We can't survive on a continuum of utter chaos, but a good jolt now and again can renew our lives. Death of loved ones, loss of jobs, divorce, deteriorating health, change of environments, devastation to personal property are typically one-time occasions; but they ripple throughout our lives and reverberate in twists and turns that interminably keep us on edge. We are rent asunder and yearn for the familiar again, but those twists and turns bring all our survival skills back into play and enlighten our being. It's when the sameness of an exact schedule runs a flat line into eternity, like the mechanical heart monitor line of the deceased, that we enter the glide path of death ourselves. We need an occasional spike in our lifestyle to be fully alive.

Dawdling and Gawking

You best include a measure of dawdling and gawking, the world's oldest relaxation techniques, in your daily regimen. Every construction project needs a couple of sidewalk superintendents to question the whys and wherefores of the job for misguided workers. A perusal of neighborhood gardening projects is in order, along with a talk to the appreciative gardeners about the beauty of their project and some salient considerations for enhancement. Shopping is another of the great crusades for the dawdler who reads every label and compares every price. Of course, gawking, especially subtle gawking, is an art form for, say, women to study a male flamenco dancer in tight leather pants as he taps his way across her line of sight or men to enjoy the unobstructed cleavage of a wondrous set of mammaries on a bikini-clad woman. It adds years to one's life!

Chilling Out

Back in the day, the word "chill" was used with reference to weather, not a state of mind. Farmers would lean over their pasture fences and say thankfully, "I'm glad the corn's in the crib and the hay's in the barn. There's a chill in the air, the frost is coming, and winter's on the way." Chill in the air, the silence of winter—quieter than a closet full of coats. To walk on a blanket of crunchy, newly-fallen snow across a 25-degree-Fahrenheit virgin landscape without tracks is like being reborn. Your cheeks redden, your breath vaporizes into the surrounding air, and your nose runs like a faucet. If you're lucky enough to be in a sylvan setting, all of your senses are engaged in the sweetness and vitality of life. The silence may be deafening, but the smallest sound, say the call of a blue jay or hawk, reverberates on the cold air like the sound waves from striking a crystal glass. Your pace quickens as the exhilaration of living acclimates you to the infinite possibilities remaining.

Glib

Among the common signs that mark our culture are those less obtrusive signs that show that we are individuals. As the old-time song implores, when dealing with fellow humanoids, always "accentuate the positive, eliminate the negative." People not only become what they expect from life, but they also become what other people expect of them. Children are known to act badly because that is the expectation for their behavior. Conversely, the power of positive praise motivates positive behavior. We all know mediocre students pursuing advanced degrees because someone said they were truly smart individuals who've just never reached their full potential. Some of us eventually go beyond our real capabilities to reach higher-than-capable goals, and some of us adjust to more reasonable goals for our abilities and interests. My ex-wife's Aunt Buddy once said to me when I was just out of military service, "You need to find a job where talking is required for performance because you have the gift of gab." I am at a loss to convey how hard I have worked to fulfill that prophecy. I've never been much for deep thinking or substance, but I can get diverse personalities to talk about their interests and talents, not because I'm inclined by gift or interest within myself, but because a caring lady in the long ago years said that I had that talent.

The Gift of Gab

Haven't we all sat down on a bus or in a theater next to chatty people who blather on absentmindedly about every minute detail of their life? These people are pitiable and enviable in the same breath. You have to wonder why they would divulge their most private and sensitive information to a total stranger. Yet, your ego is assuaged by the confidence that they have placed in you. They can talk endlessly, seemingly without drawing a breath, but almost with photographic recall. *"God,"* you mutter to yourself, *"I can't even remember the birthdays of my grandchildren, and this person is giving me dates of childhood soccer games!"*

If you ask about books they have read, they usually retreat to the one or two of their acquaintance, but they remember the details of people and events so obscure as to make you marvel at their mind—the migration routes of the Arctic ringed seal, the date Angelina Jolie got her private pilot's license, the twenty-first President of the United States, the Red Sox player roster for the last ten years—you name it! You wonder if their brain is somehow disconnected from their mouth and they are spewing random esoteric and historic facts from some bionic computer lodged in their brain cavity. They are compulsive talkers; and, even as you nod off from time to time, they talk on and on and on. Do treat them kindly and with the deference they deserve, but be cautious about what you share with them, for you may be sure that they will recall every tidbit you offer as fodder in future such monologues.

What's in a Name?

Everything. It's the light bulb of love to have someone, anyone, call you by name. It reduces the impersonality and numerology of your existence. You have been called as surely as God would call to you from a burning bush. We need each other. We relish the touch and voice of those reaching out to us. It's why the elderly blather on and on about the unending details of their life in the hope that a listener will care and confirm them as important. We get detached from others, especially in old age; and we must remain social with friends and relatives, indeed even strangers, to keep the spirit from withering. The waitress who kids you by name and remembers your usual order, the former coworkers and neighbors who you meet accidentally and who give you a big hug and delight in the details of your current life, your friends and family who maintain a pattern of phone contact from afar, and those nearby who send invitations because they want to socialize with you—these are the nourishment and salve for the soul.

Nicknames

Of course, the word "nickname" is derived from Nickolopoulous Cerniglia Krikstolaitis, who could not spell his name in kindergarten for lack of time and skill, so his teacher shortened it to Nick Krik, now Knickknack—and the rest, as they say, is history. Well, it's as good an explanation as any other. Who actually knows the possessor of the first nickname? Uncle Laz, who was raised from the dead by Lord Jez? Ivan the Terrible? William the Conqueror? Mary-Mary Quite Contrary?

The real thing is that a nickname, except maybe for Ivan, is an affectionism. In my childhood family, we three siblings were nicknamed by our father in keeping with his observation of our most prominent traits. I was Windy because, evidently, I never stopped talking. Fred, from his early assessment of all food offered him, was Stinky. And the fair princess, Martha, who regularly balked at any suggestion to do or eat anything, was Perversity. Now, with the passage of time, Freddums and I have remained true to our childhood nicknames. I tend to use verbal diarrhea as my weapon of choice while Freddums…he don't cotton to nothing but simple folk, simple eats, and simple living.

The extended family are called names like Bo Peep, Pumpkin, Peaches, Lamb Chop, Miss Priss, Mister Moopers, Maddie Moo-Moo, Scooter Bean, Bugs, Rosebud, and Wee Waddie Woo-Woo. Grandchildren should never be called by their given, formal names, but by that affectionate nickname known only to the special few. In my family, Bena and Hawk are the parents of Boomer and Stinky-Clinky; Pee-Pie and Gear Head are the parents of Keepsie and Bubba Bullfrog; Blondie and Veggie Might are the parents of Tootie and Black Jack; and Waggleman and Raz-A-Ma-Taz are the recent parents of Cada, two-thirds of a good bug.

Impatience

We all know those people whose belied tranquility can go to outright hostility in less than a nanosecond. They are the quintessential essence of impatience. Freddums' impatience with anyone or anything that smacks of needless complication is legendary. By his own admission, he doesn't easily suffer fools or witties. He is bighearted, larger than life, and wonderfully gregarious for the required five-minute introductory dialogue; but beyond that, step aside because he's—as we say—out of here. His impatience manifests itself from zero to one hundred in less than a minute. The signs are evident: his head jerks from side to side looking, I presume, for an escape route. His face reddens like an Irish barkeep, his brow furrows, and he becomes belligerent toward any proposal currently annoying him—shopping, for example, which he detests, or tourist attractions. He will walk rapidly for exercise, but most of his sightseeing is done from a car. Grocery shopping with him is a sprint, since he has a prepared list from which he never deviates; and he knows the layout of his store. I, on the other hand, will frustrate him no end when I linger, reading labels and turning new grocery items over in my hand with the possibility of substituting them for traditional fare.

Only occasionally do I prevail upon him to visit a museum or notable attraction with me, e.g. the *USS Constitution* moored in Boston Harbor's Navy yard. He refused to go aboard with me for the guided tour, so I left him seated alone on a wharf bench as I ascended the gangplank with the other tourists and our guide. During my absence, his moment of comeuppance came at the hands of an elderly woman who, as I noted with glee from the cannon deck during the tour, was seated beside Freddums, earnestly regaling him with trivia whilst gesturing toward an open plastic accordion-style picture holder. The droll vision of boredom upon his red face was worth a thousand words. I laughed heartily throughout the remainder of my tour and on many occasions later, recalling his suffering without recourse, as I reminded him that he would have been better off on the *Constitution* with me.

Fellowship Begets a Pelican King

Above the lowest survival rung on Maslow's ladder are those lighter-than-air aspirations that endear us to others of our own species. Churches, clubs, schools, fraternities and sororities, lodges, military units, the workplace, and unending esoteric organizations provide us with access to extend ourselves into common interest groupings. Such has been the history and pride of our Naval Aviators in their uncommon heroism, reflected by squadron names like VMA-214 Black Sheep; VFA-113 Stingers; or VMFA-235 Death Angels. Such is also the similar history of our over-the-road truckers with their shortwave handles like Mama's Boy, Hilltopper, Texas Tornado, Easy Rider, or Roadrunner. Yet another broad common interest grouping is the legion of serious section-and-thru hikers on the Appalachian Trail (AT). Their bond is also reflected in a great diversity of appropriate trail names like Monologue, Blistah, Mudflap, Bear

Bait, Green Bow, Faith Walker, Fly by Night, Brother B, or Pelican King. The last one, my own, was derived from years of exposure in the Florida Panhandle to that homeliest of all birds, yet most graceful in flight and most efficient at diving for a meal. You may recall verse written by Dixon Lanier Merritt and often credited to Ogden Nash:

> Here's an ode to the Pelican,
> Whose beak can hold more than his belican.
> He can hold in his beak
> Enough food for a week;
> And I'm damned if I see how the helican.

The pelican is my trail moniker.

Smug

Just every now and again, when the celestial cylinders align with your life, quietude and supreme cerebral joy overpower your consciousness and senses. You may be reading a riveting book, drinking a cup of exotic java in a sidewalk café, smoking a Dominican cigar on a park bench as tumultuous crowds of humanity scurry by, or hiking some remote trail. Suddenly, you feel as though you've escaped from the wheel of madness, been granted a reprieve from your attainments. God has lifted you up momentarily out of the race and allowed you to view it with indifferent suspicion and smugness and to marvel at the wonder of it all.

Naked Women

Now, if there's any kind of index associated with these squibs, or if this ever ends up in print and readers everywhere are thumbing through the titles, then all the gents will automatically stop at this title first and foremost for a read. It's a grabber, like our scandal sheets that pump out porn to sell papers—"Oversexed Woman Takes on the First Marine Corps Division." Guys just naturally gravitate to news of naked women, which accounts, at least in some measure, for the popularity of The Barenaked Ladies singing group. In the former all-male combat military, while briefing pilots or special ops units on enemy weapons capability and inventory; locations of gun and missile emplacements; damage assessments from incursions or air strikes; and other such boring stuff, using slide and overhead projectors, briefers would routinely flash up pictures of nude women to break the monotony of all that military hardware. It's our bane, our downfall, our truest happiness, our greatest pursuit, our greatest failure, our greatest success, and our best poetry. Bikini-clad ladies have saved *Sports Illustrated* (remember Cheryl Tiegs in her net swimsuit?), sold sports cars, added luster to boxing matches, and have generally been the social wonderment of males forever. Even in the workplace, against the grain of sexual harassment charges, men will ponder what their female contemporaries look like inside those double-breasted suits.

Of course, this whole scenario works as well in reverse, since females are not averse to what men look like under their bulging pants and fully-buttoned shirts. "Naked men," they say with more than a hint of interest!

I've Got an Ace in my Hole

We are all a wee bit anal in our own way. Some of us are just out-and-out assholes. And all of us assholes also have a few redeeming qualities, as well. As every teacher knows when assigning negative attributes, some positive traits must also be assigned to fairly balance the hand. Nobody's all bad or, for that matter, all good. Us assholes also have a few aces. You could righteously label us aceholes.

Words that Sound Their Meaning

Diarrhea. Vomit. Pustule. Dead. Rancid. Bereaved. Blather. Berserk. Snazzy. Hornswoggle. Jack shit. Now, the last one I just threw in because I don't know jack shit about word sounds, but anyone reading this, come on folks, you can take umbrage at my declaration.

You Feckless Bastard

Not all words sound their meaning, although I think we all know their general intimation, whether positive or negative, by the tone of the voice speaking them. I have a fair vocabulary, but I've also stumbled over a lot of words in recent years that I needed to look up in a dictionary. When Tom Hanks used the word "rapacious" in *Sleepless in Seattle* to describe emotional, love-starved women, I had to look it up. The same with "feckless," which my brother has generously assigned me for lazing about during my retirement years instead of taking on a serious hobby or building another house in the wake of Hurricane Ivan. I understood the "bastard" part right off, so I should have been able to pair worthless or irresponsible with it.

That Dog Don't Know Sic 'em

"That dog won't hunt" is a disparaging country colloquialism for dog or human. It was popular in rural America to denote a vacant-headed animal or person of little worth, with minimal training and less motivation. It was regularly assigned to us farm underlings for our many failures to successfully complete assigned chores. "Jimmy don't know sic 'em about backing a hay wagon into a barn," or, "That dog's only good for a family pet. It don't know sic 'em about herding sheep or hunting pheasant." Even our aunts and mother joined in its' usage with their offerings: "That woman don't know sic 'em about canning fruits and vegetables," or, "For a person of her considerable means, she don't know sic 'em about home decoration." Thinking back to that label during my farming adolescence and forward from that time down the diverse paths that I've traveled in so many different directions, I can't actually remember a time when I did know sic 'em.

Writing Something Pithy

If you can't write a novel, you might consider something concise and memorable such as what Ben Franklin wrote under the pseudonym of Poor Richard. You know, "Early to bed, early to rise makes a man healthy, wealthy, and wise," or, "The early bird gets the worm." Stuff like that. Cute stuff that rings true in real life situations. Pithy, not pissy! If you get pissy with people, they'll rain on your parade. There's a big difference between telling someone to go to hell and telling them to go to hell but have them looking forward to the trip. Besides, the one who is late to bed can capitalize on that quiet time to, say, scour a dew-laden lawn for the night crawlers that return to ground before dawn. And as any fisherperson will tell you, the best catches come during twilight feeding at dusk.

Common Man

Real men don't eat quiche! That's a familiar battle cry of the simple palate. Because America is the world's melting pot, there are obviously palates and kindred restaurants as sophisticated as any on the globe, but we are probably better known as a country for the common hamburger and milkshake than for the more urbane dishes like Swiss chard with poblanos and hominy, stir-fried bok choy with miso, Duck l'Orange, or potato frittata with prosciutto and Gruyere. Sometimes, reading an upscale restaurant's menu makes you feel as though you just stumbled out of the woods into civilized society. It is a special language, and it does make you uncomfortable to ask, "Are those real potatoes in that frittata?" or "What even is a frittata?" It's easier, and more familiar, to hang your head out the cab window of your truck and shout into the microphone, "Make that a double cheeseburger with bacon, fries, and a chocolate shake!"

A Load of Hooey

It's hard to separate fact from fiction in American advertising. The blatant, unfulfillable claims of our commercial product hawkers have numbed the collective consciousness of the world public. No reasonable person can believe anymore that there's truth in advertising. "Fresh from the bakery to your table" is assured on the wrappers of prominent baked goods, whether sold as week-old bread or just stale and hard from long transit and storage. "Guaranteed for life with the following conditions" usually means if you use it and break it, the guarantee is void. "This treated wood (or this Western Red Cedar wood) is impervious to termites" will be translated in the South to mean that you've got up to three years before the fence falls over from termite activity. Twenty-year shingles. Miles per gallon. Whitening power. A full head of hair within two weeks. The patent medicines of our early healers—e.g., Dr. Tichenor's peppermint antiseptic, originally marketed as useful for a wide variety of complaints for both internal and external use for man and animal, now mainly just a mouthwash and topical antiseptic. The exaggerated claims haven't changed, but the years of unfulfilled dreams have made us gun-shy.

I See What You're Saying

This declaration is wrong, wrong, wrong! Given that we fully understand about twenty-five percent of what we hear and fifty percent of what we see, it is safe to say that we seldom understand another or are understood by them. Communication is a delicate thing and requires much repetition, even at the elemental level. Nothing is more humorous than listening to a conversation between two people desperately trying to hear and be heard without either succeeding! I am always reminded in this foiled exercise of the following poem by John Godfrey Saxe:

> "The Blind Men and the Elephant"
>
> It was six men of Indostan
> To learning much inclined,
> Who went to see the Elephant

(Though all of them were blind),
That each by observation
    Might satisfy his mind.

The First approached the Elephant,
    And happening to fall
Against his broad and sturdy side,
    At once began to bawl:
"God bless me! But the Elephant
    Is very like a WALL!"

The Second, feeling of the tusk,
    Cried, "Ho! what have we here
So very round and smooth and sharp?
    To me 'tis mighty clear
This wonder of an Elephant
    Is very like a SPEAR!"

The Third approached the animal,
    And happening to take
The squirming trunk within his hands,
    Thus boldly up and spake:
"I see," quoth he, "the Elephant
    Is very like a SNAKE!"

The Fourth reached out an eager hand,
    And felt about the knee.

"What most this wondrous beast is like
  Is mighty plain," quoth he;
"Tis clear enough the Elephant
  Is very like a TREE!"

The Fifth, who chanced to touch the ear,
  Said: "E'en the blindest man
Can tell what this resembles most;
  Deny the fact who can
This marvel of an Elephant
  Is very like a FAN!"

The Sixth no sooner had begun
  About the beast to grope,
Than seizing on the swinging tail
  That fell within his scope,
"I see," quoth he, "the Elephant
  Is very like a ROPE!"

And so these men of Indostan
  Disputed loud and long,
Each in his own opinion
  Exceeding stiff and strong,
Though each was partly in the right,
  And all were in the wrong!

Moral:

> So oft in theologic wars,
> The disputants, I ween,
> Rail on in utter ignorance
> Of what each other mean,
> And prate about an Elephant
> Not one of them has seen!

Rock-Paper-Scissors

King Solomon's fabled wisdom reportedly solved many trying issues in his time before the birth of Christ; e.g., settling an issue of land inheritance between two quarreling brothers by suggesting that one divide the property and the other have first choice. Modern times don't seem to have embraced the talents of a single wiseman or wisewoman, perhaps because we don't have one or perhaps because our issues are more complex. In the United States, our highest courts favor the disposition of three to twelve judges/justices in rendering decisions and/or awards, seldom unanimous, many most notable for their dissents. Among children, evaluation of premises is usually based on Eeny-Meeny-Miny-Moe, while adolescents retain the time-honored Rock-Paper-Scissors method of awarding judgments.

Life is Like a Game of Solitaire

You shuffle the deck and then shuffle it again and again, hoping for the best seven-card face imaginable: a couple of aces and a couple of kings with multiple moves before proceeding to the remaining deck. You know in your heart that you've won; but somehow, even with this amazing start, you exhaust all your chances. Then you go back to shuffling and shuffling again, placing the top cards over and over in their seven assigned piles with no aces or kings showing and few preliminary moves. You fear in your heart that you've lost; but as you proceed through the deck, placing available cards in their alternate red-black descending order and then ascending order by suit, you slowly, haltingly, work yourself into a winning position.

Our Vehicle is Our Tomb

Look at us, Americans. Frozen in our mechanized boxes, staring bleary-eyed at endless concrete and asphalt corridors, throwing our trash—Happy Meal boxes and their contents, beverage cups, cans and bottles, cigarette butts, and every other form of disposable waste from a disposable society—out from tinted, motor-operated windows onto sidewalks (if there are any), roadways, and the natural surroundings. And don't forget that the roads are for vehicles, not pedestrians, cyclists, or the hapless animals that wander clueless into oncoming headlights. A walker who assumes pedestrians have the right-of-way will die believing it. Occasionally, some good soul behind a wheel will motion a pedestrian forward on the WALK light, but they are rare and, one would think, as rare as the Americans who depart their vehicle in favor of exercise.

Truck Stops are America's Wellsprings

After a long stretch behind the wheel, with mental fatigue and outright exhaustion plaguing your senses, the neon lights of a twenty-four-hour truck stop are a welcome beacon. The bathrooms are clean and cheery; service is comprehensive; and the variety of sales merchandise is fun for tired eyes, like logoed ball caps with embroidered sayings like, "This is not a potbelly. It's a gas tank for a sex machine!" or, "Sex is a misdemeanor. The more I miss, the meaner I get!" And the freshly prepared food and desserts are delicious. I remember my mother saying in the fifties that truck stops invariably made the best coffee and pies to boost the morale of our nation's over-the-road truckers. She was right then, and the truck stops have only gotten better with time. For the traveling public and working truckers, truck stops are an oasis in a long mirage of emptiness.

It Ain't Nothing But a Thing

The famous Appalachian Trail switchbacks in Georgia are nothing if not arduous. Even the descents are often physically challenging. The ups and downs mirror those in life, with sprains to the body and morale; but at the end of the day, the sacrifice boosts the ego beyond all understanding. And so, standing together with sons Paul and Sean at the bottom of some impressive mountain eminence on the AT, Sean would invariably say, "It ain't nothing but a thing."

Wanna Look Thin? Wanna Be Loved?

It's the oldest of proverbs: "If you want to feel and look thin, hang around with fat people." Conversely, if you want to tap into your well to find forgiveness, generosity, and goodwill, keep the company of bighearted people, many of whom are fat. Imprinting from a role model, whether positive or negative, is still a major catalyst for personal action and change.

Jim Sharer Bentley

Great Danes are Wussy Pussies

Speak of unique collective traits in humans, and you also have to acknowledge the same in the animal world. Dogs, for example, differ in their mix of traits almost by breed. Some hunting dogs will stand immobile in the field for hours at a rigid point to fix the location of a game bird for their master. Other hunting dogs, too impatient to stand still, will swim long distances in the water to retrieve fowl shot by hunters. St. Bernards gained fame when TV portrayed them as dogs transporting brandy through snow-covered mountains during frigid storms to save travelers downed with cold and hypothermia. Pit bulls, which have short hair that won't survive frigid temperatures, are great fighters and guard dogs. Great Danes, more than one axe handle high at the shoulder, will fight off grizzly bears to save their masters, but cower under tables at the sound of wind or thunder. The littlest and most defenseless dog, the Chihuahua, which cannot fight, swim, run through high grass, remain immobile, or survive the cold, is nonetheless totally without fear in the face of thunder and lightning. Yes, we animals are an eclectic collection of diverse traits!

The Anorexic Anemone

Poor little guy! He was dwarfed by a bigger brother and outmaneuvered for the silverfish offered to him by a horde of other crustaceans, fish, and snails also occupying his saltwater aquarium. He grew pale in color and his tentacles seldom emerged from his body. I was tasked with feeding the aquarium society when Bena and her human family departed on a vacation cruise to Mexico. I worried some about the little anemone's survival and took to putting pieces of silverfish directly on his mouth. Still no eating action as the other inhabitants devoured each morsel. One morning as I approached the aquarium with a saucer of silverfish, I noticed that the little anemone was in full bloom, with a profusion of color and a partially digested aquarium mate in his mouth. Beware the hungry bottom feeders in an aquarium and in life for they may eat you!

Finding Yourself

Supposed normalcy is enjoined with the early battle cry of finding yourself. Mothers are awash with the conviction that their children are budding geniuses who will no doubt turn out to be great actors, athletes, doctors, lawyers, orators, scientists, or Indian chiefs because of some notable attribute like talking for hours without drawing a breath, running like the wind, singing as delightfully as any nightingale, or remembering everything within a field of vision with but a single glance. Of course, most of this is drivel; erroneous; and overstated (God bless our mothers anyway.), but it is our earliest guidepost pointing to the eventual occupation of our time. Most of us seem to end up in jobs that we never gave a thought to in childhood and for which we are totally unprepared anyway. My mother used to say, quite lovingly, that I had the long hands of a surgeon and the bedside manner of a minister, so I should be prepping for med school; but I washed out in my undergrad years with organic chemistry and physics.

One can hear teachers, psychologists, coaches, and employers remarking in conferences and interviews that Clifford or Sally's poor progress results from not finding themselves. It's not about finding yourself. It's about making the most of the few skills we have inherited or accumulated, and being open to learning additional skills as they are called for in whatever occupation besets us.

So Close and Yet So Far

Never give up on your dreams! Keep taking those conscious steps toward fulfilling your aspirations, but understand that the big payoff can be slow in coming.

The Great Yawning Abyss of Time

If you don't have any time, you lament its absence; but if you do, you have to tame it, work with it, make it your own. He who doesn't make good use of his time is to be as pitied as he who has none. The former wastes what could be his salvation in renewed exploration, while the latter won't make time for more reasonable pursuits.

Time in the Sun

"Every dog has his day, but there are more days than dogs," is an old expression. Still, when you're tilting against the wheel, it doesn't always seem like the hellish sameness will ever end: wash, dress, eat, work, do the chores, clean, eat, undress, bathe, sleep. Then, blessedly, the weekend comes or vacation or the celestial cylinders align with your life in some other way and you are off the wheel in a garden beyond recognition. Afloat on the pond.

Horseback riding in the park. Building a Habitat House. Disney World. The Appalachian Trail. You are free to expand in another dimension. It's your up time.

You Don't Always Have to Color Inside the Lines

Of course, it's one of those kindergarten rules that stay with you, like holding hands when you cross the street. Obeying traffic signals becomes an imperative to a healthy life; but why, in an empty parking lot, will some people drive around the whole perimeter to avoid cutting diagonally across painted parking lines? Life is an adventure that beckons us to walk on railroad tracks to see what's around the next bend. Our inner voice calls us to ford a few rivers and climb a few fences during our passage. Don't be afraid to cross a few lines.

Time Ninnies

It's been coined time travel on *Star Trek* and *Back to the Future,* but it isn't any different than good-old-fashioned being on time. We're all acquainted with the heady rush of events prior to the modern airplane trip, from waking up to last-minute packing to scheduling a ride to calculating time in transit with traffic, weather, check-in, and security inspections before arrival at the gate. While anything can go wrong at any step, easily the most important piece is getting a time ninny to transport you to the airport.

Holy Smokes! I'm on Fire!

Smoking a good cigar is a reverential high, mellow,

contemplative, and downbeat. But don't smoke one in a hurry—say, in traffic where the flash of vehicles mesmerizes you and is apt to cause the cigar to fall into your lap. The resulting low can range from scorching your privates to causing an accident. Always pick a quiet, unhurried environment for a contemplative event.

Never Smoke a Cigar on an Empty Stomach

Otherwise, you'll become dizzy; disoriented; and nauseated. A good cigar, like good wine or conversation, requires some preparatory thought and time. You should smoke slowly on a full stomach when time abounds to savor the experience, just as you should sip, not gulp, a good wine and always give thoughtful attention and advice to a good friend.

NO TRESPASSING! Violators Will Be Prosecuted to the Full Extent of the Law

I'm not sure why these signs make me so uncomfortable. Probably because they're so inhospitable. When you're walking through wealthier neighborhoods, the signs are usually mounted on decorative iron fencing, suspended between brick or stone piers, with additional signage that reads, "Protected by the Advanced Laser and Video Technology of Bojangle's Security Systems." In the poorer neighborhoods, this same message, secured to a chain link or chicken wire fence, is usually enhanced with its further warning—"Beware of Dog," always accompanied by an ill-bred mastiff with high forequarters, a bristling nape, torn ears, multiple scars from fighting, long incisors, and slavering jaws that foam as the dog leaps, barking at you the entire length of the fence. Both messages scream, "Stay away! Don't touch me! I don't like you! For that matter, I don't like myself, either!"

Veritas

Or, in Latin, "truth," the most misappropriated word in my life. It has, in fact, been the bane of my existence, especially since my ex-wife of forty years began calling me—even in her most affectionate moments—a lying sack of shit, all because of her interpretation of the word "truth." It has always been my bent to view truth as partial only, the whole and absolute of which we are not ever privileged to know in detail; but we each do enjoy a measure of the whole truth, a separate view from the bridge—but the whole of it is, more often than not, like the six blind men of Indostan describing an elephant. I'm not talking about mathematical and time certainties for which there is but one answer. I'm talking about our perception of fact in a multi-stimuli world against a background rife with nuances and misinterpretations. We're all aware of the storyteller's license to bend the truth in fish stories, UFO sightings, and feats of athletic or sexual prowess; but we're also part of hurtful gossip of wrongdoings later found to be untrue. It's hard not to sensationalize, and I've been guilty of stretching the truth and passing illicit gossip in which I had no confidence.

Still, there is some entertainment value in the storyteller's tale if the audience is otherwise knowledgeable or suspect of the story's substance. Most of us develop a kind of filter to believe a fourth of what we hear and a half of what we see. I feel sorry for those people who don't have or can't develop that filter. They will exhaust themselves in attempting to frame an exact dimension, which is as elusive as quicksilver. Our general information flow, as we interact with each other and with our environment, is simply too shadowy and vague for exacting detail. My ex-wife continues to say that my rationale is as flawed as my perception of the truth. "There is an exact truth to be known and related, and you shouldn't deviate from it," she laments. I do love to hear and tell a good story, and I am given to embellishing with abandon. Perhaps she's right, and I am nothing more than a lying sack of shit. Still, wherever I go, I'm in good company; and I almost never expect to hear, "The whole truth, so help me God," so I'm also not disappointed to learn later that first tellings were riddled with error.

Pants on Fire

This squib's got nothing to do with lying or elevating restaurant menu fare to uncommon heights, although the otherworldly foods from the Sushi Zone Restaurant in Bothell, Washington, such as sesame balls, miso soup, coconut prawns, calamari sticks, and yaki soba noodles, and from the Racha Thai Cuisine Restaurant in downtown Woodinville, Washington, e.g., tomka soup, green curry, and padh thai, are certainly upscale. This is a warning to unsuspecting culinary adventurers who don't read the fine print on the menu or don't ask their host restaurant waiter or waitress about the spices in an unfamiliar culture's food offerings. Just as you wouldn't order five-alarm chili or flash point spicing in a Mexican restaurant unless you're inured to it, you don't order native Japanese or Thai cuisine without discussing the standard use and type of spices. Otherwise, you will indeed incur Montezuma's Revenge and the Burning Pants Syndrome.

Virtual Reality

I've always been confused by terms defining modern day technology and by the exercise of employing it, and now I'm both old *and* befuddled by our virtual reality world. I understand well enough the reality part of, say, hiking the Appalachian Trail—the slips, trips, falls, blisters, bruises, cuts, unforgiving rocks, roots, and water courses; mice in the shelters; the overpowering stench of a summer's moldering privy; and the equally overpowering beauty encompassing it all—but that virtual part created with computer hardware and software presented to appear and feel like a real hike on the AT? Really! Are we headed for or already in a world of hikeless hikes, safariless safaris, and travelless travels? May our real God save us all.

The Lamp of Joy

As a global citizen, I was intensely proud and affected while listening to my President Obama's 7th and final State-of-the-Union address. The all-encompassing speech was wonderfully written and beautifully delivered by a joyous man of optimism whose undeserved legacy, by his own admission and apology, has been fraught with rancor and distrust. Never, I thought, has any worthy leader, fighting so valiantly for his people, been beset with so many naysayers hanging onto his coattails. Nonetheless, our president eulogized his many accomplishments and still-unfulfilled dreams for the future: e.g., closing the background check loophole in the gun control law; sparing and wise use of our troops in coalition with other countries instead of enjoining all global conflicts alone or at maximum input; extending a multitude of environmental protections including global leadership to reduce carbon emissions and elimination of our dependence on oil; improving the coverage and tenets of our new National Health Care Act; attacking our monumental national debt; decrying cultural and religious bigotry particularly against Mexicans, South Americans, and Middle Easterners during immigration reform, given our historic open-door ideals; and greater support for education overall, even to offering free college tuition during the entry years, to name but a few. He lauded the American people's spirit of giving, helping their neighbors during time of crisis, and volunteering in so many different ways to make life better for all. "That's America," he said, with more than a little pride. I was, as was any coherent citizen of our great nation, deeply affected by his charisma. He said that our government should assure a "fair shot" for all Americans seeking education; training; and work opportunities and rewards, especially the middle and lower classes where small business owners operate and minimum wage people try to survive. It was a glorious speech, and the president beamed with joy at our prospects for the future. "Who could disagree with the majesty of his words," I thought. And then, as President Obama's final "God bless America" faded from the air, the rattle of rancor from a Republican response replaced his joyous words and noble goals with their cacophony of putting more troops on the ground in Iraq and Syria, returning power to corporations and Wall Street in hopes that their benevolent "trickle down" would stimulate the middle and lower classes, reducing dollars spent on environmental issues that purportedly don't exist, protecting the sacred tenets of gun ownership in all of its manifestations for all ages in all places, deporting illegal immigrants and denying Muslin immigration at all. To me, it was a de facto redress of their grievances, retribution for perceived wrongs, instead of respectful disagreements with policy. Where have all our sage legislators gone?

In tribute to the President, and, conversely, to quell in my mind the misguided naysayers, I rushed right out the next day to perform a philanthropic act for another American citizen. The act lit my own personal lamp of joy. Thank you, Mr. President, for your inspiration; and, fellow Americans, his example to do good deeds for others *is* an American trait that, if exercised, will surely light your own bulb. It's the power of positive thinking that illuminates the world and all its peoples. Try it!

II. WORSHIPPING AT THE THRONE

Universal Truth

    Christ distilled and related the two universal truths for humanity, both involving love: Love the Lord thy God and love thy Neighbor as thyself. It is interesting that all of the passions that light and stoke our separate fires, whether for self-service or philanthropy, are for naught if we don't share them. No success is achieved or completed without another to confirm it. There is no bigger failure than the Midases who will not invest their treasure in the wellbeing of others or the givers who do not participate in the joy of their labors. We are woven together as threads in fabric, as separate pieces in a larger puzzle. It is love's pursuit, pure and simple, that binds us and makes us happy. As Christ exemplified, love has no bounds and no exclusions.

You Reap What You Sow

    Ever notice if you're rude to people, cut them off in conversation, treat them badly, or don't extend common courtesies, that they'll do the same to you? It's the age-old proverb, the Golden Rule, actually: "Do unto others as you would have them do unto you." Not much mystery here. If you want to be liked, thought well of, and welcome in the sight of your neighbors—only the lonely would think otherwise—work hard to listen to, laugh and sympathize with, help and extend only kindness to them, and your way will be paved to your reward. As Reverend Clark, a Presbyterian minister of my acquaintance long ago in Newport, Rhode Island, used to say, "Always extend the right hand of Christian fellowship during your quest for the keys to the Kingdom."

The Pure of Heart Get Extra Points Upstairs

The anger tends to flow when you've been in gridlock traffic patiently—or not so patiently—awaiting your turn to exit and a speeding car looms in your rearview mirror, passing the long lineup of cars behind you and then cuts ahead just as traffic starts to move. The urge to ram them, or at the least drag out your tire iron and break all their windows, manifests. But you smolder without action in the hope that the cutter will run out of gas and be left at roadside to the mercy of those who were cut off. This scenario is repeated daily in hundreds of such incidents that, blessedly, are assuaged by a higher power that somehow tranquilizes the potency of our anger.

While most of us have to listen to that inner, calming voice of reason as we smolder, there are those who gladly give the intruders the right of way, even smile and wave as they cut in line ahead of us. I've always wondered about the normalcy of these people. I mean, anger needs release. What's wrong with them? Yet, we all know and deep down marvel at and even envy these people, the sainted wonders. It's not right to be so collected and pleasant in the face of adversity; but we all really want to be that way, and we all really envy those people for whom goodness seems to come so naturally. Their moral compass is set on righteous. They are the bighearted people who step up to the plate and volunteer for the worst jobs, who give of themselves and their resources without measure, who work in soup kitchens, give presents to orphans at Christmas, bind the wounds, nurse the ravaged traveler, and let an obsessed driver cut ahead without malice. They are few, but their example ripples through us with positive potency. Though most of us cannot or will not sustain that high standard of goodness, our sporadic association with these endangered creatures makes us better people.

May the Good Lord Bless and Keep You

It's a Christian departure wish like the Arabic "insha'Allah" ("God willing") or simply a goodbye. It has the magical Irish tinge, as it shows our wish for an omnipotent deity to offer favor and protection to our beloved during his or her life's passage through the tunnel. Such sweet endearments are seldom heard except from our elders, much less analyzed for their deeper meanings. These phrases should be protected under Endangered Goodwill Laws that require usage by schoolchildren until they resound again with regularity among all people. To those good people who have persevered to this point in my mental wanderings, "May the good Lord bless and keep you."

Peace Be with You

Like true beauty, peace cometh from within. Perhaps, true beauty is peace. Certainly, true peace cometh only at the hand of

God. All religions invoke peace through love of god and god's word. "Insha'Allah," Arab Muslims say. "God willing," usually accompanied with a bow and hand-touch to head and heart for example. It is a striking, heartfelt greeting. The familiar Christian counterpart is done during worship service with handshakes and the spoken wish that, "The peace of the Risen Lord be with you always." Another joyous greeting, but following the precepts of God to obtain lasting peace is the challenge for each of us and our nations. To love our neighbor as much as we dote on ourselves is almost unimaginable. Still, we must work to cross that bridge, every day in every way. It's a seesaw pull of opposing forces that rage within us. How can we "be quick to listen, slow to speak, slow to anger; for anger does not produce God's righteousness (James 1: 19-20)"? In *Tuesdays with Morrie*, Mitch Albom quotes a conversation with his old professor, Morrie Schwartz, describing life as a tension of opposites…a wrestling match. He asks his professor, "Which side wins?" to which the old professor answers, "Love wins. Love always wins." I'm not as optimistic as Morrie was about humanity, but I will say that without love winning, there'll be no peace in our hearts or in the land.

She's Spiritual, But Not Religious

I've become acquainted with a delightful gay couple who've been together for almost a decade. They're bright, extremely attractive women so, chauvinistically as is my bent, I felt that their mutual attraction was, somehow, a failure of mankind for not winning them over to a conventional heterosexual union. But I was wrong and assured that theirs is a simple disposition for the same sex, not the opposite. One of the two girls was raised

Roman Catholic and pursued her faith with vigor until acting upon her gay disposition, which is not sanctioned by the Catholic Church, in spite of its ongoing scandals. Gina seems genuinely at a loss for not being able to attend mass and receive Holy Communion, but she accepts it philosophically and continues in the good deeds of her Christian ancestry. Her partner, Kelly, simply says that Gina is spiritual, but not religious. It continues to prick my conscience that so many of those manifesting the goodwill and works of Jesus Christ cannot darken, or have never darkened the door of a church. It is truly one of God's great paradoxes.

The Maiden of Dishonor

It is almost a universal truth that cheating begets disdain from the chorus around you. The hue and cry rises, if only silently, from onlookers. For all of the abrasive words and actions to stun a watching world, nothing stuns so surely or deeply as an act of wanton dishonor. We all cheer for the underdog to get ahead, but not by cheating! There's something so unsavory about the mind that would prevail at the expense of others, whether a fraudulent tax return, an errant spouse, an underhanded business deal, or just a student cheating on homework or a test. Societal pressure often sets a student's bar at an unreasonable height, which can force an inept student to consider cheating as an option.

The act of cheating will most certainly—and rightfully—be accompanied by penalty, shame, and lifetime guilt for the perpetrator. Most cheaters are caught, disciplined, and publicly humiliated; but usually the long-term result is the same, a mantle that can only be dispelled by self-forgiveness. Now, that is the thing. Society may forget, but we must continue to live with the self-inflicted image of our own dishonor. Restoration of the soul requires self-forgiveness, which is, perhaps, our hardest mental journey.

Raison D'être

What, exactly, is my reason for being; the purpose of my existence; the summary of my life; or for that matter, the purpose of yours? What did God create us to accomplish, to contribute to the balance of the universe, to give back for all that we have taken? Did we assure another's happiness in our lifetime or their unhappiness with our passing? These are the eternal questions that have, so far, eluded me since for the most part, I've been a mediocre man with a history of mediocre accomplishments. I've been exposed to and dabbled in many hobbies, jobs, schools, and pastimes with only marginal success. I've skated through the eye of the needle, as the saying goes, by the skin of my teeth. But for all my insecurities, unfulfilled goals, and lack of notable accomplishments, I've also been happy or, at least, complacent. Lower expectations make success inevitable. One daunting challenge has never overpowered me.

So what do you give back when you're trolling along the bottom, drinking life in gulps of beer, and taking your pleasures with abandon? Of course, I fancy that I made righteous contributions to my country as a veteran and to the children of Escambia County in their school feeding program. I'm also a passable nanny, if you like old-timey standards; a fair cook, if you've never heard the word "gourmet"; and a tolerable companion, if you like grumpy, uncouth old men. Still, it seems my only real accolade was given by a former brother-in-law who labeled me a Peacemaker. *"I'll take that,"* I thought at the time; and I've treasured it, even nurtured it, ever since. Granted that a peacemaker is also non-confrontational and passive; but I'd obviously rather think of it in terms of compromise, mediation, and getting disparate people together.

I've also been consoled with my multitude of inadequacies by the recurring words of Scripture, especially, the First Letter of St. Paul to the Corinthians (1 Corinthians 12: 3b-7, 12-13): "There are different kinds of spiritual gifts but the same Spirit; there are different forms of service but the same Lord; there are different workings but the same God who produces all of them in everyone. To each individual the manifestation of the Spirit is given for some benefit." I may not be in the giving league with Ted Turner and Bill Gates, but I give my paltry ten- and twenty-dollar gifts to various charities with some pride. I may not be able to write successfully like C.S. Lewis, J.D. Salinger, Hunter S. Thompson, Jon Krakauer, or William Sydney Porter aka O. Henry; but I can amuse myself with these dribblings. There can only exist a higher level of accomplishment when there is a lower level like mine to compare it with. As Garth so nicely sang it, "I've got friends in low places." If I end up further down there somewhere with them, at least I'll be in lively company.

Blue Funk

We all have down days. It's a quick and easy descent from our natural complacency and optimism to the doldrums of depression, self-loathing, and pity. A backbiting acquaintance, a failing grade in school, bad news about your or a loved one's health, whatever—as noted in the overture to a popular and always relevant Kingston Trio song, "These are the times that try men's souls." Life's a test, and it's the black patches, not the high ride of success, that show us what we're made of. Bouncing back from the bottom is what it's all about, and the surest elevator to the top is your support group and your faith in God. To feel good and worthy, you must hang with those people who see you in that light, who admire your soul, eulogize your talents, and treasure your company, especially under the cloud of failure. That's why, as the Golden Rule of the Good Book says, "Do unto others..." Never miss the opportunity to tell a friend, in some way or another, that you love them, admire them, and that they mean everything to you. The same is true in your prayers to the Father, the Son, and the Holy Spirit. Amen!

Honk If You Think Jesus Is Proud of You

Remember the charismatic bumper stickers that challenged us to "Honk If You Love Jesus"? Of course, it's Scripture that Jesus loves us unconditionally, but do we love Him likewise? More importantly, do we emulate Him, do we live His Word, do we make Him proud? Words and honks are one thing, but true emulation is another. Honking a resolution is a no-brainer, but an objective evaluation would mellow out our exuberance. It seems, at times, that objectively honking only our true goodness would almost completely eliminate traffic noise.

Why I Go to Church

Church attendance goes back to my earliest consciousness. In the beginning, as the Old Testament of the Christian Bible is wont to state, my whole sense of morality, reinforced by many close relatives, was borne first through the First Presbyterian Church of Lapeer, Michigan, and then later through Annapolis, Maryland; Newport, Rhode Island; and Coronado, California, in sync with my father's U.S. Navy duty stations. During his second tour of duty in Newport, I became an Episcopalian to take communion with my parochial classmates at St. George's. After commissioning from the Naval Officer's Candidate School (OCS) and entering active duty myself, I converted to Catholicism before marrying a Roman Catholic girl from Pensacola, Florida.

Throughout my childhood and adult life, I was either taken to Sunday church services, or I went of my own volition. My first Bible of memory was a small, navy-blue, generic Bible awarded me at graduation from the USN Anchorage Sunday school in Newport at about ten years of age. Thereafter, I acquired a Presbyterian Bible, an Episcopal Book of Common Prayer, another generic Bible at commissioning from OCS, and a Catholic Bible for use in the Navigator Course that my wife and I took to study our religion. Of course, I lost all these Bibles during Hurricane Ivan, not that I ever read them diligently, anyway; but I did not lose my faith. The thing with me is the need for first-person accounts within the press of community. I was raised in the Christian tradition of getting the Word firsthand as it's spread to the greater congregation. I've never been a big reader, and I'm resigned to never reading the Bible on my own, often struggling alone to determine deeper meanings. I'm better suited to going to church, listening to the Epistle readings and the Gospel after them and then looking to the homily as gravy to point the way. Some personal thought and prayer is satisfying, communion is sanctifying, and then I'm out in the world again to practice what has been preached to me firsthand.

Plunk Your Magic Twanger, Froggy

Of course, conscience is merely God calling, like a perennial Jiminy Cricket sitting on your shoulder. The guilt from wrongdoing comes from actually knowing the difference between right and wrong, which, in turn, is honed from biblical teachings, e.g., the Ten Commandants, reinforced by your support group. Many of us have taken the biblical route up through Sunday school, in parallel with our formal education and in cadence with the beat of family and ancestral teachings. Others have followed their own unique routes to develop their own honor codes. While we have all been honed differently into our moral beliefs, we are all still replete with guilt for wrongdoing out of sync with our credo. When I stray too far from my beliefs, I can almost hear God saying to the frog on my shoulder, "Plunk your magic twanger, Froggy," i.e. Andy Devine's famous catchphrase from the children's TV program *Andy's Gang,* circa 1955-1960. In this day and age though, He might more clearly say, "Prick that dude's conscience, homeboy."

III. BIRTH RITE

The Slaughterhouse

"Slaughter" is another word that sounds its meaning. It has an ominous, foreboding ring about it. Of course, it's the side of meat production seldom pondered or seen by the majority of consumers shopping among the vast array of animal products offered for our consumption. Nevertheless, as a boy of nine, an unexpected and unwelcome view of calves being slaughtered left an indelible impression upon me.

My brother and I were frequent visitors to a residential institution's farm, which was for patients with special needs, managed by our Uncle Fred. It was a self-sufficient operation with multiple barns encompassing laying hens, dairy and meat production herds, breeding stock, draught horses for plowing or pulling the wagons between a bakery, fields and gardens that supported inmates and livestock alike, a laundry, a school/administrative building, maintenance shops, and inmate cottages. Our grandfather managed the maintenance facility, while his son managed the farm. Our post-WWII memories of roaming the buildings and grounds of the Lapeer State Home and Training School are still vivid, including the day our laconic Uncle Fred invited us to view the slaughter operation. I can still hear the bleating of the calves before and while they were stunned with a hammer or pipe—these were the days before more humane shooting methods were introduced and required—and as their throats were cut, and I can still see them afterward as they were chained around the hind legs and hoisted up to convulse while bleeding to death. It was horrific, and I vomited and cried until I was limp. Typically, Uncle Fred went about his business dispassionately; but I was deeply affected and, to this day, will never consider eating veal and have never been a big fan of beef cuts of any sort. Such is the residual trauma from a stressful experience in childhood.

Reverend Mothers

The bond of motherhood is as primordial as our earliest cave ancestors. Mothers' routine sacrifice for their children transcends all other traditions and is legendary. Even the most heinous of our criminals has a mother attesting, even unto her son's execution, that he was a good boy who never forgot a Mother's Day. Abandoned children return years later to discover that their mother loved and prayed for them daily. Such unconditional love is surely one of our greatest offerings and sources of strength.

My own sainted mother, who made my brother and me clothes; enrolled us in dance classes (Yucky!) and parochial education; engineered dates for us with friends' daughters; lauded our every effort no matter how menial; and generally, cooked-cleaned-shopped-existed for our greater welfare, was always fond of saying, "Nothing is too good for my boys."

Black Sabbath

It was a Sunday morning, and two American children were

playing together in a field near their houses when the mounting crescendo of bass reverberations caused them to start crying and cling together. Finally, their mothers came, frantically embracing them amid the deafening roar of countless Japanese Zero fighter planes diving overhead and the widespread explosions of bombs all around them. As the two women ran with their children back through scattered debris, fire, and smoke toward adjacent houses, the Japanese mother, holding her daughter Suko Higuchi, beckoned her neighbor, who was holding her son, to join them in the bomb shelter beneath her house. For the rest of that December day in 1941 on the Island of Oahu in Hawaii, a Japanese doctor, his wife, and daughter shared their bunker with their neighbors during the attack on Pearl Harbor until they could all flee to safety in the hills above Hickam Field. The only remnant of memory from that three year-old's day is the droning of planes similar to simultaneously pushing a dozen keys on the bass end of a piano, punctuated by the unnerving percussion of bombs. There is also the lingering curiosity about Suko's and her parents' fate at a time when our Japanese citizens were incarcerated in concentration camps of our own making because of their ancestry.

Impetigo

It's not a word oft spoken or remembered, but it flashes back into my consciousness when 1941 Pearl Harbor days are mentioned. After the attack, our father went to sea aboard the USN destroyer *Cummings*, not to return until the war's end in 1945, and our mother evacuated with my brother Fred and me up into the hills above Pearl City. Our mother's occasional mention of staying in the caves still lingers in my memory. After the all-clear was given and WWII declared with Japan, we returned to the heartland by way of a Liberty ship to San Francisco. All I remember from that traumatic passage through U-boat-infested waters was the enforcement of blackout and quietude aboard ship and the festering, pus-filled blisters on my baby brother's body. He had a bacterial skin infection known as impetigo, and treatment at the time meant swabbing the blisters with gentian violet, which turned Freddums' affected skin a purplish-blue color. During the blackouts, with dark cloth covering the portholes, I would attempt to distract eight month-old Freddums while Mom removed the scabs from his dried blisters with tweezers and swabbed him anew with purple lotion.

It Takes a Village

In her book *It Takes a Village,* Hillary Rodham Clinton taps the proverbs of the diverse African cultures to conclude that a child is not raised in a single home by a single family, but, rather, is also the charge and responsibility of the entire surrounding community. Certainly, it is the influence of many people and institutions that inspire our dreams, aspirations, and ultimate direction. In translating this credo to my own life, I recall an instance back in fourth grade at the Second Ward School in Lapeer, Michigan, of behavior modification made by a very collusive community that came at the hands of my fourth grade teacher, Miss Edna Murphy, and my grandfather Henry Roy, otherwise known as Gramps.

My best friend, John McBride, and I were in Miss Murphy's class; and we were prone, as outside the classroom, to

Light Flashes in the Tunnel

misbehaving with our antics and noisemaking. Miss Murphy, as most successful teachers are, was a loving, patient, and long-suffering woman who employed many strategies to curb and correct our ill behavior, like separating our seats to opposite sides of her desk, giving us titles of importance to coax responsible behavior (I was the Fire Marshall, and John was the Hall Monitor), sending us to the principal for further admonition, keeping us after school to erase blackboards, etc.; but nothing seemed to slow our disruptive behavior. At the time, post-WWII, Freddums and I were living in a farmhouse with our grandfather Roy and his older unmarried daughter, Aunt Jean, while our mother was tending our sick sister, Martha, at a rental house in downtown Lapeer, and our father was at sea as the executive officer of the heavy cruiser *Columbus* (CA 74). One evening, Grandpa Roy called me over alone to his easy chair, where he folded the newspaper in his lap, reached out to grasp my shoulder, and looked me squarely in the eyes as his irritated voice spoke the following words of reprimand:

"I understand that you've been acting up in class with your friend John, so much so that your teacher is spending valuable instruction time trying to control your bad behavior."

"No, sir!" I replied indignantly, albeit dishonestly.

"Don't lie to me, boy!" (In the substrata of our family, you were always a "boy" or "girl" when under adult tutelage.) "Edna Murphy is a close, personal friend of mine; and when you're bad, you make me look bad. If I ever hear the slightest word about any more of your shenanigans, I'm going to put the razor strap on you! Furthermore, I want you to apologize to Edna for your disrespectful behavior. Am I making myself absolutely clear here?"

What could I say but, "Yes, sir."

I was dismissed with a wave of his hand. "That will be all for now. Don't forget the apology!"

Thereafter, I did straighten up in class, and though it was one of the hardest things I've ever had to do, I did apologize to Miss Murphy, who I was told also taught my father (a model student, of course) and invited him while he was on leave from the US Navy to come to our classroom and talk to us about his WWII experiences at sea. As for my grandfather, Freddums and I were with him in the Cadillac Market, the first grocery store in Lapeer to have an electronic beam on a pole that automatically opened their doors when a customer passed, when he stopped to pay his respects to his old friend, "Well, Edna, good to see you. How's the boy doing in your class? I hope he's not giving you any more trouble."

There I was, sweating profusely between the two communicants, when Miss Murphy started stroking my head while saying to my grandfather, "No, Roy, Jimmy's turned into a real gentleman." As we left her, she looked intently into my face and winked as she smiled that community smile from across the village.

The Purple Wristband

I'm sure Freddums and I weren't happy at the prospect of another sibling sharing in the bounty of affection being showered on us by the homefolks during WWII, but we got one anyway. Martha, a blue-eyed spitfire with blonde ringlets, must have been conceived during one of our dad's infrequent liberties from Navy destroyer sea duty, because she was born during October 1944 in

Flint, Michigan, near our grandfather's heartland farm in Lapeer. There was much ado in our family and greater community about this firstborn girl. All the attention formerly lavished on us was diverted to her.

"Martha this," and, "Martha that," was a tough pill for three- and six-year-old brothers to bear. Her every whim was indulged, and she was pampered at every turn. We thought her bratty and insufferable for stealing our spotlight, not to mention our toys and favorite things. Nobody seemed to favor us over her, so we naturally resented her presence. We simply couldn't understand the blatant favoritism unanimously offered her at our expense until the color faded from her countenance and she began to wheeze and gasp for breath. She couldn't run with us or play tag without stopping to inhale and cry. It was one doctor's appointment after another, including forays to Johns Hopkins in Baltimore, then the most advanced medical research facility for cystic fibrosis. She began to falter and fail at the simplest exertion, so we began to slow down, to take her hand, to carry her. She became bedridden, and her last year was spent in a clear plastic oxygen tent boxing her upper body in bed. During a time of scarcity after the war, many local providers managed to supply the expensive oxygen bottles at no cost to sustain her last months of life.

As she lay pallid, motionless, and expressionless against her pillow, we could only attempt to beguile a smile from the corners of her mouth. We would try to touch her through the plastic enclosure to no avail. My only good recollection of those times was the baby squirrel I brought her that would lie on its back and drink milk from a doll bottle pushed up with its hind legs. She smiled, watching it, and then a resounding, though muffled, laugh emanated from within that suffocating tent. She formed the words with a silent mouth, "I love you. I love you. I love you." I wanted to rip that plastic off and carry her outside into the fresh air and sunshine, but that wasn't an option. It was the last time we were to see her alive, for we were staying at our grandfather's farm in the countryside while Martha was living with our mother in downtown Lapeer, near medical help.

The day came in 1947 when our Aunt GeeGee dressed us up in our Sunday go meeting clothes and drove us to our sister's funeral. I can still remember the communal affection showered upon Freddums and me as so many people reached out to touch us during our approach to Martha's open casket. The smell of gardenias was pungent. It was, of course, horrific to see our sister lying wax-like on white satin in a metal container, her blonde ringlets pressed perfectly against a colorless complexion, her cheeks rouged to mimic life. I have cried often and long since that day when thinking about my little sister, and I wear the purple wristband in promotion of continued cystic fibrosis research, which has now advanced light years toward the ultimate and lasting cure.

Out of the House of Many Windows

Where, pray tell, in literature can children make early friendships with nature's creatures and become entranced by their homeland in the forest? Why, that's easy. Surely, no Story Teller did a better job of wishing little ladies and gentlemen of all ages "the happy quiet of the Deep Woods, and the pleasant peace of the Hollow Tree" than Albert Bigelow Paine with his stories about The 'Coon, The 'Possum and The Old Black Crow. Their book was the literary bible of my childhood, read and re-read to Freddums and me by our mother and, in later years, read to myself for comfort and then to my children, Sean, Lisa, Shannon, and Paul, for their bedtime adventures into slumber. It evokes all the poignant lessons of love; creativity; forgiveness; the opposite sex; fear; dealing with untenable situations; and, most of all, the binding communion of friendship. The dog-eared copy that I carried with me out of my childhood and read to my children was lost in Hurricane Ivan, but my Missouri caretakers thereafter, Sean and his wife Robin, found me another on the Internet. I still re-read it occasionally for comfort and for the life lessons it evokes. Like the Little Lady and the Story Teller, I have often wished that I lived in a Hollow Tree.

Siblings

Brothers and sisters are blood of blood, flesh of flesh, soul of soul. They are who you are, and above all others, they know who you are. You came from the same clutch of eggs in a solitary nest and bubbled up together, defining and refining each other's persona and humor in the same cauldron. They are your well. When you get too far afield, lost in the maelstrom of life's bumps and grinds, you simply return to the well, and they will smooth you out again.

Siblings Know Who You Are at the Core

It is a curiosity of modern day celebrity that every act and habit of celebrities' lives are examined and reported in detail: childhood experiences, high school activities, academic records, early jobs, loves lost, troubles encountered, what neighbors and teachers thought of them, and their big break. The more menial, the better. Of course, we want to shadow famous habits to emulate them: toiletries used, automobiles or motorcycles driven, clothes worn, and words uttered. Their phrases become common idioms. Their clothing styles set the common fashion. Their natural mastery of public image projects to us what they want us to see, with an occasional faux pas. Overall, they are who they want us to believe they are, except that their siblings often paint a different picture, better or worse.

Your siblings were in life's cooker with you during the formative years when you sang badly, missed easy grounders, couldn't dance or get a date, had a splotchy complexion and unruly hair, drove a derelict car, dressed badly and had a boorish personality, didn't read, couldn't write, and had nary an exciting thought or job. Your siblings were the ones that goaded you out of your subhuman rut into early successes and, eventually, the fast lane. You know in your heart you can't fool them with your hero image thing. Blessedly, you relish this microcosm of reality where the few love you in spite of your celebrity, where you are still known as the dirtbag who overcame the adversities of life and has a notable lack of talent for reaching a higher plane. While they applaud us, they're not overly impressed with our celebrity. To them, like everyone else, we're just plain folks.

Family Taxi Service

My brother and I were ruminating recently about the difference between our outdoor childhoods sixty years ago and the indoor childhoods of today's youth. Yes, we spent time on a farm where outdoor work and play are synonymous, but even in the city or suburban neighborhood settings of our youth, it seemed we were always outdoors from sunup 'til sundown with only intermittent forays inside for food or bladder relief. Of course, computers and television were not on the horizon then, and reading was considered a nocturnal pastime. Today, the physical counterbalance to passive computer and television time is, of course, the youth sports culture, organized in our communities by age groups. Parents are responsible for meshing family schedules to include individual sports activities and then ferrying their kids to practices, games, and tournaments or working out a collective taxi service to meet their several kids' transportation requirements. It's a complicated, sophisticated, and impressive process to negotiate and fulfill carpool schedules, which was not a factor in earlier American life without such youth athletic leagues. We created our own competitive games in a local hayfield or on the street with a bat and ball or just a stick, a rock, and a sewer opening for a goal.

Party Line

This squib does not refer to your political party's raison d'etre or your cajoling words of flattery to stir up romance. It alludes, instead, to our earliest, widespread, landline installation of Edison's telephone into the American culture, when multiple users at different locations were clustered together into a "party" that used the same circuit. Operators were employed at a central switchboard facility to answer "receiver pickups" and redirect calls as requested or to send unknown requests to "Information" for further research, since early telephones saw limited use. Those on a rural party line were usually a half-dozen or so of your neighbors; and when someone was using their phone, the line was not available to anyone else. Of course, you could pick up your receiver and listen in to another's conversation; but that was considered to be most impolite. The common courtesy was to keep your call as short as possible so others on your line could have their turn, too. If you picked up your receiver and heard another talking, you were supposed to hang up and wait until an operator came online to request your number. Long-winded neighbors often had to be interrupted and reminded that you were waiting to use the line. My grandfather was proficient at upholding party line etiquette: "Mavis, you and Estelle need to quit your gabbing and wait 'til church on Sunday. You've been on this line for forty minutes, and some of the rest of us would like to use it, too!" And, of course, almost everyone listened in to each other's conversations, often chiming in to add their "two cents worth," in those days before private lines existed. For a teenage boy, asking a girl for a date on the party line was an indescribable mortification, a sort of communal bashing from the entire village:

"Miss Bleaker, it's Jimmy Bentley, and I'd like to use the phone."

"Jimmy, you're not going to call that Seaton girl again, are you?"

"No, ma'am."

"Good thing. She turned you down flat the last time. That girl's going places. She doesn't need you hanging around. Who are you calling now?"

"Well, I'm going to call my friend, Julie VanDusen."

"Those VanDusen girls are lovely. They've got no truck with the likes of you! Better that you just tend to your own affairs and wait until you've got something to offer her."

"Yes, ma'am; but I'm just calling to accept Julie's invitation to a pool party."

"Well, I swear. What is Betty thinking to let her daughter invite a bunch of ne'er do well boys like you out to their farm for partying? I never! Well, Okay, you can use the phone; but you behave yourself at the VanDusen's spread and don't reflect poorly on your grandfather!"

"Yes, ma'am. Thank you."

So much for enjoying the community party on a party line, much less developing any pride in your own reputation.

Black Sambo

The 1950 covenant of my brother's and my idyllic early teen passage was held with the neighboring Flynn brothers, Vince and Mike, who corresponded with our respective ages, and their shaggy black, knee-high dog named Sambo, probably named from the popular children's story of that era, *Little Black Sambo*. During our daily walkabouts to downtown Coronado, the local golf course, the beach, the youth center, or simply to school and back, we were never without the company and goodwill of that canine companion. Of course, almost sixty years later, after the long-overdue advance of black, female, and other minorities' rights, it would be offensive and unconscionable to parade that name in public or, for that matter, in private. Most of my African-American friends and associates have taken umbrage at the perpetuation of black stereotypes in such books as *Gone with the Wind*, *Uncle Tom's Cabin*, and *Little Black Sambo*. They fervently denounced the lowly portrayal of their race in the popular Disney saga, *Song of the South*.

While I often listened with embarrassment to their objections, I was still wont to counter them with the loving, grandfatherly image of Uncle Remus, portrayed in the movie by actor James Baskett, the greatest of raconteurs who also spun adventurous tales of the diminutive Br'er Rabbit. Stories of the protective Briar Patch, the reverse-endings from the Tar Baby, and rope snare traps were larger-than-life for me and millions of other children; certainly the equal of tales from the Brothers Grimm, Hans Christian Anderson, or Mother Goose. Mr. Baskett, in addition to a marvelous portrayal of Uncle Remus, also did the voiceovers for the butterfly, Br'er Fox, and Br'er Rabbit in *Song of the South*.

To my mind, the image of Uncle Remus was the highest compliment of humanity, boding well, not only for the black race, but for all the globe's people. It's worth mentioning that James Baskett, who played Uncle Remus in *Song of the South*, rightfully won an honorary Academy Award for his portrayal; so did Hattie McDaniel, playing the part of a handmaid in *Gone with the Wind*, who was the first African-American to be nominated for and won an Oscar as Best Supporting Actress. Not too shabby for a couple of supposed underlings! I'd trade places with them in a heartbeat.

Don't Overdo a Compliment

It's the old story of the shepherd who cried wolf without cause so many times that no one responded when the cry for help was genuine. Those good people in our lives who have spent interminable time slathering us with compliments become almost invisible when objectivity is necessary. Of course, your mother thinks you're perfect and you can do anything. You are the embodiment of ancestral perfection from the cells of her body and vision of her mind. On the other hand, the boss, coach, true friend, minister, neighbor, honest parent, sibling, or teacher who has patiently tracked the litany of our errors, mistakes, and transgressions with cues for improvement and who refrains from praise until the last resort will be the only satisfactory source of righteous elation. Their subdued compliment, on the order of "Not bad" or "Good job," will fall on our thirsty ears after we have strived hard and achieved much, and their honesty in appraising unworthy efforts will save us many moments of embarrassment down the road. Objective criticism comes only from those with our interests at heart, from those who respect us enough to make us better. Blind love is not an objective judge.

Sense of Propriety

"Have a little propriety!" shouted a neighborhood matron who caught us grade school boys tossing pepper berries at a cat on her fence. Years later, a teacher squashing a food fight in the school cafeteria echoed the same words: "For God's sake, you boys need to develop a sense of propriety!" The word "propriety" has the same feel as "statue," so it's like a death ray that makes you inert. It lays dormant in your mind awaiting adulthood, and it is reawakened when some accolade finally reverses the spell: "This employee has demonstrated extraordinary initiative and propriety." With that one password, all the childhood demons are released from your soul.

Dispensing "The Word"

Getting and giving words of love, celebration, and joy are essential to a happy and healthy psyche and a high morale. The flow of these words through our lives contributes immeasurably to our well-being and acts as a medicine to counter abysmal stress and other tugs from the dark side. Therapeutic words are most profoundly offered in written form so the sender can take appropriate time to construct a positive message and so the recipient can take continuing time to read and re-read the message for its residual benefits. We can derive unlimited and regenerative encouragement from the well of our personal, written salutations. My mother spent months before Christmas constructing messages of good will to her many acquaintances and friends and then transcribing them in her own hand onto personalized cards. She staunchly maintained that eulogizing memorable moments of love, celebration, and joy between her and the recipient with the written word was the only true way to share the word. In return, she received an equal measure of love in personal script, written from each of her many friends, all of which she kept and cherished and re-read from time to time to bolster a waning spirit during sad news or trying events.

I've taken to following her example, as best I can, at Christmas and on birthdays, and after some memorable occasions to share photographs or offer thanks. I have received many such counter messages which I, likewise, treasure, retain, and re-read as an old man living alone far from his progeny. For example, during the time of his nuptials with Brigette, my son Paul attached a card to their thoughtful gift to me with the following handwritten inscription: "Yo Pops, Thank you for all that you have done for me over the many years you have been my father. You are the best father that anyone could ask for. I am so very lucky to have you in my life. Here is to one more memory added onto the many. Love, Paul." Re-reading this note has been a salve to my soul on many a depressing occasion.

IV. THE THREE R'S

Melting Pot

Our first real venture into the wider globe beyond our first friends and family usually occurs when we enter school. We know before kindergarten that we come in different colors, sizes, and sexes, but our boundaries are expanded with exposure to the different languages and customs that meld together in our classrooms. The United States of America is a melting pot of diverse cultures because we are the world. We are strong because of our diversity. We are favored because samples of all the populations on earth are within our borders. School is our first introduction to and our lasting impression of these concepts. We learn to appreciate and cherish the individual thread of our own ethnic origins as separate but woven into the fabric of our country's multicultural whole.

Fifties Cool

Way before Peter Fonda charged our wanderlust with his Harley motorcycle in *Easy Rider*, James Dean did the same for the fifties generation with his droll, laid-back persona and palm-down wave in *Giant*. He was not hip like Louie Armstrong, suave like Cary Grant, or debonair like David Niven, but he was cool! Most of us boys attending Coronado Junior High School in 1950-52 strove to project that humble confidence and coolness of our mentor while our girlfriends gravitated to Debbie Reynolds, Elizabeth Taylor, and Marilyn. In Southern California, next to the Mexican border, cool for boys meant that we wore leather-laced Huaraches, sandals with loose cleats nailed under the heels, which tapped loudly as we walked to announce our presence. Beltless Levis rode low enough on our hips that our girlfriends would pull them down to embarrass us. Loud, bird-and flower-print silk shirts with the top two or three buttons left open to expose our few chest hairs and the tail out completed the ensemble. Undershirts and socks were out, and the hair—replete with wave and ducktail—was, shall we say, greasy. We lived in the day of Wild Root Cream Oil and Brylcreem Hair Cream. A little dab'll do ya.

We clanked as we walked slowly so our pants wouldn't drop with shiny hair combed with a monster wave in front and a feathered point at the neck bone in back. An Ace comb was ever in our rear pocket to repair the wave or tail, along with a handkerchief to wipe away excess oil melting down our face in the California sun. Like the Fonz, we bedazzled our long-skirted, lace-collared, bobby-soxed, saddle-shoed, bobbed, and ponytailed girlfriends with our beach exploits and clichéd wisdom. For their part, in my recollection, the girls spent more time laughing at us rather than with us. We met at drug store counters for Cherry Cokes and root beer floats; the park for movie dates; the beach, North Island NAS Pool, or Municipal Golf Course after a rain to swim; and the youth center or school gym for chaperoned dances, girls on one side, boys on the other. No dancing close allowed! We competed in talent shows and square dance contests, climbed the chain link fence into high school football games, and biked or walked everywhere. Always, the beach beckoned for bodysurfing or collecting critters in the beachfront tidal pools. The girls all wore modest one-piece bathing suits. We went steady, which only meant that you could hold hands and kiss, and broke up and then played Spin the Bottle at one of the more promiscuous house parties so we could go steady again. We were tasting the goodness of life and had no secrets to keep.

At the Corner of Paradise and Purgatory

St. George's is a parochial high school, literally located at the corner of Paradise and Purgatory Avenues in Middletown, Rhode Island. Needless to say, given its religious orientation, school chapel sermons inevitably gravitated to our lifelong confrontation with good and bad choices, especially with those cementing our destination to Heaven or Hell. The obvious conclusion would be drawn that, similar to the physical location of our school, we would always be in juxtaposition between damnation and salvation, so we must make our choices carefully and righteously. Other than the overpowering spin-off of guilt from a recurrence of that theme, I mostly enjoyed and benefited from my years on the Hilltop, as I related in the Fiftieth Anniversary letter to my classmates:

"St. George's meant a lot to me. The academics were tough; but, in the main, the school life and traditions were noble: the sheer visage of the Old English architecture anchored by an imposing stone chapel with colossal spires and gargoyles on a hilltop overlooking the Atlantic Ocean and its beach; the Festival of the Boar's Head ('Caput apres *dei* ferro, reddens *laudes* domino... blah, blah, blah.' I bet you haven't heard that one since SG!); dance cards; daily coats and ties; board topics; afternoon teas; the Tuck Shop (Remember Dick Gregor's call over the din for a 'Shit on a Stick' and Rev. Buell's echo in the quiet of the room, as he followed Dick in, 'Make that two'?); the Butt Room; graduated privilege and responsibility; the daily assembly; the procession to meals from the common room; the majestic dining hall with raised head table, expansive stone fireplace, country/tournament flags hanging from wooden staves overhead, sculpture of St. George Slaying the Dragon over its entry door, and our names, by class, routed into separate wall panels; morning and afternoon chapel with assigned readings; on and on. As a Day Boy (Jesus, what a moniker!), I was never truly in the spirit with the rest of you, but I did enjoy your company and sick humor immeasurably during the day. Some place along the line, I ended up with a tattoo of the SG Shield on my right arm and am strongly considering a dragon for the left; think yin and yang or, in my case, twiddle dee and twiddle dumb."

Polishing Your Balls

One spring break from St. George's, my friend Mike Cottrell invited me to work with him at his parents' historic cleaning and renovation company in Newport. Among its many projects, the Vernon Company prepared Newport's famous mansions on Bellevue Avenue to receive public tours during the coming summer, as they were closed for the winter. Mike and I were assigned the project of cleaning the dining room chandeliers at The Breakers, a summer home built by Cornelius Vanderbilt II between 1893 and 1895 during the Gilded Age at a cost of more than $7 million, now equating to over $150 million when adjusting for inflation.

Everything about the place dripped of ostentatious wealth and craftsmanship. Built on a thirteen-acre estate along the famous Cliff Walk overlooking the Atlantic Ocean, The Breakers is five stories high and constructed of Indiana limestone with massive Corinthian columns, resembling a sixteenth-century Renaissance-style Italian seaside palace. The lavish seventy-room interior, 65,000 sq. ft. of living space, is decorated in French and Italian styles with priceless tapestries, fine mosaic work, irreplaceable paintings, and ornate furniture. The waterside circular colonnade within the Great Hall, incorporating multiple shades of rare marble from Italy and Africa, enclosed a flared staircase of white marble backed by a hand-sculpted marble swan that could spew champagne into the sculpted marble scallop shell basin beneath it. Vanderbilt guests had only to hold their flutes over the shell basin to receive champagne from a stream flowing out of the swan's beak. The music room was built and sumptuously decorated in real gold by artists and artisans in France and then disassembled, shipped across the Atlantic Ocean, and reassembled in Newport. The attic contained staff quarters and the mansion's innovative cisterns, along with general storage areas connected by a wooden catwalk/bridge, soaring a full story above a stained glass skylight mounted over the Grand Staircase. A smaller cistern supplied hydraulic pressure for the 1895 Otis elevator, still functioning at that time, though wired for electricity in 1933. Two larger cisterns supplied fresh and salt water to the many bathrooms in the mansion.

The dining room, where Mike and I were each employed to clean two chandeliers from separate scaffolds, was equally ostentatious. In addition to the two intimidating glass chandeliers holding, perhaps, one thousand balls and cut crystals each, the parquet ceiling tiles had individually-carved scenes on them, e.g., fox hunters on horseback with hounds running out front, mountain top stags silhouetted against a setting sun, ducks flying over marshland dotted with blinds, and the great expanse of windows held velvet curtains so massive as to require special equipment to remove them for cleaning. Thus it went for the two weeks of that spring vacation, each of us atop a scaffold, dipping our chandelier's balls, one by one, into a cleaning solution, drying it off with a cotton cloth, and returning it to the chandelier frame swaying there so high above the dining room floor. We amused ourselves by describing the small scenes depicted upon each ceiling tile, which were all but invisible to spectators on the floor below.

Quaffing a Brew with Me Mates

Slim Dusty, the venerable Australian country singer, recorded the popular drinking refrain, "I Like to Have a Beer with Duncan, 'Cause Duncan's Me Mate." Surely, there is no type of drinking in college that compares to crowding into a booth at the local beer garden to eat hot peanuts, listen to a fledgling band, and drink a cool one with your mates. For years, while I attended Michigan State, my parents thought that my checks written to the Coral Gables were for a food plan through the university. You should have seen their double take as we drove by "the largest watering hole in East Lansing" on my graduation day.

V. BEARING ARMS

Military Service

One of the great—and perhaps only—commonalities among the diverse USA population is military service to our country. It provides us with the opportunity to put aside our many differences and be forged into a common purpose. With military service, we concentrate not on what divides us, but on what we have in common. Then we put our lives on the line in unison to protect it.

Low-Water Bridge

Part of my active military duty included a stint with the Naval Investigative Service (NIS) doing background investigations on active duty U.S. Navy personnel in need of security clearances. These investigations entailed trips to each applicant's hometown to visit local law enforcement agencies, schools, churches, places of employment, and neighborhoods to develop a profile of his or her character traits, trustworthiness, loyalty, and patriotism from those individuals who knew the person best. In other words, could this citizen be tempted to betray her or his country by divulging national secrets? I am pleased to relate that we are quite nationalistic, no matter the cultural offering.

During my only trip to the Ozarks deep in Arkansas, confused about directions in the days before GPS and Map Quest, I wheeled my government car into the lot of a country store, which had smoke curling from the metal flue of a potbellied stove inside. It was cold, and as I entered wearing the prescribed topcoat, gloves, and tie, as no uniforms were allowed during investigations, the dozen or so men around the stove, all wearing denim coveralls with wool Pendleton shirts, stopped talking and turned to face me. I remembered earlier days during my youth when I would wear coveralls and patronize Gibb's Gas Station in my own hometown farming community; and when some doll or dude in a fashionable dress or coat and tie would enter, we would stare at the person's other worldliness. One of the Ozark patrons broke the silence, "Can we help you, young feller?"

"I'm looking for the Beagins' residence," I answered after removing a glove to point to a map in my hand.

"Map's no good around here," retorted my host to a chorus of subdued chuckles. "Gotta drive down to the old Tilton place, turn right onto Mayfair Drive, which winds around Limerick Hill, right again at Three Stumps Road, and then cross the low water bridge in the holler. Clem and Mattie's place is just beyond, on the left."

After repeating the directions, accompanied by many corrections, overlays, and chuckles, I asked, "How will I know the Tilton place?"

"Well son, the house and barns ain't thar n'more, but the chimney's still standin'." As I took my leave to the nods and smiles of my rapt audience, I swear I heard a hushed whisper exclaim, "That boy couldn't find dog shit in a kennel," accompanied by another chorus of unrestrained laughter that drifted outside on the cold night air.

Of course, there was no chimney at the old Tilton place or, for that matter, any sign of past human habitation at all. Mayfair Drive was anything but fair, described only by two ruts through choking forestation. Limerick Hill was a mountain with scary passage over an unimproved road. And Three Stumps? Let's just say the route was devoid of any stumps recognizable to the human eye. Neither did the valley present me with any bridge over its broad river. I was stymied and drove aimlessly forward and then backtracked until an old man in a truck, squinting at me through his window, stopped to offer the community salutation, "Can I help you, young feller?" After describing my plight, he agreed to take me across the bridge, which ended up being no bridge at all, only a built-up creek bottom. He pointed out the stone guideposts and then crossed first in his high-wheel truck. Of course, he made it without a soaking, but my lower government car wasn't so lucky and almost stalled out. He was very amused by my anguish and drove away smiling as I was left to walk the last half-mile or so uphill to the Beagins' cabin, hugging the mountainside.

When I arrived—out of breath and lugging a briefcase with interview forms—the clearing was empty save the cabin, barn, and several sheds. Tire tracks ran here and there, but there was no sign of auto, truck, or tractor. Still, a curl of smoke emanated from another metal stack, presumably over a potbellied stove. An old hound on the porch rose, tail wagging, to greet me. I knocked and then knocked again and again. As I was about to leave the porch, a female voice from behind a crack in the door uttered the now-familiar greeting, "Can I help you, young feller?" with the additional inquiry, "What's yer business up here?" I displayed my NIS badge to the crack and explained my purpose to clear a neighbor's son for top-secret duty.

"You ain't no revenuer?" she surmised.

"No, ma'am!" I said emphatically.

The door flew open, and she greeted me warmly. The cabin was dimly lit by a familiar potbellied stove and the glowing embers of an expansive stone fireplace. There were several cuts of cured and smoked meat hanging from open rafters, which gave off a pungent, but sweet, barbeque smell. I was ushered to a rocking chair near the fireplace and asked if I'd like "drink or vittles?" Though hungry, I declined politely with some concern for the condition of the meat. She whittled off a piece of meat for herself and poured a glass of clear liquid from a jug. I got out my interview forms; and we bantered congenially back and forth about her neighbor, her life, and my life. As we talked, the shadows of other people, sitting around the perimeter of the room, appeared on the walls. There were no introductions and no noise as they seemed to glide in from nowhere to an invisible seat. Eventually, at least ten people were present in a conversation being held by only two of us. At some point, another man's voice joined the dialogue and then another; and, finally, there was a whole vocal symphony from a cabin where, at first, no life appeared to exist. We had the most splendid time. Against all investigative conventions and good judgment, I did have a few pieces of smoked meat and a glass or two of 'shine. The barbecue was probably the best I've ever eaten, and the 'shine would set you free. Around midnight, they packed me a basket filled with barbecue, a Mason jar of shine, and homemade apple dolls and walked me, with flashlights, back to my car; jumpstarted it; drove it across the low water bridge; and escorted me in their several vehicles back to the paved highway. I've never enjoyed greater hospitality before or since, but you know they're probably still saying I couldn't find dog shit in a kennel; and in the Ozarks, they'd be right.

Jim Sharer Bentley

Demolition by Plastique:
The Remains of the Hotel Victoria
in Cholon, April 1, 1966

Aftermath of the Hotel Victoria Bombing, Cholon, Vietnam, April 1, 1966.

April Fool

I was an American Fighting Man in the military service of my country, sent to Southeast Asia as part of President Johnson's

Light Flashes in the Tunnel

infamous troop buildup in Vietnam from 50,000 in June to 181,000 in December 1965. My experiences in that theatre were detailed for my children in a 35-page University of West Florida term paper in Spring 1989, entitled "Tiger, Tiger Burning Bright: A Vietnam Collage from a Tiger in SE Asia during the Year of the Horse."

Upon arrival in the country, I was assigned a room in the Hotel Victoria in Cholon, a suburb of Saigon, an easy walk down Tran Hung Dao Boulevard to the MACV II compound where I worked with the Studies and Observations Group (SOG). I narrowly escaped death three times—a holy trinity. The following paragraph, taken from my term paper, describes the third time. Aside from myself, the other cast members were my roommate (Frank); another junior officer; the Marine Sergeant, who I worked with at SOG; and an old, female resident of the senior living facility behind the Hotel Victoria.

The dawn came on April 1, 1966, accompanied by the *Ack! Ack! Ack! Ack!* sound of submachine guns. As I started awake, Frank yelled at me from the bathroom, "Get up and come on in here!" I was tempted to look out front to check out the noise, but decided, instead, to heed Frank's call. We crouched down on the bathroom floor, pulling our knees up under our chests, and covering the back of our heads with our hands. Then it came, rumbling slowly up from the street, increasing in sound intensity, violently shaking the building, an explosion of enormous compression and magnitude. Within seconds, walls collapsed and were pulverized into dust, pipes burst, and the space was filled with flying debris being sucked from the building's epicenter. I screamed for God to protect me and cried like a baby, uncontrollably. My arms and back were wet; my head was throbbing; and my face, feet, and hands were stinging from the cuts and lacerations made by flying concrete, glass, splinters, and other debris.

After what seemed an eternity, I pushed up with my back through the rubble and rose up on my knees to see, dimly through a blinding cloud of dust, the wall-less framework of our hotel. I was relieved to find that my wet spots were from leaking pipes, now running uncontrolled down the remaining support beams. I saw Frank's feet, motionless, sticking out from under a door. I shook him. No response. I lifted the door. He looked at me, dazed, and said, "Hell of a bang!" We heard moaning and screams. Frank staggered up and said he was going out to investigate. I started to follow, but turned when I heard a ghastly "Ohhhhh" sound coming from a neighboring room—another occupant on hands and knees bleeding from a cut on his head, reaching out his left hand, fingers extended, his dog tags swinging rhythmically from his neck as he rocked back and forth. He was not speaking, only groaning from the pain of his lacerations. Instinctively, I grasped his extended hand and lifted his left arm over my shoulder as he rose up on rubber legs. I put my right hand around his waist as we moved together, picking our way along the catwalk, poised open above the lobby that had been the hallway to our rooms, covered with cement dust and debris. I heard the occasional explosions outside of Claymore mines, randomly scattered by the terrorists around the hotel, detonating as they were triggered by escaping Americans or by innocent bystanders, some children. I heard sirens, saw Military Police (MP) vehicles arriving as I moved with my charge, who was slowly regaining his composure, down the skeletal structure that had been our central stairway. Someone cleared a path through the lobby ahead of me as I proceeded past the sentry stand, seeing the body of our MP lying dead within it, and then to the outside. Blessedly, my passenger was able to proceed on his own to a cleared medical area where other wounded occupants were already gathering.

I was too shocked to view the specter of this scene for long, so I walked to my office in blood-soaked underwear and sat transfixed in my chair. I don't remember how the day progressed from there—only that my boss, an affable, always impeccably-dressed Air Force colonel, said in jest when he first viewed me, "Bentley, you're out of uniform!" I vaguely remember being shuttled about by the omnipresent Marine sergeant who regularly baby-sat me en route to Tan Son Nhut Air Force Base. He took me to the dispensary for medical attention; to someone's billet to get me a fresh change of clothes; and, when I could face up to it, back to the Victoria to salvage what I could of my possessions. Interestingly, when I first stepped back into my room, lighted there on the floor in a dustless circle as if someone had blown it clean, there was the framed picture of my wife and the crucifix she had given me, both undamaged. The rest of the room was rubble. I rooted around for a couple of hours, bagging up salvageable clothing and other possessions, placing the debris in a trash heap. I stared at an oil painting I purchased for my wife; it was the winner of the Asian Esso Exhibit, highlighted in greens and yellows, showing junks clustered in some distant harbor, the canvas now hanging in shreds from the frame. I started to throw it away, but looked again. *"The hell with it,"* I thought, *"I'll keep the damn thing and see if I can get it repaired."*

As I limped from the building for the last time, stiff and sore all over, the sergeant helping me along, one of the old folks came through the open lobby from the back of the building, carrying the manger scene of the Christ Child that my wife had sent me to celebrate Christmas. I have no idea how she knew that it was mine, since there was no name on it and she had obviously recovered it from the ground after the explosion. She bowed politely and offered it to me. I held it momentarily and then impulsively handed it back to her. She smiled a toothless smile that went around her head several times. She bowed and then hugged me. It was a devastating moment, the first time that I had been touched with love in seven months; and, for that short time, I was no longer the stranger in a strange land. We had enjoyed true communion of spirit, me and my Guardian Angel, my Tra, my Uat Luy Good Spirit of the Apricot Trees behind the Victoria.

Welcome Home

Perhaps the most repugnant element of military service during the Vietnam Era was the growing antiwar movement that spawned virulent demonstrations against veterans returning from the war zone. To return from the recurrent trauma of battle, blood, and death to an angry mob of your countrymen booing you, holding hate signs and throwing objects to denounce your role, was almost worse than the war itself. So, from all of us sent out to protect your freedoms—including speech—in a foreign land, here's a fond little return message for our beloved antiwar protestors who so warmly greeted us upon our return from Southeast Asia to hang on the doorknob above your welcome mat: "Eat shit and die, you crass, low-life c&#%!@!" Instead of confronting us, you should have had the decency to petition (another freedom) the officials you elected to office that sent us as your pawns into battle.

To the woman who hit me on the head with a Coke bottle as I stared at your cavernous, open mouth in disbelief, "I hope you get sucked into a gang war inconsequential to you without police protection where both sides think you are the instigator. Have a nice day! Don't stain my life with your existence."

Here Come Da King

During my Navy duty at the Joint Strike Command, which controls US military response to crises in the Middle East, there was much ado and a lot of advance planning around a visit by King Hussein of Jordan and his entourage. As a junior officer on a staff of mostly senior, multi-service officers and civilian personnel, I was normally always nervous. But, in this instance, I was extremely nervous. I was assigned to be part of a four-hour briefing for the king and his entourage on tactical readiness amidst a cluster of other country analysts/briefers. All personnel at the Command received schooling in royal etiquette and in the expectation that no junior officer, or other such underling, should address the king directly. Rather, if he approached, we were ordered to step aside and brace ourselves at attention with eyes forward until he had passed. In spite of my meticulous preparation for the briefing, I was in a state of near-shock when my turn to speak came. Even with notes in front of me, my mind went blank, and I fumbled with the words and the map pointer in my hand. To make matters worse, senior military and State Department officers interrupted me to correct some of my many blunders and misstatements, and there was the usual snickering and ribbing at my expense.

When the questions and laughter had subsided, I took my seat again, wet with perspiration, never so glad before or since to be through with an embarrassing situation. The briefings droned on and on for hours on end, all in deadly earnest after the mirth that I had afforded them. I was left to wallow in the misery of my failed effort, still sweating profusely, while the other briefers pretty much ignored me. I realized during the introspection of those moments that I was never going to make or couldn't make the Navy a career. A great burden was lifted, and I instantly stopped trembling. After the briefing had concluded and summary remarks were made by ambassadors, embassy and State Department officials, admirals, and generals, everyone arose with King Hussein in unison. He paid his customary respects all around and then strode over to where I was standing at attention. After looking at my nametag, he said, "Mr. Bentley, where do you come from in the U.S.?" "Well, King, Your Honor," I replied, "I'm from all over the U.S., anywhere that there's a naval base—Annapolis; Newport; Coronado; Norfolk; San Francisco; New Orleans; and Lapeer, Michigan, in between."

"You have no regional accent," he observed, and we carried on about prep schools and colleges and other topics, the way people do in introductory conversation. I was completely at ease with him, and the moment was a welcome respite from my earlier stress during the briefing. At some point, I noted that everyone else in the chamber was quiet and attentive, so I began to sweat again. Eventually, the king stuck out his hand, shaking mine vigorously as he said, "I enjoyed your briefing. If you are ever in Amman, please stop by the Palace for a visit." *"Right!"* I thought, *"Me, at the Palace door in Amman, Jordan, pulling a velvet bell chord and saying, 'The King asked me to call.'"* Of course, I was reprimanded for flippancy to His Royal Highness, not Your Honor, as I had addressed him, but, you know, he was the coolest dude in the whole chamber, taking his royal time to resurrect the defunct morale of a lowly junior officer. I hold his memory in highest esteem.

VI. LOOKING FOR LOVE IN ALL THE WRONG PLACES

The Perfect Man, The Perfect Woman

Ask a teen what they're honestly looking for in a mate and you get physical dimensions—no intelligence or personality qualifications—like tight abs, a nice ass, a twelve-inch waist and thirty-six-inch bust, nice body in a bikini or Speedo. Who has these dimensions except the select few? Do they breed these people on some kind of special farm? Who knew any of these people growing up in mainstream America? Although fashion photography still clings to these images, the definitions get blurred as people get older and want—instead of abs and boobs—a loving companion with a distinct measure of intelligence and personality. Still, all things being equal, I would like my companion to have some cleavage; and I'm sure she'd trade my potbelly for a ripple of abs. A little eye candy is an elixir for the soul.

Love at First Sight Is a Cruel Hoax

True love is based on initial hormones and a lot of long-term satisfactory time together. The operative word here is satisfactory.

If the sex is great but you fight over everything else, the hormones will eventually wither and die. Without friendship and respect in the bond, divorce is inevitable. Please remember that there is a thin line between love and hate which, seemingly, can be breached during but an instant of marital discord or inattentiveness. Good unions require constant attention and are a profession of two within themselves.

Two Minuses Don't Always Make a Plus

You remember the multiplication of signs rule in algebra, but you can't apply it to human nature. It's better chemistry between couples if opposites attract, not two zany, psychotic harpies that will tear at each other until the relationship implodes, if one ever existed.

You're OK, But I'm Perfect

I acknowledge your intellectual mastery, social standing, and physical superiority over me. Nevertheless, I am unwilling to admit that your demeanor exceeds mine in any way.

Eye Candy

The physically beautiful woman is a goddess of delight to wearisome men; but the well-composed, attractive woman of intelligence and letters brings that sparkle to her beauty that provides ultimate and lasting delight.

True Beauty

True beauty cometh from within our being. It's a bit scary

that glamour modeling for adolescent girls has evolved to an image of big boobs; flawless faces and teeth; long, willowy, hairless legs; and invisible waists. They're adorned with designer clothes, exotic haircuts, exquisite makeup, and expensive jewelry. They are always shown inhabiting the drawing rooms of those equally good-looking and presumably wealthy men who have adorned their own lives with them. A perfectly-matched set of beautiful people. Where do these models come from, and who decreed their visual prominence? No mention of physical accomplishments or education is ever made for us to applaud in addition to their manicured exterior. Is the inside of a mirror the outside? Are they bred in a special lab through some gene-alteration project? What happened to the hale and hearty farm girls with deep-dimpled cheeks and engaging personalities who bubbled out of a stocky frame; sat next to us boys in school, usually making better grades; and tried everything and did everything the boys did—who could spit further, punch harder, and laugh longer? I'm talking about the girls with grit and grandeur, women who could drive a tractor and back a hay wagon into a barn, herd cattle and shear sheep, then throw on a dress and perfume for a dance at the Armory. These girls were your friends who could tell a dirty joke and smoke a cigar without losing their femininity. These girls went to college to pursue their dreams and, frequently, to move on to corporate America, politics, medicine, or the space program. They are the truly beautiful women of America! I'd like to see a fashion magazine presenting a line of designer clothes on accomplished female models that are currently cowgirls, astronauts, CEOs, scientists, or medical doctors. They may not be thin or willowy, their hair and makeup might be nonexistent; but their intelligence and humanity would radiate like the sun. Now, that's true beauty!

Girls That Are Friends, Not Girlfriends

One of the great, although mortifying, gifts that our mother gave to Freddums and me was her insistence that we take dancing lessons. Against our vehement protests, she enrolled us in teen dancing classes offered at the Officer's Club aboard the Newport, Rhode Island, Naval Base by a husband-wife dance team known as The Champlains. For a price—which I'm sure our father resented, albeit quietly—Mom was able to take us to the Navy Base Club weekly for several months so we could get our dose of humiliation on the dance floor. The Champlains paired us with different partners at each outing as they floated from couple to couple, lifting arms, adjusting chins, coaxing better posture, demonstrating the dance without music, and then demonstrating it with music, before setting us off as couples in motion, again and again. Our initial embarrassment wore off as we got to know one another and, more importantly, as we gained confidence in our abilities on the dance floor. Most of us were eventually able to perform the traditional ballroom dance steps of the day, circa 1952, when Fred was in sixth grade and I was in ninth grade: Cha Cha Cha, Foxtrot, Rumba, Samba, Tango, Viennese Waltz, even the Bunny Hop, the Hokey Pokey, and the Jitter Bug.

Beyond dance instruction, Mom would routinely set me up with blind dates, usually as an escort to a dance being held at the Officer's Club during holidays, when her friend's daughters were home on vacation. Her admonition to my resistance was always the same, "It's just a date. You're not getting married. You'll learn something more about women and doubtless, whether you like her or not, come away with greater insight to the opposite sex. She comes from a lovely family and is very accomplished in her own right. Whether there are sparks or not, she will advance you as a human being. Learn well!"

I never completely understood this message, but I did learn a lot about the female gender and did come to respect women over men as I made many female friends. At a time when women's independence was limited and phoning men was taboo, I was proud that my female friends were comfortable phoning me to ask for rides to dances and other venues. I specifically remember, when I had the only driver license, being organized by my lady friends on many occasions to chauffeur them en masse from Newport to Sakonnet during the summer dance season. Employing another maternal admonition, when I picked up girls for these trips, I went to their front door; rang the bell; and met the parents. As Mom emphasized to me, "Look steadfastly into their eyes, shake their hands firmly, explain where you're going, and when you expect to bring their daughters back home. Change your plans accordingly at their behest."

Because of those damn dance lessons, I was always the first to be asked to start dancing with one of my female friends, where the sexes were usually gathered separately on opposite sides of the ballroom, starring at each other in frozen gridlock. Because of this imprint from my mother, I was always in the know about social happenings, as women communicate better than men; and God knows, I have always loved women! Thanks, Mom.

Women

What man will broach the subject of women with authority?

It's the mystery of their elusive behavior and thought patterns that has perplexed all mankind throughout time. Most guys will admit to knowing a little or a lot about many subjects, but nothing about women. That's why you'll hear some men say that they enjoy pussy, but not what's attached to it. A Navy Chief warned his Officer Candidates at OCS, "Nothing is more overrated or punishing than a piece of ass!" We apply all of our acumen to their pursuit and conquest, only to find ourselves under their control and domination. Equality is not an option. Women rule! A teenage female cashier at Walmart, upon hearing an old male customer say, "Men should never argue with women," smiled beguilingly and countered, "You're lucky to have learned that before it was too late. Some men never learn it." It makes me wonder what too late means. And please don't say that God is an unforgiving woman!

Enough Is Enough!

Ever been shopping with some doe-eyed lovebird who's looking for the perfect gift for his lady? Well, I was invited, or rather taken along, on such an excursion. Generally speaking, men's gifting for females is a blind swing at a piñata, except for a few creative types who seem to have a knack for it. Well, Paul is creative and did seem to be moving mentally toward choosing the perfect handbag for Brigette. We traversed patiently—or, should I say, Paul traversed patiently—through several department stores and women's shops looking for the one bag that would open her heart. As I mostly sat idly by staring at the marvelous presentation of cleavage confronting us (women actually do shop en masse in women's apparel stores), Paul would converse with sales women and hold up this or that bag for my inspection. Frankly, they all looked the same to me: a large compartment with carrying strap in different colors. I continued to nod incoherently until Paul suggested I hold each bag on my arm so he could see them in use. Well, as I began to model the bags, the atmosphere changed and women began to frown upon me with disdain and to walk away from us in a huff. "That's it," I said, "No more cleavage, no more holding bags!"

Women Always Take the High Road

It is wrong, of course, for men to put women on a pedestal, because there are some dirty and underhanded scoundrels among the female sex as well; but, as a class, women are generally more noble, big-hearted, and long-suffering than men. Most men recognize this from infancy because of their mother. It may be the chemistry of childbirth, whether executed or not, that makes women generally more communicative and insightful. Women seem more suited for leadership because they can enjoin wider viewpoints from traditional networking without threat to their persona. Men sometimes make decisions too quickly without wide consideration and tend to defend untenable decisions longer to preserve ego. Women communicate exhaustively over the widest issues (think shopping); change quickly from untenable positions; and consider a "no" as the first step in a negotiation that will, ultimately, change to a "yes." Most men will wilt away from a "no" without further pursuit, perhaps because their mothers so thoroughly acclimated them to this response. In any event, most women will persevere toward noble ends that male counterparts abandon early.

Jim Sharer Bentley

Grace Kelly Loved Me First

 I believe it was the summer of 1956. I had just graduated from St. George's School in Newport and was employed again as an alley boy at Hazard's Beach on the Atlantic Ocean. My daily trip to and from the beach was made on a Hawthorne bicycle along Bellevue Avenue and Ocean Drive, famous the world over for their ornate mansions surrounded by manicured grounds. Each mansion is an audacious display of pomp and wealth to the extreme along the entire length of the avenue that parallels the famous Cliff Walk fronting the Atlantic Ocean. None of the mansions was more audacious than The Breakers, built by Cornelius Vanderbilt II, or the Marble House Mansion built by William K. Vanderbilt. The latter is enclosed by a tall marble wall, complete with a set of ornate gold-tipped cast-iron gates facing Bellevue Avenue. It was at these open gates, during production of the movie *High Society*, that I was stopped one afternoon by a cavalcade of limos entering the grounds. After the gatekeeper stopped me while beckoning the line of limousines forward, I sat on my bicycle and blankly watched the procession from my close vantage point. Suddenly, the whole shebang stopped as the limos were, apparently, backed up from the front of the Marble House. The limo stopping directly in front of me revealed the blonde locks of a woman engaged in animated conversation with a gent seated beside her. As I watched, she turned abruptly to look out the window into my eyes. Never had I been confronted with so beautiful a visage then or since; and, as I must have appeared wide-eyed and open-mouthed to her, Grace Kelly simply smiled and blew me a kiss from a gloved hand as the cavalcade started moving again. Needless to say, I have never washed off that kiss; and the story of her kindness to an ardent teenage fan has reverberated to any ear with the patience to listen. So many times have I recounted it, along with my meeting King Hussein of Jordan, that son Paul suggested I identify them as Story #1 and Story #2 so, when feeling inclined to retell them, I can simply mention the number and everyone present will nod knowingly without being tortured by the lengthy details.

Free Love Is an Oxymoron

The practice of copulating without benefit of clergy is no less free of charge or obligation than a free lunch. Any act or commitment of love-giving or lovemaking requires an offering from the soul as well as the body. Aside from the physical exertions of lovemaking, even platonic love-giving in friendship exacts a toll in anguish, contemplation, energy, time, and resources. We offer our health and ethereal qualities to our family, friends, and lovers in exchange for a similar return. Like tending a garden, each piece of ourselves we give away requires constant nurturing, just as our support group nurtures the piece of themselves that they have invested in us.

Western Dating

The hormones rage, and we follow the fads of fashion and talk, chilling in pretended nonchalance, stepping outside ourselves to be noticed, to get dates, to be on the in crowd. We sort amongst each other, trading glamour traits like playing cards, like we actually had them. Life is a stage, especially teen life where so many princes are looking for the celebrated Queen Olivia in a

Grease movie and so many princesses are kissing frogs to find their one true love and live happily ever after. Given our fifty-percent divorce rate and the costs associated with traditional Western engagements and weddings, with the subsequent division of children and property, it would seem that the nuclear family would fare better under the ancient precepts of prearrangement by the families and community. The chastity belt and vows should be returned to tradition and a Common Good Law should require all couples to be certified friends before lovers.

The Dichotomy of Love

    Love's impatient, love's *not* kind;
    Love can easily blow your mind.
    It boasts the most tormented state
    The mind or body can relate,
    And, as for pride's cosmetic part,
    Resentment in a lust-grown heart,
    Comparing yourself against your brother
    To garner points with which to cover
    Up the promise of another.
    Envious, boastful, arrogant love,
    The kind *not coming* from above,
    It's bad.

    And, yet, one taste of love inspired,
    Heaven-sent that is required
    To be so patient, truthful, kind,
    So all-embracing where one finds

No envy, boasting, pride or wrong;
Only rejoicing in hope and song
That perseveres as we travel along.
Now, that's the love that bears defending
And lights the way for love unending.
It's good.

Love Is Not Always About Making Love

The two walked hand-in-hand, arms around each other, laughing, smiling demurely, and gently nudging each other in playful affection. Their progress along the city's darkened streets was in the semi-still of evensong, very little traffic and fewer people, only lovers kissing on park benches and under street lamps. But on they went, the man tenderly pulling up his lady's collar against the cold, the woman slowly, methodically stroking his back. When they came to a shadowed doorway under an aged marquee, their vapored breath intertwining in the frigid night air, they traced the building's side alleyway around to the rear where the man, temporarily removing his arm from his companion's shoulder to grope in his pants for a key, opened the door. They entered upon some dressing rooms en route to a stage; but, before advancing, they stopped in one of the dressing rooms with a bed where, watching him intently, she removed her scarf and slowly unbuttoned her coat, which he removed while kissing her lightly on the forehead. Coyly, she began unbuttoning his coat, casually tossing it on the bed and hugging him as he enfolded her in loving arms. After what seemed an eternity, they slowly parted and entered into the dark arena, clasping each other, feeling of silhouettes in the dark, her holding tight while removing her shoes and him running silent fingers over a silken surface and down a fluted leg, finally lifting the cover and racing his sweaty hands over the dim whiteness, feeling every curve and crevice and, finally, bending to assume a bowed position as she began to twist and turn before him in the waning light, her breathing increasing in intensity, lifting her legs, bending her torso and exposing her radiant whiteness to his steady gaze. He then flipped a switch and turned a knob. The dimmed stage lights grew slowly brighter as the ballerina continued practicing her pirouettes and undulating dance steps in sync with the melody arising from her father's fingers as he played the old theater's grand piano in celebration of his daughter's return to her first love (ballet and dance) after years of childrearing. He had, after all, been her long-time mentor and pianist, not to mention her biggest fan.

VII. CHASING THE DOLLAR

Success Is Not a One-Answer Quiz

Contrary to what your successive math teachers taught you through grade school and high school, life itself does not present just one answer for success. Each individual pursues a different course by accident or intent to find success and, more importantly, happiness. It's talent, training, motivation, circumstances, or all of the above that will lead one, usually blind and stumbling, into that end of a satisfying work life.

Damaged Goods

We jump in early and eagerly, trying to make a name for ourselves at this or that visionary task, whether a profession, a marriage, a home project, a hobby, or an educational opportunity. But, somehow along the way, we can get diverted, derailed, and defunct. Mistakes or shoddy workmanship, sickness, slacking, inattentiveness, or inactivity cause disruption and failure. We become marked, as if with the scarlet letter *F* for failure. We grow into the moniker, and our lives assume this direction. We are damaged and remain so until diverted again by some positive catalyst, a person with faith in us or some errant success, that changes our mindset to an *S* for success.

Let Someone Else Share Your Pride

We all champion the underdog who, justifiably, is proud to have surmounted incredible odds and prevailed at the challenge. Furthermore, we must have some pride to support our own self-esteem, which is paramount to a normal equilibrium. However, overt manifestation of pride—that is to say, bragging and challenging equal accomplishment by others—is tantamount to treason. Modest pride is laudable, but boastful pride goeth before a fall. If you are good, people will know it, applaud you, and share your success with others; but if a swollen pride in yourself is your only lamp, others will avoid you and your disease as if it were leprosy.

Black Velvet Gloves

The District School Food Services Director participated, along with each principal, in most school cafeteria manager appointments; and the district was blessed with a significant number of outstanding black managers during the regular school year.

One spring, Susan, a notable black manager of a large inner city school cafeteria, visited the director to inquire about summer manager appointments. Summer feeding was accomplished by only a few base kitchens that transported packaged meals to numerous small programs, mostly at school sites. At the time, summer base kitchens were chosen solely by virtue of their satellite experience during the regular school year. The director explained that only those base kitchens satelliting meals during the regular year would be used during the summer. "But," said Susan, "regular year bases all have white managers, and our black managers feel that we are being purposefully shut out of summer employment. I personally don't think it's true, and I respect you too much to let that rumor circulate."

It never dawned on me! Of course, she was right; and of course, we then developed satellite bases with black managers and established a manager rotation schedule during the summer that ensured equal employment opportunity. It was my first experience with Affirmative Action, and I loved it that Susan handled me with kid gloves rather than let the injustice fester and descend into the widespread ill will bred by formal grievance hearings.

Two Cents Worth

During the time when I was laboring in the vineyard of food services, I was requested to attend the district's often virulent school board meetings as an informational resource. Like professional baseball, these public meetings were largely boring, with routine business; budget discussions; and education presentations, occasionally laced with fevered activity and outbursts. Agenda outlines were published before each meeting, so there were few attendees and an almost formal pall under the dim boardroom lights when a noncontroversial litany of subjects was offered up. In contrast, proposals of new pay schedules, school closures, department consolidations, or any school issue peaking badly with any individual or group would enliven the meetings exponentially. For a widely debated issue, the crowds would swell to standing room only, often overflowing into outside halls where wall speakers broadcast the proceedings.

The public forum, my favorite part, came at the start, after prayers and pledge. Forum speakers filled out an introductory form with their name, organization if appropriate, and intended message for future meeting minutes. No personal attacks by name were permitted, three minutes was allocated to each speaker, and the school board's attorney moderated for compliance. No response was to be solicited or received, but district representatives were often assigned future liaison duty with speakers or board members might answer a simple misunderstanding. The crowds often punctuated passionate speeches with booing or cheers, which created an electric atmosphere. The crescendo rose and fell based upon the issue or the speaker's ability to incite agreement, with some citizens refusing to leave the podium at their bell. During these contentious times, the sheriff's deputy assigned to the meeting would escort malcontents from the room.

The public forums never failed to arouse passion, to provide focus from the many onto the plight of the few, to change opinions and incite debate. I loved it! You couldn't come up with these kinds of diametrical opposites in a soap opera. Every manner of minuscule and major concern was embraced in a wide-ranging discussion that allowed every interested party their two cents worth of advice. It was the best of America, and it beats anything on TV.

Yammering and Clamoring

During my stay with Paul and his then girlfriend, now wife,

Brigette in New York City, it became apparent that Brigette enjoyed her job and the people related to it, while Paul was miserable doing his job and dealing with an exacting and difficult boss. Taking photographs of commercial properties for real estate multiple listing services (MLS) will often challenge some individual's perceived right to privacy. Paul was frequently embroiled in explaining the legalities of privacy to commercial property owners when taking his photos or explaining the nature of his art to a boss that had never done it. He told me that he had become immune to the caustic remarks, which he never seemed able to diffuse. His words struck a chord in my soul, causing me to recall, in sympathy, my years of public service in school feeding where an ever-present timbre of naysaying rose and fell in a daily crescendo of complaints from an unhappy few. I agreed with Paul that naysayers can become invisible, even within adjacent spaces, and their words while yammering and clamoring can eventually fall on deaf ears. Blessedly, most human interactions are uplifting; but unfortunately, one only remembers the clutch of antagonists that, like small dogs with sharp teeth, grab your ankle at each meeting and never let go until you drift mindlessly away.

The Macro-Micro Combo

Surely it's as much of a dance as the Macarena or the Electric Slide. We shuffle through a human wonderland of skyscrapers whilst tripping over our beer cans and other disposable waste on the ground. Remember the wall signs in kindergarten? Unless you stop-look-listen, you'll miss seeing the forest as you avoid the rocks and roots on the path. While the city skyline is beautiful from the water, we are mostly consumed with meeting agendas, grocery lists, and electric bills, otherwise known as narrowing the gap. It's a challenge to see the whole from the sum of its parts!

Home Is Where the Heart Is

Not quite! It is where you make and share your memories with loved ones, where you pursue dreams, where you entertain and insulate yourself. But home is also where you store your food and take your meds; escape the cold, heat, and wet of inclement weather (sometimes for months at a time); assemble your stuff; and lay down your head. Home is your touchstone, your well, the display case of your life. In his Spring 2007 *Ocean Conservancy* article on the return of the ringed seals to their same pupping grounds every year, Noah Buhayar defines home the best for me as, "a sentiment of habit, familiar actions centering on a place and tied to the most primal of necessities: food, shelter, kinship. Even the most temporary or rudimentary home—whether built of wood, stone, or carved out of snow—is a nexus for satisfying these needs."

Small Towns

It is a famous track from John Cougar Mellencamp and, more so, a mental track from the majority of humanoids on the globe. Small towns, lacking in all the sophistication and diverse culture of the big cities, are nonetheless the breeding ground for self-identity and confidence. As I said to son-in-law Dave's New York City attorney colleague from the U.S. State Department while sitting at the bar of McGuire's Irish Pub in Pensacola, Florida, "When you get tired of big city multiplicity, come down here; and I'll cure you with some sameness."

The Small Town Is Our Womb

Even big cities are reduced to their composite boroughs or counties to offer, in some measure, the familiarity of neighborhood living and services. We like our ice cream cones hand-packed and our barber to be our friend. It's reassuring to see your doctor, banker, neighbors, and relatives at church, while shopping, or at the community watering hole. It's important to anchor your life to the traditions of your forebears—their schools, their jobs, their playgrounds, their cemetery. And, of course, there must be a Main Street to seal the deal.

Bagelheads

Talk about a warm fuzzy! It's one of those places that click in time and space, where everyone can eat and be comfortable with a newspaper in solitude or chatty with friends, family, business associates. There are old people, babies with their parents, teenagers, mid-lifers, whole families, coats and ties, board shorts and flip-flops, gorgeous people, and dumpy people. Its primary offering is coffee and bagels; but there is a host of bottled, upscale beverages and sandwiches, something for everyone, plus a stunning view of Pensacola Bay and the three-mile Pensacola Bay Bridge to Gulf Breeze. The fans whir, the patrons talk and read and stare as they eat and drink, and the owners and their retinue of young employees treat everybody grandly while the doors open and close continually with the draw of it all.

The Dirty Whore Social Club

As Lisa tells it, she and Brigette were talking about a common acquaintance, carefully describing her underhanded social traits, when Brigette blurted out, "She's nothing but a dirty whore!" A later telling of the story made me laugh so much that I began to refer to the Wednesday morning gathering of family and friends at Bagelheads as The Dirty Whore Social Club. The moniker has spread far and wide in spite of the fact that its authoress has never joined us there for coffee, company, or a bagel—not to mention bragging rights.

Key Lime High

Of course, the way to a man's heart (actually, any living entity's heart) is through his stomach. Even plants are charged during photosynthesis by adding a little sugar to their water. It's rare to meet people who don't relish desserts or some other confection. The horizon of sweets, and the purveyors who offer them, is almost limitless. Stirring arguments debate the merits and demerits of this or that cookie, cake, cobbler, pie, candy, sauce, ice cream, roll, or pastry. Freddums and I were raised by a mother who always included dessert with each meal. Her confections were divine to say the least, coming from a repertoire of recipes collected from many sources over forty years, including a hand-written recipe for Tollhouse Cookies from Ruth Wakefield, who originated it at her New England restaurant of the same name.

Many of our mother's pie recipes came from truck stops while en route coast to coast between Navy duty stations, including her coconut creme, lemon ice box, and lemon meringue pies. My brother and I had an enviable childhood education in confections, succeeded for me by MeMa Nickelsen's mouthwatering pecan balls, by Aunt Teresa Banfell's delectable calamondin pie, by MeMe Garrison's complete dining presentation and perfected in all its glory by the dessert chef ("What is that masked woman's name?" That'd be Trina.) at the Fish House in Pensacola, Florida, with her tart key lime pie. Its consumption is a little taste of heaven! Hopefully, you deserve it.

VIII. SPAWNING GROUND

True Love is Fifty-Fifty

Of course, there's love at first sight, love in the later years, love between the old and young, love within the sexes, and unconventional love. The first strike to the heart is usually physical with a touch of personality to stir the fire. Lasting love, all those metaphysical qualities binding honor, fidelity, and good will, take time for the mind to discover and savor. Deeper love's treasure, like good wine in an oak cask, gets better with time. The one-hearted companionship of a supportive mate enhances and transcends the physical and eventually, in the twilight years, replaces it completely. True love is fifty-fifty—fifty-percent heart and fifty-percent mind. The body is just along for the ride.

Throwing Down the Anchor

Kids today are smarter. Not only did the age of technology bring infinite information to their fingertips through the Internet, but historic soaring divorce rates have slowed the progress of marriage as the only family institution. Living together and enjoying children without benefit of clergy is a lifestyle largely promoted by our celebrities. Adoptions are up among not only opposite and same sex couples, but singles, as well; and adopting the world's parentless children may be nobler than the romantic image of marriage and a conjugal family. Those who opt for children now appear to be limiting their number to one or two for a quality versus a quantity experience. Nonetheless, whether one or a dozen, in or out of a conventional marriage, child rearing is a time-consuming, full-on experience requiring all the energy supporting adults can muster. As a child invokes the family circle, supporting adults must throw down their anchor, for single life as they knew it will be over forever after. No blissful ride into the sunset here, just falling exhausted into bed—albeit with pleasant dreams, for nothing is as self-satisfying as shaping the destiny of a child.

Why Stay-At-Home Parents Are Predisposed to Alcoholism

Certainly, this is no revelation for anyone who has wrestled with a teething baby, not to mention a grade schooler or teen. Kids are full-on from the get-go! Nothing is more exhausting or painful than a contentious baby who is sick or teething—worse, if both. The bloodcurdling cries go right to your inner ear; and simple chores like changing diapers, dressing, rocking them in your arms, or play become nigh on impossible. Holding the wiggling child is like trying to put a leotard on an octopus. You must pity the red-eyed child with a runny nose and irate disposition who needs both medicine and sleep; but pity more the parent who has to administer the Rx elixir or put the child down for a nap. Changing a poopy diaper with kicking legs, hitting a flailing mouth with a medicine dropper, remaining sane and calm with a screaming baby who won't eat, nap, or be distracted with play—we're talking Herculean child-rearing talent here, not second in energy to competing in a triathlon or running back-to-back marathons. Women are better at it than men. They went through the labor, so their threshold for pain is higher; but both parents are subject to mental paralysis. It gives you true understanding of why some forlorn parents despair and drop their kids off at a convent or orphanage with a note stating, "I don't have it in me anymore to raise this kid." Still, if you don't have it in you to purge yourself of your plight, a little early afternoon alcohol does take the edge off child rearing.

Period. The End.

Child rearing is a series of confrontational situations between the world's longest-standing adversaries, parents and their children. It is the child's job to test and continually push the limits of acceptable language and behavior. It is the parents' job to set and maintain those limits, from their personal palette of cultural and religious values and usually within societal norms.

Contrary to the scores of child development classes at all educational levels, the multitude of books and the plethora of ongoing magazine articles on the subject, the professional lectures, and videos for rent, child rearing is not an exact science. It is instead a custom job that differs by culture, laws, religious persuasion, and situation and, mostly, by the influence that parents or trustees can wield over their charges. No two childhood destinies, even within the same family group, are shaped in quite the same way.

Children are wily and persistent at gaining the widest possible berth in their freedoms. Adults are equally persistent at confining their charges to acceptable behavior and curbing, if they can, life beyond the limits. Of course, within the control group, infractions of the behavior code, and associated punishments for violating it, can differ from total intolerance with brutal punishment to limitless negotiation with no punishment. Since it takes a village to raise a child, it is often the village that must exact control of wayward children. Some parents are so permissive that their child's only modification comes from neighbors, teachers, and officers of the court. On the other hand, the controls within some family groupings are so regimented and unforgiving that all creativity and free expression is removed from its individuals. Dire consequences can result in heinous punishments for going awry: beatings; the shame of ridicule that can cement entire generations against each other; confinement to attic, basement, or closets; and arduous chores. Permissive adults try to influence behavior through negotiation while strict parents set a web of rules around their expectations and punish in accord with the degree of violation. One adult cajoles the child with candy or other rewards for helping with household chores, getting good grades, performing well in sports. Another adult threatens spankings, more chores, and house confinement if poor grades or performance befall the child.

Thankfully, children seem to thrive under all forms of child rearing, in spite of some scars and mental aberrations, which begs the conclusion that the key to it all is consistency.

Whether you tediously explain the horizon of outcomes to the child's question, "Can I...?" with the hope that he or she will not pursue it or whether you simply say, "No...because I said so! Period. The end," the health of the child remains the same.

And, to any reader who happens to have made it this far

through my hallucinatory tunnel of random thoughts, I can assure you that your health will also remain undiminished as a result of suffering my mental aberrations. Period. The end.

Captain of the Turd Patrol

God doth have a sense of humor, given our chameleon-like color changes in roles and stations during a varied life. You might be or have been a storied executive supervising hundreds of people, a fabled actor or musician with enviable credits, a surgeon of longstanding and lifesaving prowess, a professional athlete known the world over, a Nobel Peace Prize winner, or a Teacher of the Year—whatever—but at home, among your family and true friends, you are just plain folks. You share the home and child-rearing duties like everyone else. It's your week to take out the garbage, do the dishes, vacuum, change the baby, pick up groceries, take the kids to soccer practice, mow the lawn, walk the dog and, oh yes, pick up those dog turds during the walk and in the backyard so nobody steps on them or you don't sling them on yourself while mowing. Captain of Industry to Captain of the Turd Patrol. It might just as well be, and appropriately so, inscribed on your name plate and office door under your other title, say, Director of School Food Services.

Anything for Pumpkin

We all have that short list of people for whom we would jump up and run. It can be the widest spectrum of people whose magnetic field keeps you coming back: a favorite uncle, a loving mother, a sibling, a friend, a teacher, a child. Paul was the youngest child, born when his father turned forty years of age, seemingly at the last stop on life's commuter line, who singly turned that life back into the great adventure of catching turtles and eating ice cream.

Why the Turtle Is My Friend

For one thing, I don't work at the speed of light, so slow and easy is my life. What other animal more closely emulates slow and easy than the turtle? For another thing, Paul was born during my change of life epoch. It's that time runners call hitting the wall, when you realize or suspect that you've wrung as much out of life as you're going to in terms of fame, success, income, all of that. What are left are the bit parts; the slide into retirement; and, of course, doing the stuff at hand that gives you joy. Well, there isn't more joy to be had for a forty-something man than to have a child around to take turtle hunting.

Paul and I had every kind of net, up to a monster twenty-foot-long, telescoping, wide-mouth, fine-mesh aluminum dip net, available to hunt and secure the elusive turtles in our West Florida neighborhood. We caught mud turtles, red-and-yellow-eared sliders, alligator and common snapping turtles, the exotic Florida soft-shells, endangered gopher tortoises, and the famous Eastern box turtles (Terrapin Carolina). We made separate pens with ponds for them in our live oak grove and tended our friends religiously. Paul even tended a blind turtle named Bates, whose eyes had been shot out by kids with BB guns. He obtained a reference book on turtles and their care from a local pet store as a trade for some of his adolescent sliders. All in all, we accumulated and fed perhaps 150 to 200 turtles, which we eventually released back into those wild places we'd like to live if we were turtles, remote swamp and water wonderlands removed from kids with BB guns.

My last turtle—a Florida soft-shell named The Man, who was caught by Paul when he worked at the local Tiger Point Golf Club—was in my second-floor bedroom on Santa Rosa Sound when the house was demolished by Hurricane Ivan. Paul and I never found The Man's twenty-gallon aquarium in a debris field that sprawled a quarter-mile into the woods across Soundside Drive. Our hope was that, since he had grown from three to nine inches in diameter over his ten years in captivity, he might have ridden the tidal surge to an inland swamp to survive.

Bridging the Communication Gap

My attending a parochial high school was my mother's idea and was initiative for her and our father to make the supreme financial sacrifice to send my brother and me to St. George's outside Newport. I was a Day Boy, or non-boarder, there for my four years of high school. Although I was not, strictly speaking, in the mainstream of school life, as I was missing the residential experience during evenings and weekends, I was nonetheless proud and fortunate to graduate from St. George's in 1956. Its campus and traditions were ennobling; and its crest, which we wore on our blazer pocket, was eye-catching. The only body jewelry adorning boys in the fifties anywhere were ID bracelets, wristwatches, and finger rings. This entire prelude is to say that, years later, when my last child Paul was eighteen and I was approaching sixty, Paul threw down the generational gauntlet. It is one of those communication moments frozen in mental time.

We were at Olive Garden in Pensacola, Florida, eating dinner with his mother and Aunt Teresa Banfell. To rev up the waning conversation, I asked Paul if his recent ear piercings meant he was getting too much in touch with his feminine side. He said, "You wouldn't understand, Pop. It's a generational thing. Something you'd never do!"

We went back and forth, with Susan and Teresa goading us on, until I said, "Okay, I won't do both; but I will get one ear pierced just to show you that fifties guys can be cool, too. Where can we go to get it done?" We went directly from the Olive Garden to Spencer's in Cordova Mall, where another teenage boy, charged with doing the piercing, kept saying, "My grandfather would never consider this! Are you sure you want to do it?" In fairness, I must say that I almost chickened out several times after thinking about repercussions at work; but I finally got my left ear pierced and purchased a small loop earring to put in the hole.

That single act changed the way I was treated and the way I viewed life. I have become younger at heart and more acceptable to youth, more attuned to the vitality within me. Neither was it a surprise, while I visited Paul later in Jacksonville during his time at the University of North Florida, that we visited a local tattoo parlor frequented by and in company of Paul's friend, Joey Puzy, to get our ceremonial tattoos. Mine is the St. George's Crest. It is personal, ennobling, and it adds to my youthful demeanor and vitality. I asked the tattoo artist if he could inscribe the words, "St. Jimbo for Hire—Saving Ladies from Dragons" around the crest. The half-naked biker sitting in the next chair, a 300-pound, long-haired behemoth with tattoos covering most of his arms and torso—one, notably a cobra with a flared hood and red eyes crawling through a steer skull—said without hesitation, "Don't add any words. They would detract from the beauty and simplicity of the crest itself." Paul and the tattooist agreed, so the crest remained pure. Once more, I was saved from myself by an angel in the next chair.

When It Is More Blessed to Receive Than Give

It's important always to thank those who support you in their myriad of ways with cards, flowers, and gifts, but I'm always put off guard by someone who gives me a gift out of the blue because I'm immediately conjuring up what I've done to deserve it. We all do without measure, and with infinite pleasure, for our children, expecting only a good citizen for the world in return. Can there be a better gift for a parent than an unfettered offering from their child which says, over and over, as you read the inscription while turning it in your hand: "May you keep your dreams alive and real. Here we go, then, while we may, through the iron gates of life."

IX. THE FALLOUT FROM A NATURAL DISASTER

The Magic of Wood

Wood is a gift from Earth's great patriarchs in the forest. It has sheltered and warmed us for centuries. It has fueled our stoves, inspired campfire songs, comprised our early ships of exploration, formed early machines and modes of transportation. Wood was even used to fashion false teeth for George Washington. Working with wood provides one of our greatest art mediums and artistic expressions, whether as a carpenter, novice, or sculptor. Handling wood is even a spiritual passage and strengthener. Both Joseph and Jesus were carpenters by trade.

The Temporalosity of Our Existence

Now there's a word for you! Temporal. Worldly, instead of spiritual. Stuff. Toys. Cars. Houses. Estates. A bigger and better mousetrap. The perfect dock. "My dad's stronger than your dad, and my mom's more beautiful. I'm better than you; and to prove it, I'm gonna whip your ass!" It's a competition to go further, faster, in more directions. No mention of failure or humility, the two major attractions on the road to wisdom.

In my time living on the inland waterway of Florida, with much help, I built three magnificent docks, each four feet wide by 200 feet long, with a ten-foot by twenty-foot end deck that included back benches and a fishing pole support shelf. Each dock was taken by a hurricane that left no water trace of the dock's existence. This became successively more discouraging, since building them was a weekend project spread over many years. The second dock, completed just before our second daughter's wedding, took ten years to build and lasted two years until Opal took it out. The last dock, completed only two days before Ivan's arrival in 2004, took eight years to build. Our neighbors, watching my slow labor over multiple projects preceding major hurricanes, grew increasingly superstitious and begged me to leave off at least one board, lest a completed dock beckon another hurricane to our shores.

Now the waterway is empty again, and I am broken. Yet I yearn to build another dock. I am delighted that my family, friends, and neighbors enjoyed using the docks to boat, fish, sun, swim, and socialize' but that's not my thing. My only forte was in building them.

Ivan the Terrible

"Don't you pay a never-no-mind to this hurricane fuss," I said over the fence to my neighbor, Kathleen Kagan, as her husband was boarding up their house for the first time in the path of Hurricane Ivan. All the local and national newscasts were touting the strongest storm since Camille hit Biloxi, Mississippi, in 1969. "All we'll get, maybe, is a little water to leave a sprinkling of debris on the beach and a little wind to take a few

Light Flashes in the Tunnel

shingles. Not worth boarding up for, and probably not worth leaving for. These news people go berserk over the smallest amount of wind and water! Most likely, it won't come close to us." Nevertheless, Paul and I installed two sheets of plywood over his upstairs bedroom window and my bay window, both accessible from the porch balcony, to appease the nervous mistress of the house. It wasn't a custom fit like Jon Kagan's and was a far cry from the commercial metal panels set in metal tracks bolted to the brick house of my other neighbor, Jack Lowe, but it was secure. Also at her urging, plus the mandatory evacuation order issued by our local Gulf Breeze/Pensacola Civil Defense EOC, we left our Soundside home for a rented room at the Ramada Bayview on Scenic Highway overlooking the Interstate 10 bridge across Pensacola Bay. Paul and I packed light: a few changes of underwear, socks, shirts, and pants and our shaving/Dopp kits. *"Why bring anything else?"* I thought, *"This thing will be over tomorrow, and we'll all be home raking tidal debris or phoning for roof repairs."* As an afterthought, I pushed the lock shut on the two-drawer filing cabinet in my bedroom closet before tossing my canvas handbag into the old '89 Chevy S-IO for a caravan ride with Paul across the Pensacola Bay Bridge toward Scenic Highway.

We arrived at the Ramada Bayview before dark on Tuesday, September 14, 2004, and I worked a half-day on Wednesday delivering USDA commodity food to school shelters preparing for Ivan's projected arrival. When I returned to the motel around noon, I concluded that the best place to park would be next to a sizable oak tree with its elongated root system and sturdy, wind-resistant profile. Paul parked next to me, after which we hunkered down with other members of my wife's greater family who had re-located there as well. At 3:00 p.m., the motel's electricity went out—an ominous sign of things to come. We gathered in the motel lounge with candles and emergency lighting to listen to a local piano man play renditions of all the universally familiar songs while we sang along or danced, shades of the orchestra playing as the Titanic sunk slowly into the frigid Atlantic Ocean. Eventually, the crowd dispersed back to their separate rooms as the wind increased in intensity, locking outside doors, drawing curtains and listening, listening, listening throughout the night to the deafening howl of a vengeful wind and the clatter of storm debris loosed by it.

At morning's first light, Susan looked back from the curtain to say nonchalantly, "Oh, I've got some bad news. The oak tree fell over your vehicles, but I don't think they're damaged." Paul and I rushed to the glass door in dismay. Since the wind had abated some, we charged outside to see that the oak had crushed the truck's cab roof to the seat, blowing out or breaking all the windows in the process, and had broken the front window and dimpled or scraped the whole roof of Paul's car, which was almost invisible under the tree's upper branches. Since neither vehicle could be moved without some serious woodcutting, we commiserated for much of the day before Susan finally admitted to having a double-handled wire chain saw she hesitated to tell us about for fear that we would set about freeing Paul's car in order to drive out into Pensacola streets crisscrossed with fallen trees and live electric lines, even washed out entirely in low-lying areas.

We did finally free Paul's car late Friday afternoon, and it was drivable, though low on gas. While we were strategizing on how and when to drive back to our Sounside Drive home, we got two more shots of devastating news: First, a friend of our other son

Sean, who had remained on the peninsula during the storm, phoned Sean to relate that he had hiked around the obstacles on Soundside Drive to discover that our house was gone; and, of course, Sean reached us by cell phone to relay the message. Second, and shortly thereafter, Susan's brother Kenny, a long-time employee of the Gulf Power Company, came to the Ramada Inn with film footage he had taken with his personal video camera at Soundside that day. Because the motel electricity was still off, a Fox 10 News crew, also residing at the Ramada Inn with us, agreed to show it on their generator-operated news equipment. We sat in stunned, tearful silence as the flickering film panned our former homestead and yard, which were completely unrecognizable except as a trail of collapsed floors, walls, and roofs covered with the personal mementoes of our life. We were all in a state of shock. Indeed, this just hadn't been our week!

The trail out of this wasteland and our return to some semblance of normalcy in our individual lives took many diverse twists and turns, which is another long story for another time. However, among the typical sidelights of Ivan's aftermath, it is interesting that I never found the contents or drawers of the filing cabinet I was so careful to lock, but I did find the cabinet shell a quarter-mile into the woods across Soundside Drive.

The Anchor Is Within You

Remember the story of Dumbo's feather and how carrying it in his trunk gave him the courage to fly? Imagine an elephant flying! You know, like all of us, Dumbo had a hard time giving up that feather. We are tied, not to feathers, but to our domicile and our workplace, our house, our home, our desk, our TV-computer-cooking-sleeping spot, our office cubicle, and the places where we hang our hat. Sometimes, like the feather, your house and cubicle are taken away, and we become anxious and depressed without our shelters and our stuff. Like a fishing reef—family, friends, and coworkers float in and float out; but the reef's supposed to live on forever. Not so, my neurotic friend. When the reef is gone, you've still got your memory bank and a cozy spot in any library, park, store, café, or apartment to explore it. Your stuff will continue to proliferate disproportionately in whatever space you occupy; and if you reach out, your family, friends, and former coworkers will keep coming back to shelter your soul.

The Next Best Thing

During the year after Hurricane Ivan swept away my home, my truck, and all my personal possessions, my marriage of forty years crumbled into divorce; I retired from my school district job of thirty-three years; and I departed my hometown to live, presumably only temporarily, with my eldest son and his family. I remember inconsolably asking during the short burst of time allocated to retirement as friends and relatives gathered to commiserate with me, "What in God's name will I do now?"

My niece, Sister Sarah, also in the grip of dramatic life changes, said matter-of-factly, "Why, Uncle Jim, from among the multitude of things demanding attention, you simply do the next best thing you can for yourself, then the next followed by the next, etc." So, resolutely, I have followed that advice out of the wallows of self-pity to a better and brighter tomorrow. Our angels are with us always. We simply have to listen and comply.

Knickknacks

What is it that compels an otherwise normal human being to fill their house with useless ornaments? It's an abnormal hoarding instinct that clutters a well-ordered room with bobbles, bangles, and beads. An inclination to bad taste only exacerbates a horrific collection habit. Unfortunately, I'm one of those tasteless collectors with a penchant for eclectic statuary and logoed coffee cups. Before Hurricane Ivan, my window sills were filled with statues of shore birds, models of boats, assorted seashells, petrified rock specimens, and countless coffee cups from travel destinations. I even had the token model of The Fishing Alligator, formed to sit on a shelf edge with his feet hanging down and a pole in his outstretched forefeet, complete with line and bobber. And who could do without a guitar-playing hound bottle stopper? In the wake of Hurricane Ivan, as I was remorsefully picking through our house rubble for clothes; furniture; personal possessions; and, of course, remnants of my beloved collectibles, Paul put his arm around my shoulder and said, "Dad, if anything good came out of this hurricane, it was getting rid of all those damn knickknacks in your room. Look at it as a fresh start and a sign to quit collecting junk." Those of you reading this squib, quit smirking; I've seen those statues of St. Francis and the Virgin Mary on your lawn, those ball caps, Japanese fan and doll collections, hand-carved totem poles and trolls, and all manner of other ugly wall decor from God knows where in your homes, too! Please exempt my camel saddle stool and ceramic elephant from this discussion.

Charity Begins at Home

In addition to being a volunteer nation, America is also notable for its charitable citizens. Americans respond en masse during national emergencies from the grassroots up. You have only to experience the aftermath of a severe hurricane to see firsthand American good will and charity at its best. Americans build and care for their hometown churches, schools, fire and police departments, athletic facilities, and any communal facility for which the call goes out for help. Nationally, Americans give to their universities and a wide spectrum of organizations supporting medical research and care, environmental concerns, reduction of human suffering, and so forth. Still, support of members in the family unit is paramount. For me, ensconced in writing the drivel of this journal, motivation comes mainly from the hope of turning enough money to rebuild after Hurricane Ivan took my family homestead on Santa Rosa Sound. Thank you in advance for your contribution to my welfare, the Jim Bentley Home Replacement Fund.

Coming Through the Rye

Moving on. Detaching. Jumping, as Tom Petty resonates in his popular song, "Into the Great Wide Open." Many teens can't wait to be free of their hometown monotony and break away early. Some go to college. Some join the military. Some are forced out by difficult family situations. Some of us are just naturally on the move—the Davy Crockets, Daniel Boones, Willy Lomans, or Errol Flynns. Some of us drive away on vacations to the shore, the mountains, the Grand Canyon, New York, Chicago, or San

Francisco. Some of us move with our jobs. Some occupations, like the military, require families to move regularly every three or four years to new duty stations. Some homeless people are compulsive movers based on climate and social services, as are migrant farm workers. As I discovered after losing my house in Hurricane Ivan, there is a whole culture of motorhome and camper people traveling the North American continent from one distant campground to the next, receiving their mail after phoning a mailing service. That's now how I received my mail as I drove from one child's home to another and back to my epicenter on the shore.

I was out moving again during 2007 in the hinterlands of Interstate 65, driving my Toyota Tacoma 750 miles from Pensacola, Florida, to Lake St. Louis, Missouri, to live once more with son Sean, daughter-in-law Robin, Boomer, Stinky, two dogs, and three cats. I had been there before during 2005 while in the traveling mode after surviving Ivan's aftermath in petition-mediation-litigation at a rental house in Gulf Breeze for one year following that horrific storm. I had made the long day's drive to Lake St. Louis (LSL) and hunkered down in the American heartland's big-city suburbia, licking my mental wounds and skewering up courage to return to the devastated shore. I shared my anxiety and quarters in LSL with our family cat, Banjo, also saved by Sean and Robin, who also survived the storm when so many other neighborhood pets were missing. And, after nine months and a stint on the Appalachian Trail with sons Paul and Sean, I had returned to Pensacola during 2006 for another year in a studio apartment, with the hope of rebuilding my life on a newly purchased waterfront parcel. Alas, it was not to happen. The real estate market was stagnant, and we could not sell our hurricane lot at Soundside, thus allowing me to regenerate at Sea Pines on the Garcon Peninsula facing East Bay, so I had to drive north once again on Interstates 65, 24, 57, and 64, back to LSL. These interstate highways pass through small towns whose citizens use them as local streets. You'll have your speed control set for 65 or 70 mph when you arrive behind two local farmers in pickup trucks, driving side-by-side and doing 35 mph. You'll drive off at exits advertising gas only to find no buildings within ten miles of the exit. Service varies, along with the cleanliness of bathrooms.

After thirteen hours and three minimal stops for gas, there was a detour off Highway 64 in St. Louis, which caused another hour's delay while a host of good people, including Sean (on his cell phone like usual), tried to guide me through the city's detour back onto Highway 64 for the final leg. Through all of this continuing transition in my life—the false starts, the setbacks, the detours, the failures—I recalled the credo of Henry Shires' Ultralight Tarptents, "...let you focus on the joy of the journey, not on the pain of getting there."

Standing Ovation

It's a glorious moment for all of us to participate in or witness a standing ovation for some celebrated individual or occasion. It is spiriting to honor our country and flag before athletic events with the pledge and a warm round of applause. Athletic events themselves stimulate many ovations for individual or team performances. Oft-times, it's simply the goodwill of the crowd that results in an eruption of applause, no matter the award. We also demonstrate approval through our applause, as when an elected official is speaking on a favorite subject or supporting a favorite project. While it's a feat to deserve, much less get, a standing ovation from the crowd around you, most of us will have to be content with the goodwill and few hugs from our support group. Say, a son and daughter-in-law, a few grandchildren, dogs, and neighbors gathered in your driveway to welcome you back from a long hiatus and return trip.

American Home Base

"Home" is a word that warms the spirit, just as the word "pustule" repulses it. Paul Simon's haunting dirge *Homeward Bound* resonates with allure to the heart chords. After all, home is where the heart is. For me, in the wake of Hurricane Ivan's devastation to my life and property, as I travel itinerantly between my children's domiciles and separate lives, my only connection with a historic home base in Pensacola, Florida, is the mail service representing me. Every few weeks, I phone the American Home Base to order delivery of the mail they have collected for me, and more importantly, to chat idly with friendly voices about the happenings in my hometown.

X. IRRECONCILABLE DIFFERENCES

Marriage and Divorce

Marriage is the completion of an interview process conducted by one's hormones and, only occasionally, one's intellect, which is cemented by clergy, common law, and, only occasionally, God. The union bound only with hormonal passion is always in danger of disintegration, as is a relationship threaded with intellect that mutates into a loving disrespect. Well, depending upon the particulars of the divorce, the loving part may be subject to debate. The endangered true love marriage has ingredients that include hormones and intellect, but always the blessing of God and always no option for divorce. Divorce is, in fact, the absence of God in marriage.

The Last Happy Couple

Divorce humor is kindred to death humor. In fact, divorce is the death of marriage, so at family or other gatherings, divorcees routinely spear former spouses in conversation; and divorced men resort to bumper sticker humor such as, "My wife told me that it was either her or fishing. God, I'm going to miss that woman."

In our greater family, several men have formed the Has Been Husband's Club (HBHC), which meets irregularly at undesignated places, except Bagelheads and Uncle Skip's backyard deck, for unknown purposes with no formal agenda. Drinking alcohol, smoking cigars, and commiserating about our unsuccessful ventures with women seems to be our major occupation. We are not discriminatory, so the club contains both men and women. Some are still married, but frequently on a discordant verge. At the first note of hostility between marrieds, we always rush to patch up their marital discord with the simple conclusion that yes, you are the last happy couple.

"Pelican King on the AT in Full Gear, April 2008 (photo by Sean)"

Light Flashes in the Tunnel

"Pelican King (aka: JSB) and Brother B (aka: BB, Paul) Dallying Atop Springer Mountain, GA, as Paul Takes Landscape Photos, Prior to the Official Start of Our AT Hike, April 6, 2006 (photo by Sean)"

"Brother B (aka: BB, Paul) and Fly-By-Night (aka: Sean) Dallying Atop Springer Mountain, GA, as Paul Takes Landscape Photos, Prior to the Official Start of Our AT Hike, April 6, 2006 (photo by JSB)"

Jim Sharer Bentley

"Fly-By-Night (aka: Sean) and Brother B (aka: BB, Paul) at Their AT Campsite Near Blue Moutain Shelter, April 13, 2006 (photo by JSB)"

"Fly-By-Night (aka Sean) and Pelican King (aka: JSB) Next to an AT Pictorial Sign of 'The Ever-Changing View' in Front of the Wayah Bald Stone Observation Tower, April 13, 2008 (photo by a passing hiker)"

XI. ROAMIN' IN THE GLOAMIN'

Foot Traffic

We start life immobile until, at first, we crawl, then stand, and then tentatively walk out into the world. Afterwards, we travel by tricycle, bicycle, motorcycle, and motor vehicle until our stress is compounded by the rush of our schedules and the motorized traffic around us. Then, we return to the silence of the natural world and the meter of walking again to absorb it.

Walking for Sanity

Of course, walking is good. It is the earliest and most conventional mode of transportation and probably the single, biggest reason that Europeans are thinner than Americans. Our physical education teachers, trying to reduce or eliminate America's growing obesity epidemic, have re-instituted walking as a pastime and as a popular fundraiser. We walk for cancer, we walk for diabetes, we walk for heart— all good causes. Still, for all its physical good, walking remains the ultimate, and sometimes sole, aphrodisiac for the mind. Never you mind that there's no sex in your life, no support group to coddle you, no money to sustain you, or no physique to use to curl and lift with the big dogs! Just take a walk on a different path through verdant nature or city streets, take notice of your surrounds and the curious, creative flair of your fellow man, and you will return whole to face the world again.

Let Us Go Then While We May

T.S. Elliot invited us all through the *Iron Gates of Life*, which Number Two Son reiterated on a pocket watch given to me at my retirement with his Appalachian Trail salute, "Here we go then." That was April 2006, when both sons and I embarked upon the Mother of All Trails. We spent three weeks together, along with kindred souls, basking in the interlude of woodland silence and rejuvenating our good will for humanity.

Everything Else Is Just Routine: A Tribute to the Appalachian Trail

The Appalachian Trail has been a sporadic adventure for me, inspired in my menopause years by a National Geographic Magazine article "A Tunnel Through Time" in February 1987 and the encouragement of my support group, primarily my two sons—Sean, a pilot calling himself Fly By Night, and the Apostle Paul, forgoing his childhood nickname of Pumpkin in favor of Brother Bentley, or just BB—who both accompanied me on my first two outings: Amicalola Falls to Deep Gap in 2006 and Deep Gap to the Nantahala Outdoor Center in 2008. The time on the Appalachian Trail with my sons, as any parent can imagine, was probably the single greatest communion of mind, body, and spirit

Light Flashes in the Tunnel

in my life. The boys, who are eleven years apart and in two separate generations, had never really connected before their hike together. They walked with the same long-legged gait, chattered continuously like chipmunks, and usually ranged far ahead of me, although they both continued to encourage and nurture me, even as I slowed their progress on the trail. Evenings and down days in local trail towns, Hiawassee, Georgia, and Franklin and Bryson City, North Carolina, created memory fodder that continues to surface during current conversations and reunions years later.

Subsequent to hiking with my sons, I had three separate outings on the Appalachian Trail: from the Nantahala Outdoor Center (NOC) to the Fontana Dam in 2009; from the Fontana Dam to the Smokies' Clingmans Dome in 2011; and, most recently, from Clingmans Dome to Newfound Gap in 2012. This latest hike was typical of my meager progress on the trail, a total of 8.3 miles over one night and two days, averaging only 4.1 miles per day, cut short by a slip and fall off a fungus-covered log onto another log that tore the meniscus in my left knee and caused severe pain and swelling. In contrast, most well-conditioned hikers average ten to twenty miles per day, some as much as thirty, whether section hiking or thru-hiking. For me, seventy-six and in questionable condition with a potbelly, the trek was generally arduous and unforgiving, but no one out there enjoys more than me the mountain breezes, the valley bottom creeks, the pungent rhododendron tunnels, the flower-bedecked balds, the magnificent vistas, the melodic waterfalls, the parade of wildlife, and always the coy beckoning of the elusive white-blazed line into greater and greater adventure. In the grand scheme of things, we can always forgo showering for the body, but we cannot deny adventure for the soul. In my life, the Appalachian

Trail is God's aphrodisiac for releasing the Kraken in my soul. Everything else is just routine.

Skip Church. God Is on the Appalachian Trail.

It's the primordial call of the wilderness, those untamed spaces that seize our psyche unremittingly and cause disruption to our hamster-wheel existence. We are lured into the woods with dreams of adventure and incomparable natural beauty, of no regimen but survival, of stepping outside the circle binding us to the tedium of predictable routine, of a cure for sameness. We ache for challenges to define our lives, to ennoble us, to give us meaning. The Appalachian Trail looms as an image of escape on our dream horizon. We talk of it, read about it, exercise for it, make plans regarding it, accumulate gear for it, and eventually face the reality of hiking it. There are time and economic sacrifices to be made, complicated logistical planning even with all the resources available, and certainly strenuous physical exertion, especially for those of us getting along in years; but, upon embarking, the actual solitude and natural beauty are still there in definition beyond our dreams. The Appalachian Trail is a reward of disproportionately high magnitude to its reputation.

Of course, we humans are awestruck by our notable works in the name of God, e.g., the Sistine Chapel Ceiling, Notre Dame Cathedral in Paris, and my own boyhood chapel at St. George's School; but, in truth, I have only felt the overpowering presence of God in three diametric locales. The first and everlasting in memory was during the paranoia of survival in Vietnam when the daily dose of horrific events kept me ever mindful of the tenuousness of life. The second, later in life, was in the nocturne during our baby Kirk's death throes. The third, later still, occurred during my annual escape to section hike the Appalachian Trail from its southern terminus. All three venues are similar in their elements of danger and fear, but the AT adds an ethereal quality that, in spite of the labors to achieve it, lifts the spirit above this world.

My daily life, mostly by comfortable choice, has been a familiar humdrum of repetitive activities from morning ablutions to nocturnal prayers. To borrow a line from T.S. Eliot, "I have measured out my life with coffee spoons." So the beckoning of the AT stirred me to deviate from a routine existence into an adventure for the soul. Like all of us extending ourselves beyond normal boundaries, the AT provides that around the next bend adventure that we curiously seek. The Mother of All Trails, our longest national park, winds through fourteen states and eight national forests. Slogging along in modern, lighter-than-leather Gore-Tex, ankle-high backpacking boots, eyes ever down to preclude the inevitable stumble or fall on the rock-and-root-strewn trail, continuous exhilaration manifests itself in the difficulties of negotiating the terrain; the quest for available water sources; the presence of wildlife, especially potentially menacing wildlife like bears, boars, and cougars; the condition of the twelve-to-eighteen-inch trail along cliff faces and steep drop-offs; the commitment of well-being to remote almost-unreachable areas; and the ability to traverse this offering in an awkward pack without physical endangerment. To date, I have spent a total of thirty-two days on this trail during five separate years, hiking a distance of 204.7 miles, a meager accomplishment by comparison to most hikers completing that same mileage in less than ten days.

There are shelters typically infested with mice unless the site is blessed with a resident snake or two, and a word associated with AT hiking is moldering, as in the moldering privy. Now, this is upscale stuff! The privy is a three-sided box with roof on a platform over a pit below the crest of the mountain shelter, opposite the water source, of course. On the platform is a box throne with toilet seat attached and a bag of cedar bark mulch at hand. You bring your own dissolvable toilet paper (which is questionable with hikers, especially the purists) if you use it and hand sanitizer. It's a scary thrill to pad down the privy trail during the night with your headlamp ablaze and sit, squinting into the darkness, listening to the sounds of the woods and praying that you don't see a pair of eyes peering back, at least a pair that's higher than your own.

Of course, only some shelters have moldering privies, but most require that you relieve yourself in a hand-dug pit within a designated dumping ground. Some have nearby springs where you can get water or are on or near upper elevations with a prevailing breeze and no bugs, but others are without handy replenishment or are in lower or valley-bottom locations with unimaginable bug swarms.

But it's not the comforts, conveniences, or facilities that endear you to the trail. It's the sheer grandeur of natural beauty and the reach of humanity to be found hiking there, a true mixing bowl. It's mostly people at crossroads in their lives, seeking answers to or direction from their plight of recent divorces, deaths, graduation, retirement, layoffs, or job changes. Evening campfires, even catch-your-breath conversations when passing hikers on the trail, are rife with thirsty soul-searchers transcribing information from other's lives. God, moderating it all, translating between the unknowns, is uniting dispirited souls into a common bond, pleased with the fellowship of goodwill prevailing through bounteous beauty.

Judged by the Company We Keep

If we are truly judged by the company we keep, then my AT reputation must range from being affable to being zany. Among the diverse characters populating hiker ranks during my time on the AT, I offer six here beyond myself as a representative sampling. As you will see, the poignancy of trail monikers usually reflects some essence of its designee, for example, Green Bow, The Ole Man, The Dumbbells, Faith Walker, Preacher Dude, Almost There, and Pelican King.

During our first outing from Springer Mountain, affable Dave Brown, or Green Bow, a burly bar and restaurant owner from Newburyport, Massachusetts, took mercy upon my wrenched knee and offered to trade me his lighter, forty-five-pound Osprey Backpack for my sixty-five-pound pack during the next two days in the Georgia mountains before reaching Woody Gap, where I was expected to lighten up. Indeed, at the Hiker Hostel there, an aging veteran of both military service and AT hiking, The Ole Man, relieved my pack of thirty pounds of unnecessary weight, which I sent home, so I could hike on in parity and dignity with Green Bow. The Ole Man's wisdom was lifesaving, and Green Bow's generosity was a living act of Good Samaritanism.

The Ole Man's message rang loud and clear: "Buy light and don't pack it if you don't need it!" He further recommended that I replace my three-pound, three-ounce synthetic-fill North Face Mammoth Sleeping Bag with a one and a half-pound goose down

Western Mountaineering Mega Lite Mummy Bag, which I did, sending my North Face Bag home. And between hikes, also at The Ole Man's recommendation, I traded my six-pound, fourteen-ounce Gregory Palisade Backpack for a three-pound, five-ounce Gregory Z-55 Backpack and my REI Quarter Dome Tent at four and a quarter-pounds for a Henry Shires Contrail Tarptent weighing just one and a half-pounds. When you're on foot with your life support in a backpack, it's all about the weight. Blessings be upon the carrier and the messenger.

While staying in the Walasi-Yi's Hostel in Neels Gap, my boys and I had retired to the crowded bunkroom at day's end, where, among many ruminations from a diverse assemblage, we listened to the story of The Dumbbells, a husband-wife team who had made ten consecutive thru-hike starts on the AT with varying mileages before quitting for the year, only to return the following year to Springer Mountain for another start. The rapt audience almost asked in unison, "Why would you restart your annual hike at Springer Mountain instead of where you left off the previous year?" to which came the obvious and only reply, "That's why we call ourselves, 'The Dumbbells.'"

Faith Walker wore oversized leather boots inherited from her deceased grandfather, in whose memory she was hiking the AT. She carried a store of Reese's Peanut Butter Cups, which she would dispense after praying over our ailments. We alternated passing each other in our slow, ever-rising progression through the Georgia mountains when, one evening at shelter, she asked me how her prayers were affecting my sprained knee. "I can't confirm the value of your prayers," I admitted, "but the Reese's Peanut Butter Cups are doing wonders for my morale." That is the true song of the Appalachian Trail, the sometimes quiet, sometimes loud celebration of the human spirit. God blesses all abundantly who enter that sacred space.

In the spirit of AT lore, where Trail Magic—a kind of anonymous hospitality from mountain locals and sundry others who leave food, drink, and gifts along the trail for weary hikers to discover and enjoy—is almost reverential, let me share a few words about Preacher Dude. Andy, as in "James" Bond, was called to an evangelistic ministry on The Trail from the corporate world where he worked as a business consultant with an MBA. We saw his Styrofoam cooler while approaching the base of Kelly Knob. In his handwriting on the cooler was this message, "Trail Magic from Preacher Dude—Help Yourself. Tonight at Deep Gap Shelter will be beef stew, fresh fruit, bread, soft drinks, and coffee. Tomorrow morning will be a breakfast of scrambled eggs, bagels, cream cheese, sausage, and coffee." We each had a cold Coke and then tackled the hike to Kelly Knob from Addis Gap, 1.1 miles of torturous ascent that rises 965-feet or approximately six feet every thirty feet. It's a renowned bitch, and we walked it with the toes of our boots at a forty-five-degree angle above the heels. Every time our eyes would meet a ridgeline, we would have only to climb further to find that it was a faux peak. With my lungs exploding from lack of oxygen, I could only count out a twenty-five-fifty-step cadence and then stop and blow for a few minutes as the boys ranged further and further ahead of me. When we got to the water source before Deep Gap Shelter, it too was full of Cokes and fruit drinks. As we approached Deep Gap Shelter, we could see a large lawn tent pitched in front with a food prep table inside it. An unshaven man wearing a porkpie hat, sandals, and a Georgia Bulldogs T-shirt stepped out from the tent to welcome us with a wide grin and joyous attitude. He greeted each of us separately as we staggered into the shelter's clearing, inviting us to eat and drink in the name of the Living Lord on this Easter Sunday. He had chairs for us to sit in; a water bag shower with sprinkler attachment and cutoff valve set up behind the shelter; and, as promised, a delicious beef stew dinner accompanied by lilting Easter music from a radio/CD player. Here we were, a global citizenry of differing ages and occupations in the wild woods below Kelly Knob enjoying hospitality not to be equaled, or sometimes even found, in some of our most notable hotels. The AT is, indeed, a spiritual place where anyone can reach into their soul to find and touch the face of God. Amen!

Almost There was a ghostlike apparition with disheveled hair sticking out in every direction and teeming energy, flitting about during her sleepless night in the shelter (she said she required only a few hours of nightly rest), talking and praying to herself in a continuous murmur as she read her Bible and tended the fire for the rest of us. Her wild appearance and zany demeanor made us all think that she was still a long way from being there. She and her husband had operated a Spartan-like fish camp in the Maine woods; and after his demise, she embarked upon the AT with an inventory of heavy, outdated camping gear and a spirit embracing the intrinsic generosity of humankind to share their stores with her. She said that the Lord provided her sustenance through His Angels, who were seldom disappointing. I won't certify that any of our trail companions in attendance at the shelter that night would qualify as an angel, but good-natured sprite that she was, we all eagerly contributed to her food stores. Be careful in judging from whence the Lord's blessings flow.

Pelican King, my own Trail name given me by my neighbors

on Santa Rosa Sound, was derived from the faithful attendance of that bird on the pilings, cross-ties, and stringers of a dock that took me ten years to build and finally cover with decking.

That's a Lot of Words to Describe a Stick

Appalachian Trail hikers, or for that matter all serious hikers walking any trail, are notable gear heads. What used to be simply shirts, shorts, socks, and boots is now described as Coolmax, Sahara, Thorlos 3 Lt. Trekking Wool/THOR-LON Midwt, Crew, and Montrail Torre GTX. The old walking stick has been replaced with Leki Super Makalu Long COR-TEC AS Trekking Poles. It's not uncommon during conversations at trail shelters to overhear a baffled hiker ask, after five minutes of listening to another's gear description, "Are you talking about your boots?" Still, Leki is commercially savvy enough in its advertisements to suggest that, "Everything else is just a stick."

Outside the Zone

Whilst plying our fortunes and strength toward conquering the Appalachian Trail, my boys and I each carried our clothing, food, shelters, and water on our back. Beginning- and end-of-day meals were mainly commercially dehydrated fare in aluminum bags to which we added boiling water, e.g., Backpacker's Pantry and Mountain House. The in-between snacks were whatever items you could carry without them spoiling— fruits and vegetables, hard-boiled eggs, cheese—supplemented by nutrient bars formulated for maximum energy and nutrition. The bar we carried was the Zone Perfect All-Natural Nutrition Bar, packed with nutrients and a great taste guarantee. They are covered with chocolate and the first thirty or so were delicious, but as time wore on, even the fabulous Zone Bar lost its appeal to three starving hikers, like boiled eggs or cherry pies in one of those all-you-can-eat contests at a fair.

The Teddy Bear's Picnic

What mental tremors could interdict an otherwise euphoric passing through the solitude of Appalachian Trail splendor? A children's song comes to mind:

If you go out in the woods today,
You won't believe your eyes.
If you go out in the woods today,
Be assured of a big surprise;
'Cause, all the bears that ever there was,
All the bears and all of their fuzz,
Today's the day the Teddy Bears have their picnic.

As Sean and I were hiking along the AT on April 13, 2008, from Winding Stair Gap near Franklin, North Carolina, to Wayah Shelter (a distance of eleven miles), we became disconcerted over a sign prominently posted in Wayah Gap which read: "BEWARE: Rogue bear has been ransacking hiker's packs from Wayah Gap to Deep Gap, from whence we came, and shows no fear of humans. Ranger, Nantahala Forest." I'm not sure the word "rogue" was included in the verbiage of the sign, but it was certainly in my mind! As we hiked up, ever up, and away from Wayah Gap, we turned to glance backward more than once to see if that rogue bear, red-eyed with anger and drooling from lack of food, was trudging along behind us—actually behind *me*, since I was always behind Sean and I knew that the bear probably hadn't read the Good Ranger's sign defining his territory. Neither did it help my over-stimulated imagination for Sean to keep repeating, "All I have to do to escape being eaten by a bear is to run faster than you."

The resounding question from those unwilling to face the delirium and paranoia of a solo hike, even an accompanied hike, in bear country is always, "Why pursue an activity that absorbs your psyche with the fear of fatality?" The answer, of course, is the counterbalancing passion for adventure that, in my mind, is best expressed by "a young wilderness ideologue whose demise resulted from underestimating the harshness of nature."

"So many people live within unhappy circumstances and yet will not take the initiative to change their situation because they are conditioned to a life of security, conformity, and conservatism, all of which may appear to give one peace of mind, but in reality nothing is more damaging to the adventurous spirit within a man than a secure future. The very basic core of a man's living spirit is his passion for adventure. The joy of life comes from our encounters with new experiences…" —Chris McCandless, *Into the Wild* by Jon Krakauer.

This quote certainly captures our own vibrant spirit of adventure for embracing the AT.

Bear Bait

I lifted this title from an Appalachian Trail hiker's moniker. While it is amusing, there is also a certain sense of urgency about it, especially when hiking in areas like the Great Smoky Mountains National Park, where, according to *The Thru-Hiker's*

Handbook, "There are an estimated 1,600 black bears inside the park, one of the highest bear population densities in the country." This note further piqued my already high anxiety, especially after seeing an Animal Planet presentation on TV that listed the black bear as one of the top ten human predators, with testimony from a surviving victim to describe their ferocity. I have been, as the expression goes, on tender-hooks about meeting a bear on the trail; but my fears were somewhat allayed by a Bear Country note in the Spring 2009 *National Parks Magazine* article on Glacier National Park which said, "But keep a level head about it; the bears aren't out to eat you. If you visit in August when huckleberries are in their prime, you're likely to encounter a grizzly or black bear. Simply make noise and let the bear know you are there, but remain calm and enjoy the opportunity to witness one of the most charismatic animals in America. Speak loudly on hikes, especially in the early mornings and evenings when the animals are most active—but avoid ruining other visitors' solitude with 'bear bells.' Most studies have found them ineffective; if you're looking to protect yourself, bear spray (a potent pepper spray) is available everywhere and much more effective. Respect the animal, and it will respect you." Of course, I wondered if that last bit of advice had been shared with the bears of the Smoky Mountains.

Since bears don't read boundary markers, you can spot their scat along almost the entire southern portion of the AT. When you're solo hiking like me, the overpowering solitude can sometimes create delirium and paranoia to the point that you hear and see things that are not there, like my night alone in Cable Gap Shelter preceding Fontana Dam. I had seen a few piles of scat on the AT hiking in from Brown Fork Gap Shelter and thought I spotted a furry black critter in a distant ravine downhill. By the time I got to the shelter late in the afternoon, I was holding the trigger of my pepper spray canister and looking over my shoulder every few seconds. I carried the spray around the shelter site as I filtered water, went to the privy, cooked and ate my meal, and completed evening ablutions prior to last light at about 7:30 p.m., when I slid into my sleeping bag. As the wind from an advancing rain storm picked up and the trees began to groan from their swaying and grating, I began to hear distinct growling through the thin walls of the three-sided shelter and, belatedly, remembered leaving my pack and food bag hanging from the open roof overhang instead of hoisting them into a distant, tall tree as prescribed for bear country. Needless to say, I didn't close an eye the entire night, sitting against the back wall of the shelter with the bear spray in one hand and my Petzl Tikka Headlamp in the other. During a midnight speed run to the privy, I was sure I spotted two red eyes, far apart, glaring at me through the dark! Oddly, there were no mice at this shelter, either, which I translated into them fearing bears or already having been eaten by hungry bears. My inordinate fears that night proved to be unjustified, but I still can't shake that feeling of being an hors d'oeuvre at a bear feeding frenzy.

Birds That Stick Their Heads in the Sand

How is it possible that natives of any spot on the globe have not experienced or seen that for which their hometown is famous and for which global tourists travel and expend great resources to experience and see? I was especially taken with the charming citizens of the lovely towns along the fabled Appalachian Trail who remarked, even as we gazed together out windows of their establishments onto scenic mountain backdrops, "I've really got to get up there and visit the AT someday!"

A Classroom in the Woods

The AT grandeur of natural beauty is also a classroom dispensing life's wisdom for the high price of great physical exertion. One thing I learned is that we are all searching for something better than ourselves, outside of ourselves, that "one true thing" that eludes us: the Fountain of Youth, the ultimate experience that's the envy of our associates, a standing ovation, love, fellowship, acceptance, discipleship with God and His portal Jesus Christ, whatever!

I learned that the search might very well be satisfied within the core of our being and the core of beings that we bump against daily. Within everybody is the incalculable capacity for good, even great good, and evil. Others give to us without measure or take from us with irreverent abandon. The AT houses mostly good-seekers who give without measure and leave you filled with love for your fellow human—people like Green Bow, who carried my sixty-five-pound pack for two full days until I could get to the Hiker Hostel and Paul The Ole Man Renaud and Andy Preacher Dude Bond, who left drinks and snacks at the base of Kelly Knob and who cooked both dinner and breakfast for us from his own personal larder for nothing more than love of neighbor and dedication to God's calling.

The AT itself contains all of the elements of natural beauty, with its balds and peaks reaching ever upward to unbounded skies; trees majestically framing the shroud of mountains and forming tunnels over leaf-covered paths winding aimlessly beneath them; ravines at valley floors where streams splash loudly over elevated falls or trickle slowly through rock-strewn beds. Hawks circle ceaselessly overhead, birds sing out within the leafy tree canopy, wildflowers cluster down hillsides and spill out around your boots on the AT, and the wind moans everywhere around you all the time as it brushes your face and cools your body. It is paradise, but it is also unforgiving pain—pain from stumbling, turning your ankles, twisting your knees, sun burning your arms and legs; infesting you with ticks and assorted flying bugs; generally straining every fiber of your body as you thread through the roots and rock scrabble, inevitably pumping up and ever upward, but almost never, seemingly ever, walking down. Like anything worthy of having or, even temporarily, holding, it requires a supreme sacrifice to achieve. That's what I learned about the AT and, for that matter, about all of life.

Lastly, I learned that baby steps, one foot in front of the other, slow and steady like the turtle, will get you there every time. The chaplain at Tray Gap who took twenty-seven years to thru-hike the AT with his boys, one small section at a time, fanned my fervor to return again and again, allowing reasonable time between hikes for the broken body to heal, and pick up where I left off. It's a thing you get in your mind about finishing, certainly a love-hate relationship, but also a primordial calling of the wild to seek and soothe the savage beast within your soul.

On the other hand, if I never go back, I'll always remember the times I spent satisfying my curiosity about our oldest and greatest national trail. It's been here as a footpath since the dawn of time and will be here evermore for the following legions of hikers seeking peace and purpose along its route.

Connections

You'd think this title refers to the favorable influence one can garner with friends, relatives, or work associates to get help in one way or another; but no, this makes reference to travel connections and coordinating separate modes of transportation. I am lost in the process of overlapping travel vehicles to make a smooth whole and continuous trip; but both my sons can link together an afternoon or multiple-day trip via airplanes, buses, cabs, limos, rental cars, subways, and trains in such a way that the journey is seamless. It helps that Sean is a pilot and travels for a living and that Paul lives in New York City, where mastering the Metro and the subway system is an art form. Nonetheless, when Sean and I hiked the Appalachian Trail into the NOC during April 2008, arriving at 7:00 p.m. to discover that the registration office had closed at 5:00 p.m., Sean was able to negotiate a room at and a ride to the neighboring Bryson City Sleep Inn and, the next day, to secure a private taxi ride to Asheville, North Carolina, where he had contracted a rental car to get us back to St. Louis. His dexterity at turning random phone calls to heretofore-unknown sources into a synchronous travel plan never ceases to amaze me. And the most colorful part of his plan, the Midnight Taxi ride to Asheville, involved a soliloquy from a descendant of the infamous Hatfield-McCoy feud, but that's another story for another time. Frankly, I was just glad that we came away from that one with our lives.

XII. THE WAKE OF LOVE

Everybody Works, Nobody Shirks

This is the unfailing spirit of any commune, monastery, military unit, team, organization, or human grouping. Families, too, abide by this principle, excluding, perhaps, the very old or the very young. Exclusions from the group's survival tasks are as few as the forgiveness is little for shirking them. In an active family group, workloads shift in accord with outside-of-family demands and the ability to perform work at hand. Youngsters learn to watch younger siblings as adults shop, clean, maintain their house, tend to babies, chauffeur kids to school and sports activities, cook, feed the masses, supervise homework and chores, and orchestrate the bedtime routine. Eventually, youngsters clean, cook, wash clothes, do dishes, mow the family lawn, paint, and work for pay outside the home.

It's good for old-timers to be at the epicenter, lending a hand, supervising, or dispensing time-honored advice. Better than being alone in an old folks' home feeling sorry for themselves and commiserating over their ailments. The fast lane of family momentum calls to every participant alike and keeps old-timers feeling good about their contributions. It's adding years to my life to live in Missouri with son Sean, daughter-in-law Robin, and their kids, Boomer and Stinky, along with two dogs and three cats. One of the cats, Banjo, was brought home in Florida as a kitten by Paul from his first job as an animal groomer at twelve years old. Fourteen years later, Banjo could not be found during our Hurricane Ivan evacuation, but survived to be rescued from our house rubble in the wake of that devastating storm. Since we no longer had a home, Sean and Robin were good enough to take her with them back to St. Louis. We were reunited the following year in 2005 when I joined their zoo. Now, Banjo and I share the same quarters and are both being nurtured into senior adulthood. We get free food, unlimited love, and lots of strokes; and I get to work again alongside everybody else. What more can you ask from life?

Moving Patton's Third Army

Indeed, there is no greater puzzle in modern day, requiring the patience of Job to complete and the logistical planning of the Normandy Invasion, than packing up the family vehicle for vacation. When parents must pack themselves, their babies, older children, assorted pets, and attendant miscellaneous support gear, the act of accumulating and packing their stuff in the car is a most extraordinary undertaking. Listening to Sean explain this ordeal for a recent excursion to Florida from St Louis, which took him and his wife almost three hours alone, was comparable to setting up and then striking the entire Ringling Brothers, Barnum & Bailey Circus. Unfortunately, there were no clowns available to make him laugh through the cloud of profanity that had beset him.

Reading the Fine Print

What, pray tell, is entertaining and interactive for a nine month-old baby whose only mobility is a spring frame, jump-up sling, or walker on wheels? Swaying to the music is okay, gift-wrap and ribbon is always more fun than the present it contains; but by far and away, the most fascinating thing is to tear apart or chew on a glossy magazine. There's nothing that compares with drooling on our celebrities to help a baby get ahead.

Sticks and Stones

"Sticks and stones will break my bones, but names can never hurt me." This battle cry of adolescence almost casts a derogatory pall over two favored symbols of the infantile world. As for sticks and stones, the nemesis of all nannies, they're favored to twirl and suck on. Nothing is more fascinating to a two year old than a good stick to twirl or pebble to suck on. Stinky-Clinky has a vast collection that she regularly redistributes around her house to the chagrin of her neat-nick mother.

Chortling

It is strangely melodic and soothing to listen to the happy noises of a baby learning to talk. The varied intensity of singsong sounds in rising and falling rhythm, accompanied by gleeful laughter, is akin to bird sounds in the tree canopy of an otherwise quiet forest. It is a pleasant punctuation to the usual cacophony of noise surrounding us.

Owee Technology

The boo-boo has morphed into an owee. The childhood bumps, cuts, and scrapes of yesteryear, requiring at least a mother's hug and kiss, then iodine antiseptic, later Mercurochrome, and later still Methylade or Campho-Phenique, now require the same hug and kiss from mother; but instead of iodine dispensed from a glass bottle with skull and crossbones on the label and a red rubber stopper, they require a swipe of triple antibiotic ointment. The plaintive cry has gone from, "I've got a boo-boo!" to, "Pop, I've got an owee." Medicine and hygiene have advanced along with our communication technology, from party lines and radios to laptops and iPads. Johnson *&* Johnson Company now makes Baby No More Tears Shampoo to replace the caustic soaps and homemade lye bars of my youth. Then there was castor oil and cod liver oil for constipation, upset stomach, vitamin enrichment, or any other ailment or sign of ill-health, which caused us to never betray our maladies for fear of getting a spoonful. Nowadays, kids get children's fruit-flavored Advil, Motrin, or Tylenol; and they look forward to a dropper-full. Times in medicine have definitely changed for the better!

Three Children's Tales

The naiveté and unburnished honesty of children surpasses all understanding.

Martha, a precocious three year-old, sat daintily in her ruffled dress and bonnet between her two older brothers at an Easter Sunday church service aboard a U.S. naval ship. During the quiet of a reverential sermon, she leaned forward, hands on her brothers' knees, and exploded with a loud fart, which caused a uniformed officer in the row ahead to turn around and scowl disapprovingly. Without a moment's hesitation, Martha pointed at the officer and said at the top of her lungs, "He did it!" after which the congregation erupted into gales of laughter while the officer's face reddened as he turned back forward.

Joshua, nicknamed Boomer, another precocious three year-old, fidgeted unceasingly during the long invocation to the school district's annual retirement ceremony. As the minister droned on and on, there came a pause, during which Boomer shouted, "Boring!" Snickering rippled through the crowd around us as many people, feeling the same as Boomer, clasp their hands over their mouth to prevent all out disruption.

Boomer's sister, nicknamed Stinky, was at nine months a late teether and very contentious during that time. She drooled prolifically, licked her gums nonstop, and took to sticking out her rolled tongue while blowing spittle in all directions. She automatically did this when you looked closely into her face, so when strangers would bend down to admire her, we would rush to warn them. One such lady, who bent over Stinky's stroller while her mother was distracted elsewhere, came up quickly wiping her face after the proverbial raspberry, and proclaimed the child malevolent. Truer words were never spoken. So be it!

Babies Ain't No Pushover

The developing personality of an eighteen month-old child includes not only a fearless confidence that you will safely catch them whenever they are disposed to leap at you from a chair or table but also a growing vocabulary of one-word communiqués that embrace a larger meaning. My beloved granddaughter, Stinky-Clinky, is wont to stand defiantly pointing at the garage door with one forefinger and furrowed brow, the other hand a clenched fist resting on her hip, and then saying, "Side, Pop, side!" The greater meaning here is that she wants me to clothe her for the outdoors so we can go out and jump on the trampoline, run through the woods behind her house, or pick her mother's flowers—or usually all three. The word "park," also accompanied by the same forefinger, furrowed brow and clenched fist, means, "Dress me up, get some drinks and snacks, and wheel me to the playground in the jogging stroller, where we can while away the hours sliding on the slides, climbing on the monkey bars, or swinging on the swings." Guess who gets to push? We will sit for interminable hours watching *Jay-Jay the Jet Plane*, *Teletubbies*, or *Finding Nemo*. At day's end, when her mother or father is whisking her off to bed, I always implore her in compensation for my daytime efforts to comply with her demands, "How about a smooch for the old Popster?"

"No!" is the immediate reply.

"Well, then, how about a hug?"

"No, Pop!" she will retort, after which she presses her forehead against mine and grins in the most mischievous way while blowing kisses from her hands. I tell you that bump with those drooling grins, usually accompanied by a crumb-spattered face, and air-blown kisses added years to my life.

One Big Smacker for One Fine Baby

And I'm not talking about a twenty-something, bikini-clad hard body with an hourglass figure, stunning face, and bodacious

Light Flashes in the Tunnel

tah-tahs. This seventy year-old's baby is a contentious two year-old on the fast track of life. Independence is Stinky-Clinky's most identifiable personal trait, and "No!" continues to be her favorite word. She wants to perform and be treated in equal measure to the adults around her. This entails eating at the counter or table in a regular chair rather than a high chair. She doesn't want to be handled or lifted unless she extends a hand or both arms. Don't engage or serve her with anything until she's offered prior consent. She initiates all the activity in her day, and everything is on her terms. Our conversations might go something like this:

"Choo-choo train, Pop."

"You want to go upstairs and play with the GeoTrax?"

"Yeah."

"You want to take Pop's hand going upstairs?"

"No!"

"You want Pop to carry you?"

"No!"

"You want Pop to put all the engines on the track?"

"No! Uh-uh! Truck."

"You want Pop to put the blue truck on the track?"

"Yeah."

"How about one big smacker for one fine baby?"

"No, Pop!"

"Wha'cha mean, no?"

"Uh-uh. BB!"

"You want Pop to find your Binky?"

"Yeah."

"OK, here's your pacifier."

"La-la's, Pop."

"You want to go down to the basement and listen to your

Living Lord Jesus CD?"

"Yeah."

"You want to take Pop's hand going downstairs?"

"No!"

"You want Pop to play, 'My God Is a Great Big God?'"

"Yeah. Up, Pop. Dance."

"You want Pop to pick you up so we can dance around to the music?"

"Yeah. Again! Again! Again! I lov'ou."

Wrangling the Tee-Tot

Engaging a two year-old in wholesome, safe play with boundaries is like herding cats. A boundary like, "Don't go into the roadway!" is an open invitation to cross the line. The recurring warning-laughter-trespass-scolding is predictable and ludicrous. "Again! Again! Again!" Clinky shouts as you swing her. "Push, Pop, push! Now, Da-Da!"

"Don't lean back, or you'll fall out!" we implore her, but back goes the head and out go the feet as she screams, "Ah! Yyee! Higher! Higher! Higher!" On we go down slides, across fields, up and down stairs, into the roadway, dutifully following her while she pushes her baby carriage or swings a stick to whack stuff along the way. "Ring around the rosies, a pocketful of posies. Upstairs, downstairs, we all fall down!" Down we all go, whether on the carpet, lawn, or trampoline. The words, "Let's play Jay-Jay/Tracy," "GeoTrax." "Hide and Seek," or "Choo-Choo Trains with Thomas and James" are commands that make tired blood run cold. At day's end, after bath, bottle, and stories have put her into a peaceful slumber, surviving adults lounge exhaustedly in her wake, agreeing humorously with Sean that, "She's not a bit of trouble!"

Worn to a Thin Frazzle

The two year-old's temper tantrum rolls, like a squall on calm water, out of nowhere. A moment of happy laughter and quiet play can be changed to screaming and spasms in an instant. It's often challenging to determine what triggered the tantrum, which can be anything from a child not being understood to discomfort with a poopy diaper or exhaustion from too little sleep. Stories must be read the same way each time, and make-believe game rules must be followed to the letter, or the storm will erupt. No matter how many apologetic hugs and kisses are offered to assuage the wrong, our entreaties will be forcefully and hurtfully brushed aside like so much fecal matter.

"Jushwa wunt hav reel at his toys. Da fish eeder," Stinky declared, looking into my eyes for some semblance of understanding.

"Joshua has a fishing reel among his toys?" I offered.

"No, Pop!" she resounded in a screaming fit, flailing her arms.

"You ogre! Don't you know that she's talking about her mermaid doll, Ariel, and the clown fish, Flounder?" inquired her mother, passing through the living room with a load of clean clothes.

"Oh," I recoiled sheepishly, "You mean that Joshua doesn't want us to play in his toy castle with Ariel and Flounder?"

"Yeah," she said with an impish grin while cupping my face in her hands and simultaneously bumping my forehead with hers. "That's right, Pop."

I feel as though I have just been awarded the Nobel Peace Prize; but after fifty or more of these conversational starts during the course of a day, with their draining magnitude, I am well beyond exhaustion when my turn for shower and bed arrives at night. God bless the mothers of this world and keep replenishing their fortitude and morale.

The Backside of the Fussy Clock

Structure is the hallmark of childrearing. Children need a dependable schedule for feedings, play, nap, bath and bedtimes, interspersed with guidance, hugs, snacks, changing, tooth-brushing, more hugs, medicine, and participation in other ongoing family activities. Without expectant feedings and rest, temper tantrums spin into existence like cyclones on a dry prairie. You can see them coming like bad weather itself, a darkening disposition approaches naptime, which transcends into the thunder of contentious behavior if the nap ritual is ignored, thence into the storm of a full-blown tantrum. When the arms start flailing and the temper rises, better check your watch to see what part of the child's routine is being missed, 'cause you're now on the backside of the fussy clock.

Hunting the Venerable Wormie

Stinky-Clinky's an outdoor girl, fascinated by all things that bloom, crawl, fly, grow, hop, slither, or simply appear outdoors within her range of vision. Her only tranquil moments seem to be in study of something presented by Old Mother Nature. She is mesmerized by bugs and will spend long periods of time watching them creep along on their daily rounds; we once played with two ladybugs on her trampoline for several hours. She found her first night crawler crossing a flagstone, wet with morning dew, in the path en route to the trampoline. She picked it up and passed it from hand to hand as it twisted and writhed to get free. She carried it around until it was limp, releasing it into a flowerpot only after we convinced her it would remain there, anxiously awaiting her return. After that experience, the command, "Wormies!" meant that we were obligated to turn over all the flagstones in the walkway until we could supply her with sufficient companions for her continuing study.

The Little Engine Who Couldn't

When summoned by two year-old Stinky-Clinky to play choo-choo trains, we would repair to the loft, where the kids' GeoTrax were forever strewn about the floor. We would gather up the engines, their cars, and the controllers; fix broken track sections; and push the sound buttons atop the bell tower and tunnel. Then Clinky assumed the awesome task of placing each engine on the track in the same direction so they wouldn't collide. Next she would scurry about, her arms full of cars, adding them one by one to the tail of each moving train. Of course, as the trains got longer, the cars would fall off on the bends or the engine would simply slow to a standstill. "Baby, you can't put more than two or three cars on a train because the engine can't pull any more," I would implore her. Still, she continued to add five, six, or seven cars, and the batteries in each engine would run down very quickly.

"The poor little guy," she would echo, "he needs new batteries!" In life, that is frequently the scenario between expectation and performance. We shouldn't take on more than we can accomplish, and we need to re-energize our batteries from time-to-time.

Boogers, Poop, Monsters, and Spiders

Granted, the two-year-old vocabulary is limited and based on what the child hears from those around her. My granddaughter, Stinky-Clinky, can enunciate: "I love ou;" "choo-choo train;" "Jay-Jay;" "Barney;" "pease;" "thank ou;" "again, again, again;" "side;" "park;" "shit;" "no;" and "Mama gouchy!" without the "r". Of course, these are mostly words and expressions parroted from her parents, brother, and me, which she repeats for effect and feedback. Her comfort zone and bedtime rituals would not be complete without "BB" and "Blankie." But proudest I am of words she got from the old Popster. These are the useful words of daily discourse and imagination.

Everybody Has a Hiding Place

During the longtime passage of my daily rituals with Stinky-Clinky I occasionally heard grumblings from other family members about personal property that had gone missing. Mama, Clinky's mainstay, complained of losing favorite brassieres and perfume. Da-Da, Clinky's end-all, was looking for missing foosballs. Boomer couldn't find his toothbrush or Matchbox cars. Stinky herself continued to request that we find her Jay-Jay the Jet Plane model. One day, mid-afternoon when Ma Bear forbade snacks before dinner, I happened to spy the Clinky-Girl munching a muffin that had not been in our inventory for days. Curious as to the whereabouts of her find, I tracked her closely from afar. After finishing her week-old muffin, she surreptitiously looked around before approaching a little-used cabinet under the kitchen island. She opened the narrow door and slowly removed a half-eaten piece of rancid string cheese. I signaled her mother, who removed the hardened cheese from her grasp and, to Stinky's adamant protest, opened the cabinet door wide to expose a cache of her treasures, including all of the foregoing plus a plethora of other personal items which hadn't yet gone missing. I knew from Br'er Rabbit's tale in *Song of the South* that "everybody's got a laughing place," but I didn't know, until my granddaughter reminded me, that everybody also has a hiding place.

Kids Live in the Moment

Much is made by young parents about keeping adolescents and babies connected to people and places. I've heard Bena on the phone, time and again, entreating Boomer or Stinky to "Say 'Hi' to Pop, MeMe, or Paw-Paw." "You remember Pop, with the mustache?" or "Paw-Paw, with the horses?" Boomer will look up from his Nintendo game to utter, "Say 'Hi' for me," while Clinky races around with a balloon, mindless of who her mother is talking to or what point she is making. We want to imprint our own strong, sentimental feelings of attachment to our children; but the simple, blessed fact is, if the object or person is not in front of them, they don't engage. The very old also live in the moment, appreciative of the attention they get, but easily diverted to something else when it's gone. As I get older, I push the familiar out in front of me so I can enjoy the present while looking forward to the future. As I move on, the past is gone and forgotten until I get back. The aged and young never look back or forward.

Separation Anxiety

Sean is a pilot with Polar Air Cargo and has to leave home to work typical stints of sixteen-to-twenty-one days. He is a consummate father, so his absences generate continuing interest about his return. Stinky-Clinky, especially, is absorbed with his homecoming, after which she clamps herself to his every activity and fights going to sleep even as he lies next to her reading bedtime stories. For his first week home, she has a catatonic fit if he gets out of her sight, so she may usually be found riding on his hip or hanging around his neck. Like the post-traumatic stress syndrome of my Vietnam days, her heightened anxiety over Da-Da's departures begins to fade away with time. Still, there are those occasional flashbacks when Wee Waddie Woo Woo, as he calls her, will leap up from her nap or play, imploring the company at hand, "Where's Da-Da? Where's Da-Da?"

The Walking Scab

Two year-olds in the always-feverish running and exploring bent are prone to trip, fall, and skin their bodies. Adults can't stop them from trying to keep up with the older children in their life; so their limbs and faces perpetually display the bruises, scabs, and scars of life's first lessons. "I see you've added a few new dents to that left leg?" I'll ask Stinky-Clinky, and she'll respond, "One, two, three, five, six," while touching in succession the blue spots or rose-colored areas dotted with fresh scabs.

"How many times did you fall down today at the park?" I continue.

"Two, twice, Pop," she'll say, meaning, I suppose, she fell twice and has two new badges to glorify her outing.

Ready or Not, You're a Grandparent

This old man's mind is still young, even immature, although the body has aged S-O-M-E, but what wisdom can the young-at-heart impart, no matter the age, to those impish, adolescent faces imploring an answer to some momentary curiosity. "Pop, why do dogs bark instead of talk?" they ask innocently. "Da-Da said you'd know." My first and lasting impulse upon being cornered with such inquiries to which I have no knowledge or answer is to make up some wild story to pacify them for the time being and then research it. But, as their own knowledge grows with computers, reading, school, and TV, one has to have some semblance of fact to support a good story. This requires deft maneuvering to hedge your answer before visiting an encyclopedia or library, if you're not online like your grandchildren, to divert the festering question from hitting the perennial fan of their own research. It ain't easy being old and stupid when your grandchildren are young and wise!

A Rhapsody in Dynamic Tension; Otherwise Known as Sibling Rivalry

Never mind Eugene Field's *Gingham Dog and Calico Cat*, as I sat side by side with my grandchildren and three dogs barking in a deafening chorus at the living room window. I started to inquire about quieting the dogs:

"Will somebody see about—"

"Pop," interrupted eight year-old William, "did you know a burp is just a breath of air that comes up from the heart; but when it takes a downward turn, it then becomes a fart?"

I started again, "No, but will somebody—"

Ten year-old Madeline interrupted loudly, "Mom, William has my ball; and it's special to me!"

William shouted back, "Mom, Madeline's trying to take the ball away that I found on the couch!"

"Give it, William!" screamed Madeline, pushing her brother's face while pulling at his arm.

"Madeline hit me!" said William. "You're selfish, Madeline!"

Mother Lisa broke in, holding her son by the shoulders, "William, could you have said that any better? You're being rude!"

"No, you're rude!" said William.

Lisa said, "William, listen to me! Look at me, William! Ask her again, nicely, if you can play with her ball."

"Can I play with your ball, Madeline?" implored William as he and his sister pushed and pulled the ball back and forth in a seesaw struggle for control.

"No!" said Madeline, snatching the ball while pushing William's face. "You're such a pain!"

William screamed through his tears, "It's not your ball! I've got one, too!" and he snatched it back.

"But yours is blue!" shouted Madeline at the top of her lungs.

Their tired mother appeared again: "William, Madeline's right. Her ball is red, and yours is blue. Please give it back," she said before returning to the kitchen.

William threw the ball to the other side of the room while pushing his sister.

"I hate you, William!" said Madeline, indignantly storming out of the room.

"Mom, Madeline said she hates me!" cried William, sobbing loudly.

His tired mother reappeared. "Madeline, come back and say you're sorry to your brother. William, go and get the ball and return it to her. Both of you, stop looking for a fight!"

The three dogs continued to bark at the living room window.

"For God's sake!" I begged, "Will somebody—?"

"Pop," interrupted Madeline again, "my All-Stars Soccer Tournament is this weekend. You are going, aren't you?"

"No, Madeline! Pop's going to my game. You're going to my game, aren't you, Pop?" said William.

"Pop, who are you looking at?" Madeline said contemptuously.

"I'm looking at you," I said in the only complete sentence, albeit short, that I'd been able to utter.

The kid furrowed her brow and adamantly declared, "You're staring! Don't you know it's rude to stare?"

Lisa interceded yet again as I sat staring blankly out the window over her three barking dogs and two fighting kids, remembering the quiet of the Appalachian Trail and an earlier time in my own grandfather's living room where children were seen, but not heard, a philosophy that he reinforced with his razor strap. But as Bob Dylan so eloquently sang, "The times, they are a changin'" (and not always for the better, says I).

Lisa sat down beside me, patting my thigh, and sighed, "Your grandchildren are smart, accomplished, and independent; but they can misbehave from time to time. It's always a challenge to keep them content, preoccupied, and quiet."

"Precocious?" I said, really thinking, "*Spare the rod and spoil the child.*"

"Right!" concluded my daughter. "Precocious."

Of course, sibling rivalry is as prevalent as the common cold. We've all experienced friction with our brothers and sisters, if any. Intra-family competition and out-and-out fighting have been around since the dawn of time. Consider Romulus and Remus, Cain and Abel, Freddums and me, and Lisa and her sister Shannon. Nevertheless, this rite of passage should not exempt good manners and civil behavior toward those witnessing it. Good luck on that one!

In my mind I'm thinking that today's precocious, tech-savvy children need to occupy a world that does not always revolve around them, where their survival depends upon a fair contribution of their considerable talents and good will and that does not shine a forgiving spotlight upon their ill-behavior. At the very least, they need to pay more homage to their long-suffering and overly supportive mothers.

   "But the truth about the cat and pup
    Is this: they ate each other up!
    Now what do you really think of that!"
                              Gingham Dog and Calico Cat

Well, for one thing, I never thought I'd incur PTSD again after Vietnam.

Grumpy Old Man for Hire

The ad might read, "One Fat, Grumpy, Old, Male Nanny for Hire: By the hour or by the day. His few drawbacks include being contentious, irritating, smelly, and belligerent to a fault. Takes a bath once a month, whether he needs one or not. Believes in spanking rather than 'time out,' fear rather than reward as the proper motivator. Subscribes to the time-proven motto, 'Spare the rod and spoil the child.' Is a devotee of the philosophy that children should be seen and not heard, whether they're 'precocious' or not. Feeds a balanced nutrient diet in suitable portions for age and expects that charges will belong to the Clean Plate Club. Children are assigned age-specific chores, since 'An idle mind is the Devil's workshop' and are rewarded for early, satisfactory completion. Rewards include being first into a warm bath, where energy is saved by not changing water; dessert at dinner if any, assignment of easier chores, etc. Children will call him 'Sir' or 'Mister,' not by his given name, because this is a dictatorship; and he is not their friend. Eight o'clock bedtimes are enforced, and stories are optional depending upon behavior. Fearsome stories may be included for bad behavior because a little fear often garners a more obedient attitude. Is good at play with manual toys, e.g. playground equipment, trampolines, blocks, bubbles, chalk, GeoTrax, balls, and kites, but incapable of engaging in online or computer game entertainment. Advice is archaic and mostly inapplicable to the modern age, but sincerely given and usually received with humorous acclaim. Children in his charge will be overjoyed to see their parents again and will surprise them with new-found courtesy skills. Come one, come all; one grumpy, old man for hire as a manny-nanny or a cure for an ailing society."

Jim Sharer Bentley

Children for Sale

Two boilsome, quarrelsome children for sale,
Two pushing and shoving, occasionally loving,
But mostly incendiary, children for sale.
They kick and they scream, are seldom serene.
They rankle and tattle and trample like cattle,
Are ever-heard, at hand or unseen.
They pester their father and cry to their mother
Of wrongs committed by one to the other.
When in disagreement, they start slamming doors
And throwing vile tantrums upon local floors.
They interrupt talking of others who speak,
Wreak havoc like mavericks with no souls to keep.
Guaranteed always to be such pests
That they'll ruin an outing and drive away guests.
It's "me, me, me" and "I, I, I"
Resounding earthward to the sky;
Always "Gimme," never "Me, please."
It gives us all the heebie-jeebies!
They're rude to adults, as they challenge their will,
With stares and curt words that rapidly fill
The sainted senior with anger and spite.
Forget them for sale. They're yours outright.
Okay! I will pay you to take them away,
So I can live for another day.

The Ogre in the Basement

A grumpy, old grandfather living with an active family tends to put a slow spin on the activity around him. Kids come to expect a dance around Pop to be in quarter-time. Words are not heard at first utterance, and time is allocated tediously. I help with cleaning, washing dishes, changing diapers, watching kids, feeding animals, edging/mowing the lawn, raking leaves, emptying trash, etc. Exercise, meals, naps, shopping, sightseeing, visiting, and work are scheduled ahead for each day or week, usually by the caretakers; but adequate time can be leached from the schedule for the old guy to do a walkabout, drive to the post office, shop for necessities, dispatch mail, and travel afar as the calling arises. A cell phone keeps me in touch with my far-flung kids, and I am welcome to use Robin and Sean's computer for my writings. We visit the YMCA in O'Fallon collectively to exercise, there is a nursery/childcare facility there, and we eat out periodically to relieve Ma Bear of her self-assigned cooking burden. It's a good life, and I gain much from the close exchange with kinder. Still, I yearn for an independent life in the solitary surrounds of Sea Pines on the Garcon Peninsula in the Florida Panhandle, where my heart soars. The ogre doth need the sunshine of independence for the good of his soul.

Ma Bear's Mad Dash Cleanup

One would surmise that a loving and sweet one-and-a-half-year-old baby be docile and quiet. Wrong! Stinky-Clinky, while a most-loving and sharing baby, can turn a neat, well-appointed house into rubble, kindred to my Soundside home after Ivan, in less than an hour. She's inside and out, upstairs and down, into the kitchen cabinets (having learned early how to open the child-proof latches and garbage cans) and in the bathrooms, the bedroom closets, the basement toolboxes, the garage recycle bins, and the wondrous flower gardens of Ma Bear. There is nothing too small to escape her eye, much of which she pops quickly into her mouth: berries, acorns, flowers, leaves, pebbles, sticks, bugs, dog turds, etc. We all run breathlessly behind her, trying to anticipate and remove unsafe objects and actions. We are only marginally successful; and in her wake, debris is strewn like that pictured on TV in the path of a tornado. While she is napping or in bed, we adults congregate to crisscross the house and yard to put things to rights. But picking up is not cleaning, so Ma Bear, always conscious of the sterile behind the well-ordered, in the last hours before picking up her pilot-husband from the netherworld of Polar Aviation, rushes madly about to Clorox toilets and tubs, scour sinks, disinfect countertops, Windex mirrors and windows, change cat boxes, wash sheets and towels, change beds, Spot Shot the food and vomit stains on their W-H-I-T-E carpets, and vacuum throughout. That's right—with two children, an old-timer, two dogs, and three cats, Ma Bear contends with maintaining W-H-I-T-E carpets! God bless the world's cleaners, but especially those shoveling shit against a white tide. I stand in awe of her ant-like cleaning fervor. However, it is my sincerest advice that people with children and pets do not install white carpeting.

Monsters and Mayhem

It's the inherent job of youth to challenge the wisdom of age. While middle-aged parents are charged with guiding and shaping their progeny on the front line, grandparents and other old-timers serve to reinforce from the sidelines. The threat of power, included as a tool in the role of parentage, is absent to the geriatric crowd. However, substituting admirably for the obvious lack of physical power is the wonder of storytelling and the invention of fearsome creatures, inhabiting close-in spaces, which always watch and yearn to correct us. Old-timers have a storehouse of mystical knowledge from bygone eras and experience to conjure up a believable story from the unbelievable. While psychologists might recommend otherwise, the raising of a huge, hairy, slobber-mouthed ogre bowling with human skulls in the attic or basement brings all sorts of disciplinary possibilities to the table. Descriptions should be vivid, like slavering jaws; glowing, yellow eyes; long, smelly, matted hair covering the entire head and body; and razor-sharp claws that click on the floor as it walks upright or, preferably, on all fours. If you personalize the ogre, he becomes the more believable. "Don't make me have to call Hector up from the furnace room to deal with you!" is the obvious challenge to a disobedient child.

"Mama says there's no such thing as monsters," they retort.

"So," you respond, "you're telling me that Big Foot and UFOs don't exist? Pop's telling you that a Yeti used to take lambs from the barn when he was a boy, and I've personally seen a flying saucer in the corn field where there's now a crop circle."

Their eyes widen, and the power is yours. And don't forget to call them to the TV whenever the Mystery Channel is exploring the possibility of Sasquatch in the Pacific Northwest or the Roswell UFO landing and recovery incident.

Communing with Your Demons

Humor has been described as life's best medicine. The more you laugh, the more joy overtakes you. The louder you laugh, the more you expel your demons. When the laughter becomes infectious, the demons laugh, too, and sit with you in such blissful repartee that they become consorts and friends. There's nothing like a good laugh with the monster that lives in your closet. He's not nearly as hairy as you thought.

I'm Sweet on You

Men Are from Mars, Women Are from Venus is one of many books and discoveries that emphasize the obvious psychological differences between the sexes. My own brother, in whom I have absolute trust, has been wont to say on more than one occasion that men and women cannot live together in harmony, that there is no such thing as a happy marriage. Certainly, my own marriage, and that of our parents before us, lent truth to Fred's conclusion; so I was never surprised by the energetic yelling bouts between my caretakers in Lake St. Louis. During one such heated confrontation over some usual subject, such as frivolous spending or proper child rearing, Robin bellowed out, "Why would you say such a thing?" to which Sean responded quietly, "Because I'm sweet on you." Needless to say, the resulting laughter reverberated long after the tiff was forgotten. Peace was restored, and happiness enjoined, at least for the short term.

A Perfect Day in Paradise

During October 2008, I had occasion to drive back to my native land surrounding Pensacola. I returned to visit my several doctors and to service the truck that was purchased from a local dealer after Hurricane Ivan. Of course, some visits to family and old friends were included on the agenda; but for purest pleasure, I reserved a day to commune with the sand and water of my memory. After my usual scrumptious Brunchzone and flavored coffee at Bagelheads, I crossed the two bridges to Santa Rosa Island and parked at the Pensacola Beach Visitor's Center, walking west along the sidewalk fronting the Gulf and Soundside apartment condominiums, interdicted by neighborhood streets emptying onto Ft. Pickens Road and boardwalks stretching between high-rises across dunes to the beach. After passing through the Ft. Pickens' boundary gate, I proceeded for an uninterrupted mile along the old road to the entry station foundation. Sand had blown over the road in places; and the big roadside dunes that existed before Ivan were now gone, leaving a surrealistic aura from Gulf to Sound that reminded me of a moonscape. The sky was cloudless and brilliantly blue. The sand was so white as to be blinding to the eye. The silence, broken only by the shorebirds and occasional claxons from distant boat traffic, went on forever. I inhaled and exhaled the pure, salty air. I traced the foundation of the former park service entry station and returned to the boundary gate and then back along Ft. Pickens Road to Peg Leg Pete's eatery and watering hole for a Bushwhacker cocktail of Kahlua Liqueur, rum, and cream as well as a Key West Salad with dijon vinaigrette and a slice of key lime pie. As I returned to my truck with a slight breeze touching my cheeks and the sun baking my brow, I confirmed in my soul yet again that this was my paradise, and this day was perfect in it.

Wanderlust

True release of the captive spirit always involves travel, from a simple change of scenery to a dramatic relocation. Transport can mean walking into a different field of vision or using planes, trains, and automobiles to cast your lot afar.

My convulsed world since Hurricane Ivan has left me interrupting the life cycle of my support group as I travel between them. Always, I hope that my contributions of assistance and company outweigh the drain on their time and resources. At length, I fret that freeing them for a while is the only courteous alternative (recall Ben Franklin's admonition that, "Fish and visitors stink after three days"), so I make plans and set an itinerary in motion. This traveling saga will continue until I can regenerate on East Bay near my home city of Pensacola.

After a second active year with son Sean, my mind has taken flight again to see what's around the next bend. My caretakers also need some time free of me to return to an unencumbered family dynamic. Hearing again the train whistles of my youth, I am imagining a circumnavigation of my country on Amtrak from St. Louis to visit a niece in Raleigh, a daughter in Washington, a son in New York, and a second daughter in Seattle. I have shared my dream with Sean, who suggested instead that I travel by plane to Raleigh so I can leave my truck in his garage for safekeeping. I acquiesced, and he immediately went online to secure me a ticket. I phoned Amtrak myself to reserve separate train tickets to Alexandria in Virgina, New York Penn Station, Chicago, and Seattle. And so the saga of my wanderlust is jump-started yet again.

Packing for the Trip

In defiance of the expression, "You can't take it with you," when we take a trip, we usually do! Like the exonerated turtle of folk legend, we carry our house and stuff on our back when we travel. Whether near or far, of short duration or long, the cells of our duffel bags, packs, suitcases, and trunks are a nexus for satisfying our needs for food, shelter, and kinship. We are not only what we eat, but what we pack. If young, we pack a teddy for love and security. If old, we pack checkbooks and credit cards for the same thing. Favorite objects of jewelry that adorn our ears, fingers, legs, necks, noses, and toes always accompany us. Caps, hats, and T-shirts with the logos that identify our history and interests are packed for wear. Drinks, snacks, and freeze-dried foods sustain us. Books, gifts, correspondence logs, debt-pay calendars, and the profusion of pills that we take daily to stay healthy are brought. Our special cleaners, ointments, exfoliators, scents, conditioners, shampoos, enhancers, revitalizers, lotions, body washes, and emollients are taken along with the traditional contents of a makeup or shaving kit. Formal and informal attire is selected based upon time, weather, and our itinerary.

If you're a frequent traveler for business or pleasure, then you know from experience how to pack light with drip-dry clothes and to fill in consumables along the way. It is possible to live out of your suitcase, even for years at a time. Prescriptions for medicine can be renewed by phone, and mail can be dispatched to changing addresses. Collectibles and second-tier stuff can be mailed back to a holder for safekeeping. The cell phone keeps you ever in touch with friends and kin. Life on the run is an accommodative art. Still, longtime travelers yearn for the permanence of their own bathroom, bed, closets, and floor space to display their stuff and their own play-and-work areas to share memories, pursue dreams, entertain, and insulate themselves.

Love Can Be Smothering

"Ma Bear," I said while planning my next sortie into the world from her basement enclave in Lake St. Louis, "life is tenuous. We can't afford to waste any time!" Of course, I was talking about me wasting time, but not exactly wasting it with my grandchildren, more like not engaging the dreams harbored in my own solitary soul. "It seems a dichotomy trying to escape the goodwill and love of your support group in order to fulfill an unknown quest for adventure, but it is a fact of life. We all have those solitary calls that beckon us beyond the comfort and support of the familiar status quo. There it is; that's the best explanation I can give you. And now, I bid you goodbye."

"A person can be lonely even if he is loved by many people, because he is still not the 'One and Only' to anyone."

Anne Frank, *The Diary of a Young Girl*

He Scared the Death Out of Me

Seven year-old Jack had a penchant for running at his grandfather unexpectedly from behind doors and furniture. In this attack mode, he always added the high-pitched dual-syllable karate yell before driving his head into my potbelly and chopping at me wildly with rigid hands. Periodically, his mother would remind him, "No taking down Pop!" but the warnings usually fell on deaf ears. One early morning, as he rushed me loudly during my slumbers in bed, I awoke abruptly and blurted out, "For God's sake, Jack, don't do that! You scared the death out of me!"

Jack paused only a few seconds before replying, "Actually, Pop, scaring away death is a good thing. In other words, it means you'll live forever."

Light Flashes in the Tunnel

Of course, I meant to say, "You scared the life out of me," or, "You scared me to death," but Jack had responded correctly to my misstatement. "Jack, I'm sure you know that death is inevitable for all of us. It can be postponed through exercise and good nutrition, but not forever," I offered grumpily.

"Actually," Jack retorted, "it can be avoided because there are dudes with powers to avoid death."

"Jack, you're talking about a Wii game, and those characters aren't real!"

"Uh, uh, uh, actually, Pop, they are real and only lose power. In other words, they don't die."

"Jack, they don't have any power in reality. It's a play-pretend game."

"Actually, it's not a game, and guess what? In *Pirates of the Caribbean*, only the real dudes die, not the other dudes."

"That's what I'm talking about, Jack."

"Uh, uh, uh, by the way, Pop, did you know that there's lots of haunted houses and places where spirits open and close doors, sing, talk, and blow out candles?"

"Yeah, Jack, that's paranormal psychology, which might have some credibility regarding ghosts."

"Actually, ghosts are real."

"They're supernatural, Jack, and may or may not be real."

"Guess what, Pop? They are real. I've seen them on the *Othersiders*. And, guess what, Pop? When Captain Jack Sparrow was fighting a Redcoat dude, he threw a barrel at his head and then kicked him in the nuts!"

"Are we talking about a ghost here, Jack?"

"Oh, no, that's real. It's on my video game."

The kid's going to scare the death out of me yet!

Jim Sharer Bentley

I'm Not a Big Fan of Healthy Food

After my Amtrak trip around the U.S. ended in Seattle, I had occasion again to visit in the Woodinville home of my daughter Shannon, son-in-law Pat, and grandchildren Tootie and Black Jack. Most notable in the scheme of their daily lives is the fact that Shannon and Pat are vegetarians. While Tootie, age ten and in fifth grade, craves the occasional tuna fish sandwich, she is generally happy with her parents' prominent vegetable fare and imitation meat products made from soy. Jack, age six and in first grade, on the other hand, will not abide soy bacon, which he calls fakon, or pizza without real pepperoni. They both share my sentiment about sweets; but Jack don't truck no substitute for bacon, chicken, chops, fish, ham, hamburger, loin, ribs, roast beef, sausage products, and all the rest. Jack is a true carnivore. To placate him in those dire moments after he has made every face imaginable for his vegetarian offering, his mother brings out her reserve Yard-O-Beef Summer Sausage to whittle off a few slices for Jack, who invariably sings out, "Sweet!"

"Why do I have to eat vegetables at all?" he implores at almost every meal.

"Because vegetables are good for your health," return his exasperated parents in unison, to which Jack always proclaims, "I'm not a big fan of healthy food!"

Bakugan and Falafel

They sound like passwords to some secret, medieval society, but in reality, they're just food, fun and games in daily usage in modern times. My introduction to both at seventy-one years of age was in Seattle, where upon stepping off the plane, you are inundated, as in most major metropolitan U.S. cities, with our multicultural human landscape. Amidst the crush of derbies, Stetsons, veils, turbans, coolie hats, and saris, you'll see the world's children carrying the hexagon tin of Bakugan Battle Brawlers and adults, principally Middle Easterners, munching on fried falafel patties—ground chickpeas—for a snack. I was invited to partake of both on a play date with Black Jack and Tootie in the home of a lovely Lebanese-American mother, who served me falafel patties with hummus on pita bread and a salad composed of romaine, pita pieces, nuts, and nasturtium blossoms (red and yellow) for lunch. The latte, she said, was strictly from Northwestern U.S. tradition. As we ate, we watched Black Jack and her son Joe play with their G-Power Bakugan Gate Cards and marble-like cylinders that bounce open into various characters with names like, Dragonoid, Klawgor, Mantris, Blaze, and Rip Tide. Along with the game itself, it was also a grand day of transformation for this old man: latte and dark chocolate with cherries for dessert, a delightful hostess for company, and the song of children battling to capture Gate Cards in the background.

Slug Bug—No Tag Back!

Jack's sister Tootie is nothing if not the essence of civility and model behavior, quite amazing for any human, but especially so for a ten year-old girl. She has impeccable manners and is polite to the extreme. Furthermore, she is unerringly considerate of everyone she meets; reserved in her demeanor; conscientious about assigned chores and fifth grade homework; and the pride of her adult support community including neighbors, relatives, and teachers alike. For her fat, grumpy old grandfather who came out of the children-should-be-seen-and-not-heard generation, she is a joy to be around and, seemingly, a rapt listener of my verbal wanderings and deranged stories. Her persona is a continuum of a mature lull beyond her years, at least until she gets on a soccer field. The transformation of her character during competition from good-natured passivity to aggressive demon is quite a metamorphosis to behold. She is the bane of those opposing her, so much so that many are reduced to tears or simply limp off the field to escape her. But at the game's final whistle, she returns as quickly from the maniacal Mr. Hyde to the caring-sharing Dr. Jekyll again, with handshakes, hugs, and innocent taps on my shoulder as we pass a Volkswagen Beetle while saying, "Red slug bug. No tag back!"

A Reading and a Rendering

As we all know, the seven-book *Harry Potter* phenomenon has captivated the collective imaginations of our global human population, particularly the young and young-at-heart. This was reinforced for me during my nannying time with Tootie and Black Jack in the summer of 2009, when the kids were out of school. Tootie had already been infected with a love for reading, so while her mother pursued a nursing degree at the University of Washington and her father worked at Microsoft, she would read and re-read the *Potter* series as Black Jack played Bakugan or one of his many Nintendo Wii games. Their mother, with a bent to encourage active reading rather than passive screen-watching, required them to read each book before she would take them to

Light Flashes in the Tunnel

the movie or purchase the DVD. This mainly applied to Tootie, who at age eleven had devoured each *Potter* book in its time from second grade forward with her classmates and friends.

The portrait of Tootie's childhood, reflected here, is the habitual violation of her bedtime curfew to read on into the night. Jack, age seven, and I, age seventy-one, were wont to watch anything at any time without any such restrictions; but Shannon and Tootie held fast, and Tootie additionally imposed her own *Harry Potter* mandate that the books had to be read in the order of their publication because, "The last book, *Harry Potter and the Deathly Hallows,* is the best book, which won't make any sense unless you read the series in order." At this time, she and her mother were planning a weekend trip to Woodinville's movie theater to see the sixth film in J.K. Rowling's *Harry Potter* series. They had purchased and read all seven books, along with purchasing and viewing repeatedly, I might add, the five DVDs now available for home screening. This was a ceremonial mother-daughter event, from which their three men were excluded. Of course, we were aghast and protested vehemently, but to no avail. The women held fast again, even when I pulled out my AARP card and pled for special age consideration. We were not only off the latest *Potter* movie, we were also off the five existing DVDs until we read the books.

It was conceded that hearing the books read would qualify as a reading, so Tootie volunteered to read them to Jack and me during the day when her parents were away. She started, of course, with the first book, *Harry Potter and the Sorcerer's Stone,* and read with gusto and relish, gesturing wildly, and intoning voice inflections remembered from her DVDs. Jack and I were wide-eyed at these renderings, when Tootie didn't read so fast or intone so oddly that we couldn't make out the words, but we were also without honor in following their mandate to watch the DVDs in order or at all without first reading the book. Still, Tootie's readings and renderings were dramatic and unforgettable, prompting greater impetus for Jack and me to go beyond the first book.

A Cell Phone for Tootie

When I arrived at SeaTac Airport during June 2009, Tootie was imploring her father for a cell phone; "Dad, there are twelve girls on my soccer team, and they all have cell phones except Brooke, Rachael, and me." The petitioning continued as her summer soccer season progressed until, finally in exasperation, he offered her a tongue-in-cheek bargain whereby he would concede the phone if she would make a goal in the forthcoming Starfire Tournament in Renton, knowing that she played Stopper in a defensive position where she rarely advanced beyond midfield, much less near the penalty box strike zone for scoring a goal. Now, Tootie is a fierce competitor, much admired by her coach and teammates, so Pat and I still suspect they had a collusion during the Renton game when she dribbled the ball through the opposing team's defense to reach the penalty box and kick it over their goalie's head into the net. After the requisite number of jumps and arm thrusts, she turned, grinning, toward her father on the sideline while putting the little finger from a clinched fist against her lips and the thumb against her ear. Pat just shook his head, but later that night, he went online with her to order the purple wireless phone of her dreams.

A Kick-Back Day

Nannying can be quite exhausting for a fat, old man, as I learned during my tenure with Tootie and Black Jack. The kids were agreeable and obedient enough; but, like all children, they needed feeding, instruction, and positive distractions from a sedentary lifestyle. Fortunately, Tootie was immersed in summer soccer and Jack in twice-weekly karate lessons, so all that I contributed to their exercise were the occasional walks on off-days. Tootie was fit from running in soccer, so she enjoyed the walking; but Jack, at seven years old, balked every time we mentioned exercise or set out on a long explore. We had to coax him along with promises of stopping at playgrounds; ice cream parlors; lunch counters; or places to collect BBs, sticks, rocks, etc. He was always thirsty and emptied not only his own water bottle, but mine and Tootie's, as well. Rest stops were frequent, and the pace was tediously slow. Occasionally, to salve my and Jack's souls, I would declare a no-chore-no-exercise-no-nutrition day off where reading, computer games, TV, and eating sweets in our pajamas could prevail with abandon, a down-day of truce for the nanny and his charges.

Twinkle

Even as my fourteen year-old granddaughter Tootie was winging it across the globe with her mother, grandmother, and soccer mates, I was in residence with her father and brother in Woodinville, Washington. It was late June 2012, and the girls, with their coaches and chaperones, were invited to play in a multi-country tournament near San Sebastián, Spain, before which they would pass through Madrid and after which they would visit Barcelona before returning to the USA. To heighten their already electric enthusiasm, the national soccer teams for Italy and Spain would be playing for the World Soccer Cup during that time. Tootie and her teammates were alive with life and the sheer jubilance of living every moment. Their pre-departure banter about their European visit expectations and probable memories gave rise to my own recollections of her illustrious development from fearless infancy, when she would hurl herself off furniture backs with abandon and trust into our outstretched arms, through stellar academic and athletic soccer careers, to the accomplished youngster of her present demeanor. I had to smile at her split personality, divided between a natural composure and reticence in the school day world and a fierce, aggressive nature on the soccer field. She is the peer-elected captain of her Select Soccer Team, the peer-elected student government treasurer for her upcoming eighth grade year, and a recent inductee into the Northshore Legacy branch of the National Junior Honor Society.

While staying in her bedroom during this visit, I enjoyed the "It's Your Day" foil balloon, floating contentedly at the end of a silver ribbon, with two separate green and purple balloons astride it, that simply announced to all that Tootie was out of her oral braces and free to smile again. I explored the treasure trove of Tootie's advances in imagination and intellect as I perused her extensive library of books; listened to her dream of writing a children's story this summer; and reacquainted myself with her sentimental collection of stuffed animals, including her favorite Gund Teddy Bear, variously named Bear-Bear, Cuddles, and George—a baby gift from Uncle Paul and me—and a goblin named Pickle that I sent her during September 2008 while staying with Uncle Paul and Aunt Brigette in New York City. Holding Pickle again reminded me of the book about goblins that I also acquired at the time of Pickle's purchase from F.A.O Schwarz and also sent along to Tootie. I ransacked her library and finally found the book by Brian Froud and Ari Berk. Thumbing again through its magical, mysterious contents, I found my inscription, still prominent on the back of the title page, which reads as follows:

September 2008
Yo Tootie,
Goblins, goblins everywhere! It's hard to glimpse them indoors or out, especially during summer, because of their camouflage and size; but your Uncle Fred and I did see them in winter dancing in the snow. As Mr. Froud relates, most times it's only stinks or stains or that bubbling sound beneath your bed that announces their presence. Of course, their infernal thievery and tricks are the sure sign they are in residence. Mischief! Mischief! Your early ancestor, Gov. William Bradford of the Plymouth Bay Colony, must have been a goblin because of that outlandish hat he wore. And you may have a little goblin in you because of that mischievous twinkle in your eyes. Certainly Jack is a goblin for the same reason. And your Dad, carrying around that Sticky Vegetable Sandwich with the squash bookmark? Then there's your mother with her Wisking Statue and morning chant, "Braak fest es kumin, halde yur tamm hurrses!" Woe is me. What's my peaceful world coming to? Read up and you'll find your true lineage. I love you and I'll see you soon.

Inderwink

Good at Making an Innocent Message Either Totally Incomprehensible or Utterly Offensive (that's what I'm talking about!)

Plan B

During Tootie's and her mother's absence, her brother Jack and I remained behind with their father to pursue summer dreams and obligations without interruption from the ladies of the house. Now, Jack is the opposite of his sister's normally composed and reticent demeanor. Instead, Jack is the essence of the word "extrovert." He ain't nothing if not an outgoing, overtly expressive person. There are no strangers around Jack for very long, because he makes it a point to draw them into his circle. He'll chatter with anyone and everyone, no matter the location or occasion. It's always enjoyable to watch him interject himself into other people's lives. He's very good-natured, and everybody loves him from the get-go. He has a large assembly of acquaintances and friends from his many past and present activities and interests, even (he confided to me) a special girlfriend named

Mackenzie. While Tootie has remained almost solely committed to an out-of-school soccer regimen as her primary interest, Jack has hopped from karate (he's now a Black Belt) to soccer to guitar lessons to kendo to football. Kendo evolved from his interest in martial arts and sword-fighting/fencing. During Jack's kendo phase, while his mother and Tootie were in Spain, Pat and I regularly took him to kendo for his weekly exercises and lessons. Since it was at some distance from their house in Woodinville, we stayed and watched the banging and flailing of bamboo practice swords by their practitioners hidden under thick pads and metal headpieces. I noted during these practices that Jack was usually paired (by choice) with an attractive and personable Asian girl of about his same age. When I inquired about their allegiance to each other, Jack simply blushed and introduced her as Kyra. En route back home, I asked Jack the name of his real girlfriend.

"Mackenzie," he replied.

"But what about Kyra?" I implored. "You seem to be infatuated with her, too!"

Without missing a beat, Jack said, "Oh, Kyra. She's Plan B."

Believability

During my June 2012 visit to Woodinville, my semi-sophisticated yet still-naive Tootie had long ago passed through the age of innocence when her grandfather could beguile her into believing my fanciful stories. In fact, her cousin, Stinky-Clinky, was dubious of the old man at only six years old during my later visit to her during January 2012. This fact was re-established with Tootie when I tested the waters during our daily "Got'cha last" tag match. I submitted to her that, "You can't tag me. Old people are protected from being tagged by an invisible force field that renders it impossible to touch them," to which Tootie responded, "Sorry, Pop, I don't buy it! You're it, and you know it!"

Revisiting Stinky-Clinky

It was January 2013, and I was invited by Sean and Robin to visit them and my two grandchildren, Boomer, now eleven, and Stinky-Clinky, turning six on January 21. It had been almost three years since I departed from a multi-year residence in their home, so I was anxious to see how the intervening time had shaped them. Boomer, a fifth-grader, was a mostly quiet, introspective child with a serious bent toward making good grades in school and performing well at the host of video games he played on his iPad and Nintendo GameCube. He was generally passive and maintained a low profile at home until his sister started pushing his buttons. The Clinky Girl, on the other hand, was high-profile, with boundless energy and playtime imagination. She could play quietly with her menagerie of stuffed animals and dolls but seldom did. She was all about engaging her parents in wistful pursuits, harassing her brother, or hounding the cats and dogs. Of course, now that her grandfather was back in residence, her attention had turned to me, starting at the early hour of 6:00 a.m.

"Pop. Pop. POP! Get up. It's time to play."

"What are you talking about, Clinky? It's the middle of the night. Go back to bed."

"No, Pop! It's morning. Mom said so, and she sent me down to wake you up."

"You're kidding me. That woman has no mercy! I'm going

back to sleep."

"No, Pop! It's time to get up and play."

"What do you want to play at this ungodly hour?"

"I want to play Dragon."

"You mean that fire-breathing beast that burned all the hair off my eyebrows while flying around my bedroom during the night?"

"Pop, there's no such thing as a fire-breathing dragon that flies. They're not real. The closest thing to dragons were dinosaurs that lived a long time ago and are not alive anymore. My plastic dragons are only toys."

"What you say, girl! There are komodo dragons living on several Indonesian islands that grow up to ten feet long and weigh upwards of 150 pounds. They eat goats and the occasional sassy girl."

"That's wrong, Pop. I'm going to ask Mom."

"Whoa, let's not get hasty, little woman. No sense in riling up your mother."

Robin's voice from the nether regions: "I heard that, Pop. Don't you be telling tales that will get Madison too scared to sleep."

Pop back to nether regions: "Komodos really are dragons, even if they can't fly or breathe fire; and, by the way, if they could, they'd be more scared of her than she would of them. Just like me."

Robin's response: "Pop, no more dragon tales!"

"Clinky, if you're real quiet, Pop will tell you the story of Saint George and the dragon. Then you'll believe," I said.

"Pop, you're pulling my leg, again."

"You don't believe my dragon tales?"

"Yeah."

"You do. Good. Then let me tell you about the greatest dragon slayer of them all."

"No, Pop. I don't believe in dragons! I just said so."

"You said, 'Yeah.'"

"I said, 'Yeah, I don't believe in dragons.'"

Note: At this point, I was afraid to muddy the waters further by summoning up the old-time song, "Yes, we have no bananas. We have no bananas today."

"So, do your dragons have names?" I asked.

"Yeah." (Note: Clinky uses the word "Yeah" interchangeably for "Yes" and "No.")

"How about we call this one Fred and the other one Jimbo?"

"No, Pop, dragons are all girls. This one's Frieda, and the other one is Jasmine."

"I never heard of a fire-breathing dragon named Jasmine. You must be thinking about a lamb."

"Pop, quit pulling my leg."

"How can you tell if they're girls?"

"Because they're cute, they dress up fine, smell good, and get along with everybody. Boys are stupid and don't know how to act."

"Well, Pop is a boy, and I've got nothing but good will for you and your little girlfriends."

"Pop, you're not a boy and you're not a girl. You're just a fat, old man!"

Robin's voice from the nether regions: "Madison Rose, don't you call your Pop fat!"

"I'd rather think of myself as 'pleasingly plump.'"

"Pop, Mom's being kind. You are fat, you are old, and you

are not a boy!"

"Am I at least as cute as the dragons?"

"Pop, you're not funny either. Quit kidding me!"

"Well, I can't imagine that a dragon would be thought of as cute by a sweet-smelling girl."

Thus ended our little innocent diatribe, which denuded me of any masculine status and forfeited the cause of all boys to the cherished ranks of womanhood. So young and yet so smart! Stinky-Clinky for President!

The Conundrum of Giving and Sharing

While the light flashes in my life's tunnel continue to occur sporadically, the writing of them is even more sporadic. There's been an almost-three-year lapse in my writing regimen since Robin evicted me from my longtime residence in their homestead. After that embarrassing time, we reconciled our piddly differences and I have been invited back in favor to catch up with Boomer and Stinky-Clinky. The ostensible reason for my visit during January 2013 was to attend Clinky's sixth birthday party as a surrogate for her father, as if anyone could take his place in her heart, while Sean was away in Miami undergoing a two-month captain's training program for Polar Air Cargo. I returned to Lake St. Louis having seen the Clinky Girl only twice, for short half-hour bursts, since my March 2010 eviction. Nevertheless, ever the precocious, hard-driving girl that she's always been—albeit twice the age now than when I left her—she dutifully resurrected her past collection of stuffed animals and Barbie dolls by name to accompany us on the previous imaginary journey through her elaborately crafted fantasy world. Of course,

I had forgotten all the names of our cast and most of the rules surrounding their engagement, but she brought me up to speed muy pronto.

I also found that her rationale for life's Christian lessons is a curious study in personal adaptation. She was on board with Aunt Ro-Rose's suggestion to make personal birthday hats for all attendees of the forthcoming surprise party in Clarksville for her grandmother, MeMe Garrison; but when her aunt suggested that she and I join together to buy MeMe the *NLT One Year Bible* she wanted, Clinky spurned the idea in favor of giving her own separate gift, a handmade card and a hard-earned one dollar bill from her piggy bank. Clinky said, by way of explanation, "MeMe has always given me money, and I want to give her some money in return." So Aunt Ro-Rose and I drove off alone to the Back to Basics Christian Bookstore to purchase MeMe's birthday gift. Clinky declined our invitation to go along, thinking, I suppose, that we were taking her to another boring church service.

After purchasing the requested Bible, we perused the store's other merchandise on hand and Ro-Rose found a pink ladies' T-shirt in MeMe's size sporting the Christian message "You Are Loved" from the book of Romans. We discussed Clinky's earlier desire to give her own gift, with the thought that she could choose an additional offering to MeMe between the Bible and the T-shirt, while I would give MeMe the remaining gift. When we returned home, I asked Clinky if she would like to give one of the two additional gifts purchased for MeMe and she readily acceded. Aunt Ro-Rose then held up the Bible and the T-shirt side by side for her to examine while I requested that she choose one or the other to wrap for her grandmother. Without a moment's hesitation, Clinky said, "Both of them." So while Clinky wrapped her two additional presents in colorful crepe paper, with oodles of Scotch Tape, I wrote a note over my name on MeMe's group card saying, "We formed a MeMe Birthday Club with your bossy granddaughter as president. While I was not allowed to make any decisions, I still wish you a Happy Birthday with many happy returns."

The Raccoon Tree

Among my most cherished gifts lost in Hurricane Ivan were a photograph of Freddums and me as adults, sitting atop a marble slide in a Newport playground where we had once played near our home as children, and a drawing from my granddaughter Tootie interpreting my tales about The 'Coon, the 'Possum and the Old Black Crow. My niece Sarah had graciously taken the photograph of Fred and me on the slide and had placed two copies into artistic, filigree frames before sending them to us. I proudly displayed mine on my bedroom bookcase. And Tootie was probably a four or five year-old child when she drew and colored her scene with a bright yellow sun; blue sky and brook; hollow tree with black hole and green foliage; and, best of all, a stick raccoon with black mask and ringed tail that looked more like a sawhorse than a living creature. I thought the work splendid and greatly advanced for a mere child.

Of course, I expect that all families around the globe, diverse as our world cultures are, exert the same parental and grandparental pride in our children. Don't you know that where children abide, the refrigerators and walls are covered with their artwork and school papers? I had Tootie's drawing framed and hung it on my bedroom wall for all time, which turned out to be about two years. I then lamented its loss to Ivan long and loud over successive years until Tootie drew me a second edition as a seventeen year-old for Christmas 2014. In her latest interpretation, we are two raccoons, sitting in Adirondak chairs aside the brook on a meadow of green grass next to the hollow tree. The raccoons are in proper proportion and employment, me with cigar and Sudoku puzzle and Tootie with a hopefully redeeming book. I am in character with a mustache and glasses, although the square rims make me look way cooler than is my nature. The hole in the tree trunk is considerably larger than before, presumably to accommodate my expanded girth. The sun and sky are gone, but the close-up composition is inimitable. I offer it to you here with all the pride that a loving grandfather can muster. It is, without question, one of the world's greatest masterpieces in any century. I'll treasure it always.

Light Flashes in the Tunnel

The Racoon Tree by Tootie Edmonds (age 17) for Pops Bentley (age 76), December 2014

I'll Leave You to Your Own Devices

In the long ago days, this phrase meant, "I'll let you rely upon your considerable talents, intelligence, and opportunity to bring the goal at hand to fruition. It's now the scourge between generations, as flustered parents watch their inactive children online with assorted computers, iPads and smart cell phones. From an agrarian economy where kids milked cows and did farm chores in the country or played stick ball and hopscotch on city streets and sidewalks, the cacophony of children's noisy cries has quieted with their retreat to computer games on computers and texting on cell phones. Hundreds of program apps are crowding the screens of their devices and their physical endangerment in a Google, Facebook, Twitter, YouTube, and Craig's List world has changed from slips and falls, cuts and bruises, and broken bones to finger clawing from holding phones, carpal tunnel from keying remotes, and neck dysplasia from bending over screens and keyboards. It's a new dimension, and old-timers have been left in the dust to despair that their progeny have turned into the zombies of their popular current culture.

XIII. ADVENTURES IN THE MIND

Winning the Lottery

In my retirement travels between relatives' abodes, I stay connected by cell phone, the anathema of us old hard-wire types. During one of my cell conversations with Paul, he naturally asked what I was doing to improve my lot. I responded that, along with his brother and sister-in-law, we had invested in Power Ball Lottery tickets with the hope of securing the multimillion-dollar jackpot. "All you're doing is buying the dream," he retorted. "It's a no chance thing! What you need to do is keep writing the squibs for a book. That has far more potential for a payday than the lottery." So, after hanging up, I'm back to writing this flash, illuminated by the good will of my youngest child, but with little hope of financial gain, those of us on the dole cannot resist the temptation to invest in The Dream.

Geocaching the Sierra Madre

We're all looking for a little treasure to ease our financial burden or just guild our ride though life, whether it's shipwrecks laden with Spanish bullion, gold panning, or the less auspicious purchase of lotto tickets. Elemental to motivation and success are dreams of discovery, notoriety, and riches. Dreams promote their own adventures to take the first step toward seeing what's around the next bend. Childhood games are a precursor of future success, a treasure in itself. Early scavenger hunts provide the stepping-stone map to finding life's bounty in successive actions. In Pensacola, there is an annual Tristan de Luna treasure hunt during the Fiesta of Five Flags, with daily poetic clues to its whereabouts published in our local *News Journal*. Presumably, everyone has a chest full of riches at the end of their rainbow, which awaits only our faithful commitment to take it. So we're spurred to keep taking baby steps toward living large in our dreams until we reach the reality. Of course, modern day technology is available to enhance the age-old saga, so geocaching provides an outlet to hide and find treasure, if only a note of good will, with support from satellite telemetry and a hand-held GPS receiver. Here's hoping you find your treasure in whatever venue.

The Incredible Lightness of Being

Senior citizens, our elder statesmen and women, deserve their discounts for coffee, movies, garage doors, and all the rest. They have passed a long way through the tunnel of life; and for their aberrations and wrinkles, they deserve their few accolades. Most societies on the planet honor their elders for the wisdom and stature they possess. Only in competitive America can age pass unnoticed, but with the ten-cent coffee discount at McDonald's, that is changing. Retirees are being lured back into the workplace for their acumen and loyalty. They have already paid their stress price and, once retired, are floating free. Wisdom in the workplace among the hard-chargers adds a dimension of lightness to an otherwise austere environment.

I Gotta Be Free

The warmth and sustainability of the family enclave having already been stated as life-giving for us old-timers, it is also a fact that we need our freedom and independence from time to time to play dominos; throw horseshoes; engage in the great sexual fandango; garden; go to the Moose Lodge; or the local Irish bar, McGuire's, for some feasting, imbibing, and debauchery. Old people take college courses, dance, teach, work in supplemental jobs, go to rock concerts, surf the curl, soup-up their cars, and hike on the Appalachian Trail. The point is that, whether you are in or out of the fast lane, old-timers ain't always hanging onto the milk wagon. They have to breathe free like everyone else. Love us, but let us float. Hold onto that high note of that last-century crooner, Sammy Davis, Jr., when he sang, "I gotta be free."

In many an elder's personality, the strong call of independence means that they must live and function alone, visiting their support groups in small doses as the need for company bids them. Either way, living in or out of your support circle, the American signature trait of independence should be manifested.

Hawkers, Hucksters, and Flea Merchants

My old friend, San Francisco, beckons me to the City by the Bay. I return periodically, as if a pilgrim to Mecca, drawn by the singular entreaties of its many spells: the Golden Gate Bridge; Clam Chowder Bread Bowls at Boudin's Bakery on the Wharf;

Alcatraz; Chinatown; the Italian's Washington Square; Lombard Street; the Palace of the Legion of Honor and the Museum of Modern Art; Grace Cathedral, with its marvelous Doors of Paradise and labyrinths; the Anchor Steam Brewery; or almost any neighborhood walk with its townhouse architecture resplendent with multi-colored cupolas, dormers, gingerbread, and ironwork.

During my last trip in September 2009, I stayed at a Union Square hostel where the youth and vigor of a largely international population varied markedly from the streets leading to it. All cities are shareholders in the panorama of the human condition, from the business elite to the dynamic wannabes to the beggars and hucksters; but the streets of San Francisco, in particular, are alive with sellers of everything legitimate, plus imitation knock-offs, assorted illegal drugs, and stolen black market goods. The pandering reaches obnoxious proportions. Street entertainers perform to the relentless hordes of passersby, hoping to attract a crowd and money donations for their livelihood. The great multitude of beggars simply sit on the sidewalks or pass through the crowds, thrusting their plastic cups forward, imploring people to give them loose change. Some carry handwritten signs like the one I saw prominently parading around the Powell Street Visitor Information Center on Market Street: "Will take verbal abuse for loose change!" The extent of poverty is certainly reflective of the general economy, but its pronounced presence subtracts greatly from the face of a city and its program to help the needy. Is destitution now so widespread that we cannot or will not rehabilitate a lost neighbor? Life's needy also beg us ogling old timers to consider the truthful postulate, "There but for the grace of God go I."

There Are Signs Everywhere

In my twilight time at sixty-six, after a divorce; Hurricane Ivan; and retirement left me alone, penny-and property-less, and adrift, when I took to traveling between the homesteads of my far-flung support group and living with them out of a suitcase, I was finally en route to Number Three Son's domicile in Bronxville, New York, and Paul and Brigette began to lay on instructions for reaching their apartment. I was intermittently seized with the fear of missing one of the intricate cues to piecing the overlapping transportation means together: arrival by Amtrak at NY Penn Station, Yellow Cab to Grand Central Terminal, Harlem Line Metro-North Railroad to Bronxville, Black Depot Taxi to 555 Palmer Road. Sounds easy, but to a newbie, the links are opportunities to make a mistake. Brigette and Paul talked me through it, but a bearded AT hiker with backpack and Leki Poles handed the railroad conductor a Metro Subway card and, in punishment for not knowing the difference, paid $13.00 on board fare for a $6.00 off-peak, station-purchased ticket. The affable conductor simply smiled and said, "Same mother, different children." It was an expensive lesson that didn't include me, but that made my apprehension about city travel grow exponentially to the three simple steps provided me.

With tutoring and encouragement, I finally became adept at taking the outlying fifteen-mile, mostly above-ground railroad trip from Bronxville to Grand Central Terminal, from which I walked to the New York Public Library and the Empire State Building; up Fifth Avenue to the Diamond District, Rockefeller Center, St. Patrick's Cathedral, Central Park, and Times Square;

and then back to Grand Central for the return trip. As I wearied of investigating midtown Manhattan by train, the inevitable multi-colored and splendored inner city subway map invaded my consciousness. Of course, it didn't help that the trains for railroad and subway all looked the same. Brigette and Paul had purchased a pocket guide for my use, *Top 10 New York*, listing the ten best of everything in twelve delineated areas, along with a suggested day's exploration of each area. The guide also included a Manhattan subway map with a legend of intimidating symbols for Full Service and Part-time Service; Local Service Only; Shuttle Service; All Trains Stop; Free Subway Transfer; and the most-confusing Free Out-of-System Subway Transfer, excluding a single-ride ticket. Lines were marked with various letters and numbers and abbreviated station names.

As I mulled and read and queried, Paul said, "Dad, this isn't rocket science. Find your numbers and symbols on the map to your hopeful destination and then, when you're en route, the signs will appear everywhere." He was right, and although I was primed and pushed along the way by many good-natured people, the magic letters, numbers, and names appeared on beams, walls, and pillars everywhere for me to find my way into the netherworld beyond midtown. While it was excruciating for me to negotiate the subway maze, my niece and son, like all New Yorkers, had inculcated within their brains a mystical time and motion clock that allowed them to read or sleep in transit, then arise and exit their train at the exact moment the doors opened at their stop. While there are signs everywhere, the only real gift is that the $2.00 entry fee permits you to ride forever like Charlie on Boston's MTA, if you don't exit the system, which allowed me on many occasions to return to missed stops on another train.

Woe is me; negotiating the greater New York City subway is rocket science!

Alone, But Not Lonely

Please let me introduce you to yourself: A good person with a few eccentricities. Selfish sometimes. Sad, even morbid; but also alive, adventurous, happy, and stimulating. A thoughtful friend. Generous. A good conversationalist. Someone to look up to as a role model. Worthy in most ways. Good company always to invent and reinvent those lifelines that save the soul and help us skirt the pit of insanity.

Gourmet Food from a Box

Ever notice that the true gourmet cooks, culinary artists, are scarce in your life? Oh, your mother might have baked a good cake or batch of cookies like as not from a Betty Crocker box purchased at Walmart, or your spouse might be able to marinate meat in Dale's Steak Sauce and then grill it to perfection; but a family chef who can put together a sumptuous meal with appropriate appetizers, beverages, entree, vegetables, salad, and dessert, supported by a balance in ambiance with fine tableware, linens, decorations, pleasant scents, lighting, and music? Now, that's the thing! These people seem to be in short supply to the average citizen. We're lucky to encounter even one such talented chef in a lifetime. Most of us purchase our gourmet food from the freezer cases, vegetable pallets, and dessert aisles of Walmart and then heat and serve them on a kitchen counter. Give the real gourmets in your life a hug. They're as endangered as the Piping Plover in America's coastal regions. The Mary Lou Sharer's of

Napa and MeMe Garrison's of Clarksville who bake their crab imperial on scallop shells and their grandpa rolls from scratch and serve them on a colorful table cloth with matching napkins, candles, centerpiece, and place settings are as artistic and masterful as a concert pianist!

Muddling Through

In the fast-paced American culture, our older citizens are frequently viewed as impediments to progress. They drive too slow, they eat too slow, they walk too slow, and they speak too slow. Some are on canes or, worse, walkers. They block progress into and out of buildings, elevators, intersections, parking lots, and restaurants. They're in the way! On the Appalachian Trail, where courtesy dictates that slower-moving hikers stand off the trail for faster hikers, the twenty- and thirty-something's blow by the old-timers with nary a glance. Yet consider the great courage it takes to stay engaged in daily pursuits when your mind is not as fertile and your body not as whole as in youth. Most elders pursue their chosen activities with little confidence and a lot of pain. Imagine the fear generated by hiking rocky terrain on a walker or trying to get about a busy city without becoming too much of an impediment. On the AT, justice occasionally prevails when, during down days in trail towns, the seniors encounter their youthful comrades laid-up with injuries from traveling too far, too fast. In response to how someone so old can escape injury, seniors are obliged to share again the story of an old and young bull on a hill surveying a herd of heifers in the meadow below. "Let's run down and get us a heifer," said the young bull.

"No," replied the old bull, "let's saunter down and get them all."

Cornballs and Dreamers

You're only as successful as you can dream. It's a known fact that repeated visualization creates the greatest motivation for achievement. Who among us is not a sucker for a happy ending? The arts, particularly the visual arts of stage and screen, show us the mirror of life's unending drama. The grand musical productions of the fifties—*Carousel*, *Flower Drum Song*, *Guys and Dolls*, *Oklahoma*, *Show Boat*, *Sound of Music*, and *South Pacific*—set the majesty of life to the beat of music for us to whistle, long after the curtain goes down. And whistle we do, into and through our own drama of pursuits, trying to realize what we dream of and wanting a happy ending.

Reverie

Dream time for the weary mind is a defense against the mundane and tumultuous. We are all retrieved from our occasional reveries by the impatient stampede of loyal family and friends who unforgivably draw us back onto the flat line of life that numbs us or the heady rush of life that sets our soul afire. Unless you're the master of your destiny, reverie is your only respite and your only way out.

Dreamers Need Some Reality to Survive

Dreaming is, of course, wrapping your mind and spirit around something before it happens. Like a male erection, you can only sustain a good dream so long before some action must take place. A vacation anywhere, a new house to accommodate the bigger family, a long-awaited raise at work that's going to make you solvent, a boob job that's going to create such cleavage to make all men stare and all women hate you, a partner who's going to make you whole. No matter what your dream, take small, continuous steps toward its fulfillment, whether a change fund, a gear purchase, a research effort, or a daily practice before the mirror. Whatever. Keep your dreams alive and moving toward their fulfillment. The only time you can stop dreaming is when you're dead!

OCD and Voyeurism Are Among My Better Traits

While I get no pleasure from other people's distress or pain and am definitely too shy to watch a naked couple copulating in front of me, in the truest sense of voyeurism, I am a profound observer of life's interactions. I enjoy sitting on benches in malls, parks, airports, and train stations to watch the heady rush of life pass by in all of its diversity and purpose: businesspeople in suits with briefcases, homeless people pushing grocery carts with all manner of collectibles, and birds and squirrels scurrying for crumbs. It's as much fun as going to an aquarium, a zoo, or a museum. I relish it, and I am compelled to return again and again. Such repetitive behaviors are usually with us from our teen years and get manifestly more entrenched with advancing age. Brother Fred and I still make our beds every morning because our mother instilled that chore in us as children. In public restrooms, I religiously pick up all paper towel litter on the counters and floors because, once as a child in a gas station restroom during one of many family junkets from duty station to duty station, after washing my hands and toweling off, I wadded up the paper towel and tossed it toward the garbage can, but missed it. I was opening the door to leave when Dad called me back and ordered me to pick up not only the towel I left on the floor, but all the towels left on the counters and floors. "The attendants here have more important things to do than clean up your mess," he said. Compulsion ensued! These compulsions may not be as compelling or glamorous as repeated hand washing, talking to oneself, or stepping over the cracks in a sidewalk; but they're ritualistic, nonetheless.

The Little Sabine Meat Market

The glorious panhandle of Florida, starting at Pensacola, boasts many wonders, none greater than the Navy's Blue Angels flight demonstration team. Since Pensacola is their home base, local Panhandlers gather en masse for home shows, none more attended than those over Pensacola Beach to celebrate Independence Day. Motor vehicles of every description form a continuous line of traffic through Gulf Breeze to the beach bridge on days of scheduled air shows. Similarly, a line of boat traffic passes from the Inland Waterway through the channel into Little Sabine Bay. The bay is deep enough around its perimeter to allow passage of boats, while its interior is only a foot or two deep to permit easy walking. The bay is large, holding up to a thousand boats that anchor around fifty acres of pristine, water-covered sand. The revelers, arriving on the boats, come in swimsuits and sunglasses with refreshments, mostly alcoholic; animals, mostly dogs; and assorted playthings, mostly Frisbees. There is much fraternizing from boat to boat and sharing of refreshments, as partiers watch the air show while walking around the interior of the lagoon, marveling alike at the Blues overhead and the wondrously displayed anatomy of the opposite sex in shin-deep water.

A Man of Means by No Means

An old man retired from government service, education, and the like, divorced and splitting an already-meager retirement income even with an assist from Social Security, is, assuredly, living on the financial edge without considering the implications of poor health in our mega mucho milk-that-son-of-a-bitch health care industry. Indeed, with five children and a single income for most of our marriage, I know something about balancing to the penny. The joke in our family is that I would become totally stressed out if I were ever to receive more than minimal subsistence, say winning a lottery. I'm a coupon-cutter, a sale watcher, a minimal stuff hoarder, a clothes pauper, and a walker to avoid paying for gas. In this, I feel that I truly represent my fifties generation as sung by Roger Miller in his famous ballad, "King of the Road."

Too Much Information

Have you ever given directions to an out-of-towner who pulls up alongside you in a large sedan, cracks a tinted electric window only a few inches to keep from losing A/C, map in hand, and asks how to get to some destination or other? When I'm walking, the weather is agreeable, and I'm feeling charitable, I do my best to offer highway numbers or street names to get them where they're going. But, usually, after the third name or turn, their eyes glaze over; and you know you've given them too much information. So now I give them only one compass direction, with the first name to get them successfully en route. Of course, if they pull up on an August day in Florida when the humidity and temperature are both over ninety-five, and I'm, say, mowing the lawn and sweating profusely like a pig, and they only crack their window a few inches to prevent loss of A/C, I intentionally give them wrong directions to Never-Never Land!

The Murphy Bed

Early comedies included bits where an ardent suitor, always holding a bouquet of flowers, would be knocking at his beloved's door, while she would be inside scurrying about with another boyfriend, whom she would hurriedly fold into the wall on a Murphy Bed before primping and opening the door. Murphy Beds add precious space to studio apartments where there is none when they are open. The bed end lifts up on six hefty springs at the head as the legs at the end fold down against the frame and latches into a cabinet with doors that fold over the frame to completely remove the bed from sight. It's entirely magical, but leaves the uneasy feeling that you've just watched your life pass into a black hole in the universe. After all, there's nothing so reassuring as a massive bed swaddled in pillows, sheets, blankets, and a comforter that says, "Come to me when you are weary and I will give you rest."

Occupying Your Space

Whether you're a collector or a minimalist, we all gather stuff. We crowd the familiar around us. We can move into a 10-by-25 foot studio apartment with nothing; and within a week, the refrigerator will be festooned with church bulletins, theater schedules, favorite restaurant menus, doctor's appointments, newspaper clippings, photos, children's art, and so on. Logoed T-shirts and coffee cups accumulate. Flat-and-tableware, pots and pans, cooking utensils, toaster, cleaning and paper supplies, and that souvenir from the local art festival with your name written all over it. Stuff grows! It proliferates disproportionate to the space that you occupy, like navel lint. Even after a hurricane, when you've lost everything, you will personalize your space to the point that, after one year, it requires serious planning just to deal with all your stuff.

Don't Rain on My Parade

Nothing enhances the experience of small town life more than a parade. In fact, nothing is more representative of small towns than their parades. I'm not talking the Macy's Thanksgiving Day Parade in New York City or the New Year's Day Tournament of Roses Parade in Pasadena, California, where you'll see professionally-designed and expensively-manufactured lighter-than-air, dirigible-sized characters floating overhead, all secured by a horde of attendants pulling on land lines to move them forward. Many are block-long, self-operated floats resplendent with prominent national celebrities, thousands of flowers, intricate mechanical presentations and every scene imaginable. Rather, I'm thinking Bothell, Washington, and Gulf Breeze, Florida. However, Bothell does have a striking pirate frigate on wheels, sporting the skull and crossbones and a band of gnarly knaves with eye patches waving broad-bladed scimitars,

Light Flashes in the Tunnel

whose canon mounts discharge explosive canisters accompanied by clouds of black smoke to the appreciation of the surrounding crowds. Otherwise, they're similar to their Gulf Coast counterpart in every way. Remember, not big city—small town. Use what's available, at hand and constructible within a few weekends, with every-age and all-volunteer labor. And the only locals not actually in the parade are either resting comfortably in a cemetery or are adamantly-opposed to marching the distance or riding on a home-made float (i.e., the curmudgeon corps). Small town floats are usually pickup trucks bedecked with handwritten signs and streams of crepe paper. Beyond the pickups, you might see a flatbed farm wagon (pulled by a tractor or pickup) bedecked with more riders, bigger-lettered signs, and more crepe paper. Don't expect to shop or conduct business on parade day, because everybody and their dog is in the parade, advertising local businesses; churches; doctor's clinics and hospitals; fire and police departments; insurance agencies; radio/TV stations; dance studios; athletic teams with their marching bands (usually out of tune and out of step with one another) and their always-exuberant cheerleaders; and, of course, all politicians currently running for office. By tradition, the police motorcycle brigade leads off with red lights flashing, punctuated by occasional spritzes from their sirens, as one or two run ahead to clear the route of neighborhood revelers reunionizing in the middle of the street...But, of course, they get stopped to swap their own gossip, too. Then there's the children's bicycle/tricycle entry, with anxious parents weaving in and out to assist with accidents, ill will, and progress (sometimes even parents vent each other over the misbehavior of their children, and the deputies have to intercede). A large, well-dressed canine corps is always present to bark and sniff and pee or, for the smallest dogs, be carried by their proud owners. If the local sheriff's posse has a mounted unit, then there's an equestrian entry, complete with a following pooper-scooper unit to shovel that shit to the oohs and aahs of the crowd (some invariably pinching their nostrils while grimacing with an extended tongue). However, our equestrian unit was officially dismounted and disbanded, so no horses of late. To make up for the lack of horses, we are proud to present a children's dance entry with every child out of step and spread out in every direction, as proud viewers reach to hug this one or that one; some even carry batons that they twirl uncontrollably into the trees or the fearful crowds actually paying attention along the route. Politicians always ride standing up or sitting on an open convertible trunk, smiling insincerely and waving while nodding benevolently. Of course, the sporting and vintage car clubs are on display, usually with a restored Duesenberg or Model T Ford leading a caravan of different model-year Corvettes or Thunderbirds, all replete with families or politicians or business agents throwing bangles, beads, logoed cups, or other souvenirs. Boy Scouts and Girl Scouts appear (on floats or marching) under their separate troop banners, some in full khaki uniform with appropriately-logoed shirts, shorts or skirts, belts, caps, socks, and merit-badged sashes; but most have only one or two remnants of the full uniform. The separate entries are either congested together on top of one another or spaced out so far as to make spectators wonder if the parade is over. Bringing up the rear is always a local fire truck and crew, with lights a-flashin' and horns a-blowin' intermittently. And, of course, during the annual Christmas Parade, Santa Claus sits atop the fire truck throwing kisses and plastic toys, accompanied by a host of children who have vied for this privilege in local community benefit competitions. In my hometown of Gulf Breeze, Florida, the parade emanates from the high school parking lot and proceeds along Shoreline Drive, so the question of spacing makes us wonder how placement is decided. Perhaps it is decided by the same administrator who makes out the school bus schedules. Why aren't the slowest entries—children and dogs—at the head of the parade, and the fastest entries—mobile units—following behind to slow as needed to maintain close ranks? Anyway, not to belabor. Organization is not a hallmark or requirement of small town parades where everyone is everywhere along the route, socializing, clapping, pointing, and catching or throwing beads. The neighborhoods are deserted and the stores vacant because of the magnetism of this parade event, which, of course, makes rife the opportunity for home invasions and business robberies. But for an old man like me, it's blissful just sitting along the way in a fold-up lawn chair, catching beads and giving them to the little kids that get muscled out by their older siblings. Ain't life simply grand when things are in balance?

XIV. COMMUNION DURING THE PASSAGE

Gratitude

Every page of our lives is dripping with nectar for which we must express thanks. Indeed, appropriate expressions of appreciation for our gifts would take as long as our life itself. Even the short thank you version can run interminably. We must always be in a state of gratitude.

A Tree Falling in the Forest

We've all pondered the postulate of whether a tree falling in the forest makes a sound if there is no ear to hear it. To me, the real postulate is whether you're a person existing in real time if you have no one to confirm you. Are we really alive and fulfilled if there is no one to applaud our dreams and support our reality?

Nuances

Ever notice that it's not the purveyors of aggressive confrontation or hostility who get you down? The loud, caustic drill instructor. The barking coach. The unremitting teacher. The obnoxious friend. Your brain becomes inured to their cacophony, and they have no measurable effect on your morale or self-esteem and may even sustain them. What you see is what you get! They treat everybody the same, and theirs is a negative high. On the other hand, the insidious degradation of malignant gossip and backbiting, the double entendres in conversation at your expense, the hurtful button-pushing to exhume past mistakes—they damage the good in your reputation or subtract from your positive momentum. It's these nuances that erode morale and exhaust you with damage control. The spiteful acquaintance teaches us only that the nuances of a positive friend can be as uplifting as the vengeful person's derogatory actions are damaging. Give the latter no notice or ammunition and curry good will among your friends in countermeasure.

Friends Welcome Anytime, Family by Appointment Only

When the intensity of family life is dialed up a few notches, we can occasionally become weary of our ever-so-lowly station at the bottom of the heap, never lauded or laudable for picking up dog turds, raking leaves, mowing the lawn, doing the dishes, or babysitting the kids. After all, everybody else in the family is working harder than you. You often feel as though you've been relegated to some inferior servant status. The backbiting can get acrimonious if one of your beloved housemates feels that you're shirking your share of the chores or speaking out of turn. One must always be sensitive to the feelings and needs of kindred. Teenagers never feel that your viewpoint is relevant, that you truly understand them or their generation, and that your dreams can actually coincide. Partners never feel that you're completely aware of their needs or that you can fully relate to their place in mind and time. Distant relatives—especially your spouse's—are even more intimidating because you shouldn't have to listen to them, but they do hold partial sway over your destiny. Never borrow that which you cannot return or make reparation for within short-term memory.

The home is as political a place as any Hall of Congress. Debts of money, possessions, and time must be repaid in kind, in short time, or your reputation suffers; and no one can scald you as deeply as a sibling, partner, child, or distant relative. Even though your family holds your place in the world's hierarchy and controls the reins of your momentum, your friends usually offer the most affirmative, if not objective, interaction. Friends assuage the ego, whilst relatives are usually incisively objective about your accomplishments and blatantly honest in sharing their opinion of you and yours. Sometimes honesty is not a good expedient for momentum, so bring on the friends and distance the relatives.

Good Things Do Happen to Good People

Given all the villainous scenarios that we encounter in life, not least of which is seeing the ill-begotten prevail time and again over their adversities and, without gratitude or sharing, accumulate staggering fame, good fortune, and wealth beyond reasonable limit. Worst of all, they're quick to diminish those around them, many who they have stepped on during their mercurial rise to riches and stardom. Good bystanders who have aided or encouraged the bastards en route must then reconcile being ignored or slandered for their goodness. Life just isn't always fair! But it does happen that big-hearted people occasionally get their own break and prevail against their own odds, appreciate their good fortune, and continue to share their bounty and good will with all those impacting their life. Such a person is Aunt Teresa, divorced mother of three, one of which died in a train wreck near YMCA Camp Cosby, where she was a counselor. She is remarried to Skip Mullet Master Banfell, a former employee at Curves Fitness Center, an Oprah devotee, a singer at funerals and weddings, a laundress for the St. Ann's Parish priests, an extraordinary friend, and a parent who cherishes her human bonds and goes to any length to strengthen them. She brings food to the homeless and grieving; she drives the aged or incapacitated on shopping trips or to medical appointments; and she is my consummate friend—who, with Mullet Master, has repaired my torn ego repeatedly since the 2004/2005 nether years brought me Hurricane Ivan, divorce from her sister, and retirement from the Escambia County School District. Now she is embarked upon her own fitness enterprise with her friend Tidy T and the miracles to ensuring their success—upfront money, legal advice, tech support, appropriate space to lease at a good price, equipment, advertising, and an enthusiastic clientele—seem to be re-doubling with daily momentum for their venture, "Fit for Women."

All of the good will that she has freely extended is flowing back upon her fourfold. Best of all, not only does she deserve it, but her success will be revisited again upon her beloved support group. It's so good to see the big-hearted person flower! Recycled love is what holds the kingdom together.

Contributing to the Delinquency of a Major

The Mullet Master is formidable, to say the least. His demeanor is comparable to that of a grizzly bear in the live-and-let-live sense, accepting of others at a distance, but defensive of his own time and space, agreeable and contentious at the same time. He's a two-fisted drinker with an imposing arsenal of alcohol to loosen things up, much of it from his seafaring jobs in Africa, the Far East, Mexico, and Russia.

"Yo, Jungle Jimbo, how about a shot of absinthe before we start or after we've finished drinking to take away our miseries and put us in the right mood?" he'll implore. You must learn to refuse these early or final invitations and pace your alcohol consumption in his presence, or you'll simply collapse mentally and physically. Many a confident guest tried to match his capacity with disastrous results. Once in his graces, he is the consummate host and gregarious to a fault.

"How's about a little toddy for the body to toast that thought? Mama, our guests need another round of drinks," he'll wryly observe as we're nodding off by the chiminea fire or watching him prepare a seafood delicacy from behind an apron and under a chef's hat. Skip is a seafood cook without equal. He has an eclectic mix of interests and traits, stamped predominantly with a love for the sea from his upbringing in the local Pensacola boat-building community of Sanders Beach. His father, grandfather, and uncles built fishing boats and skiffs in their backyards to compliment other professions and have fun. Skip worked along with them building boats and then, predictably, worked on boats locally at the start of his work life before shipping out internationally with SEACOR Marine as a tugboat and overseas port captain.

Beyond his profession, everything else about him is also nautical, from his interior house decor to the boats and outboard motors that clutter his shed, yard, and life. He throws a big cast net to catch all the mullet for his famous feeds and gets his shrimp from friends fishing professionally from local boats. I've been with him in Santa Rosa Sound on one of his own boats when he'd simply pull up to a shrimper to get fresh seafood at a nominal fee or, more often, to get it free from a Sanders Beach friend. Of course, he's picky about seafood quality—meaning fresh, same-day-caught from pure beds—and he is partial to particular color, location, size, and season: gray Pensacola Bay, twenty-count/pound in the summer and fall; pink Gulf, twenty-count/pound in the winter and spring only. I've had the pleasure of tours with him through many of his favorite Pensacola haunts, including Sanders Beach, Captain Joey Patti's Seafood Deli on the Main Street waterfront, and Charlie Benbo's Seafood Eatery in the same neighborhood. On one occasion, during a fried mullet lunch at Benbo's, a table of old-timers from the area recognized Skipper and badgered him to visit them for an hour or so while they recounted memories of his childhood and regaled him with stories of his colorful relatives. It was most entertaining to listen to the frequent belly laughs rumble up from his soul after much good-natured ribbing. He was the youngest, at fifty years old, among a grizzled, weather-beaten assemblage of mostly ancient mariners.

Like many of these local stalwarts, Skip is a Master Mason 32nd Degree Scottish Rite, traditions descending from ancient times that embraced George Washington, and a born historian from the U.S.'s oldest city, Pensacola. He has relatives buried in three local cemeteries, including St. Michael's Cemetery, arguably the oldest cemetery in Florida, where he and his wife, Teresa Rose, are on the Board. The Mullet Master and his wife took us into their home and hospitality after the wrath of Hurricane Ivan had decimated our homestead. We were blessed in the aftermath of that catastrophe with such standup friends, who also found us a rental house nearby; suffered through our divorce; nurtured me beyond the divorce and my simultaneous retirement; and then fed and entertained me almost nightly until my departure from the womb of Gulf Breeze for St. Louis.

There was a lot of feasting, imbibing, and debauchery on Skipper's hand-built back deck during that time, accompanied by his colloquial narrative—unlike anyone else's. For example, he compares mankind's relationships with their women to tap dancing in a minefield with clown shoes on. When I phone him about dropping by for a toddy while my ex-wife is there, he will suggest that I'll be about as welcome as a fart in an astronaut's suit or a pork chop in a synagogue. Ever my protector in the challenge to keep a low profile during stressful times, he'll emphasize, "I don't want you to feel like a rolling highway sign in the woods during hunting season," or, "A man don't use his head might as well have two assholes," attributed to Skip's Uncle, Julian Peaker Banfell, or, "One 'Oh shit!' wipes out fifteen 'Attaboys.'" Long live the colorful Mullet Master and his Little Missy, Aunt Teresa!

Forever Amber

My support group is my sustenance. Of the many beacons lighting my life, none is brighter or more encouraging by example than my Carolina niece. Amber now works as a representative for Eli Lily Pharmaceutical Company out of Raleigh, North Carolina. Her first domicile away from home was in Greenville.

During her growing years, she was the quintessential irrepressible child: smart, proactive, and competitive, with personality-plus. She was a standout in high school and college, finishing her Bachelor of Science degree at Northwestern State University of Louisiana in 2000—during which, as is her bent, she impulsively signed onto a year-long "Up with People" tour, an international song and dance revue based in the U.S., in 1998, right before her senior year of college, to bolster her resume and have some fun at the same time. All the while, Ambo kept herself fit by jogging, which she started at age five with the Buster Brown Derby; and, never being a big-time drinker or smoker, she developed a passion for marathons at age twenty-six. I believe her first marathon was at Disney World in 2003 while living in Greenville, North Carolina, as a member of Team in Training (TNT) to benefit leukemia and lymphoma research. She has also run marathons in San Diego and New York City and then again at Disney World in January 2006, when she invited me to join the rest of her family and friends to cheer her through two successive day's runs to complete a half-marathon and then a full marathon. It was the height of excitement to trek from one visibility point to another along the course, viewing the strung-out array of runners and tracking Amber electronically with our cell phones from the chip attached to her shoe past each mile marker. Her mother, Aunt Teresa Banfell, had affixed a large, colorful papier-mâché palm tree to her umbrella, which she hoisted high above the crowd of spectators for instant visibility. As Amber appeared in the running throng, we all rang bells, beat drums, and sounded an infinite number of noisemakers to get her attention and laughter. And so it went to the end of each viewpoint in each race, after which the Mullet Master and I embarked upon our own ceremonial sampling of international beers around the EPCOT Lagoon.

Now, the real thing about Ambo is that, along the way, she contracted cancer herself, diagnosed as non-sclerotic Hodgkin's lymphoma Stage IIB. She had chalked-up months of exhaustion to long work hours, her physical training regimen, lack of sleep, and poor nutrition. It was a miracle that she didn't collapse given her hyperactive lifestyle. She wrote in the fitness magazine *Endurance* in June 2004, "The night sweats were so severe, it was as if the roof leaked during an eastern Carolina rainstorm." She endured four different types of chemo every two weeks for six months, with side effects from the medications including hair loss, nausea, and bone pain. She received her twelfth and final treatment on May 24, 2004, with PET scans reading cancer-free from that time.

Throughout this ordeal and beyond, Ambo has maintained her traditional ebullient spirit. Always the consummate hostess when I visit her, Ambo has introduced me to the eateries, products, and sights of her city, along with engaging me in entertainment and exercise. She has driven me out to New Bern to meet a realtor selling waterfront lots on the Inner Banks in the hope that I would settle there, near her, and she has shown me through the North Carolina fairgrounds, where vendors sell everything from fresh produce and honey to handmade furniture. She bought me a jar of Tupelo Honey, reputed to have remarkable health and medicinal benefits. After a day exploring one of Raleigh's fascinating museums, where she would drop me off before going to work, we would exercise by walking around the North Carolina State University's track and then have a brew and dinner at one of Raleigh's many notable eateries.

She is unwaveringly upbeat, never alluding to the possibility of a cancer recurrence, but living each day in fast forward as if it's her last. Still, as I watch her spin forward with that inexhaustible glee befitting her positive attitude, I cannot help an occasional flashback to the April evening in 2005, approaching Ambo's first-year anniversary of being cancer-free, when we participated in a ceremonial cancer walk around a local stadium track for those celebrating their conquest of this horrid disease. We met her doctors and caregivers, and she invited me to join the throng on her celebratory walk in a darkened arena where hundreds of candles and flashlights glowed on wet cheeks and choked words disintegrated into sobs. Under fire in Vietnam, we were numbed to the possibility of death in a flash, whereas, here, the indomitable spirit of human life faced death in small bites, with each drip of an IV, each burst of radiation, or each nauseating pill. Indeed, Amber and all cancer survivors everywhere are a bottomless font of inspiration. She's the reason I wear a yellow wristband.

The Sister Woman

The soundboard of those who love us enough to steer us through our vanities is a treasure trove of objectivity. Not only is my niece Sarah, the Sister Woman, a font of objectivity, but she also has an incisive, surgical wit that would do a comedienne proud. In spite of her protests to the contrary, she does have a good heart, which is faithful in correspondence and resplendent with gifts. She works for Time Warner in New York City, so I have been the recipient of many of their publications at her hand, plus a now faded red LIFE ball cap that has been with me for every step on the Appalachian Trail. During my Fall 2008 visit to New York City, she introduced me to her charming Brooklyn brownstone apartment and neighborhood and the adjacent East River Promenade, where we smoked a cigar on one of the many benches and reveled in the lower Manhattan skyline across the river. We talked affably and spiritedly, as close relatives are wont, during our first reunion since my retirement in May 2005. We discussed family news and our respective current interests and stations in life. Sarah is a dyed-in-the-wool New Yorker with unwavering pride in everything Big Apple, from the diverse cultures and food to the education and intellectual offerings in abundance. She waxed on about Central and Prospect Parks, the shopping, and the Metro. "It is a vortex of everything global," she said unabashedly, and her spirit was infectious. I continued to nod in agreement as our charisma grew from the long-time anchor of our linked lives.

In one such excited moment, she put her hand affectionately upon my shoulder and pointedly exclaimed, "You know, I've heard from Padre and Paul that you are writing in earnest?"

"Yes," I responded proudly, "I've been writing snippets entitled *Light Flashes,* and I've written one or two about you. Would you like to read them?" I queried.

She cautiously withdrew her hand from my shoulder and, brow furrowed as she studied me, slowly said, "You know, Uncle Jim, I only asked if you are writing. I didn't say I wanted to read any of it!"

Insatiable Appetite

 Sarah introduced me to a few of the diverse eateries during my visit to New York City. We enjoyed true boiled and baked bagels with a slightly woody taste and slathered with herb tofutti at Absolute Bagels, Turkish cuisine at Akdeniz Restaurant, Mexican food at Blockhead's Burritos, and Ethiopian food at Awash, all sumptuous eating experiences. With my pronounced sweet tooth, I was, from my upbringing, ever mindful of dessert after the repast, but many foreign restaurants don't include dessert fare. It struck me that the epidemic of obesity in the U.S., and the corresponding lack of obesity in the rest of the world, might have emanated from our love of sweets and our obsession with dessert (Well, duh!). My potbelly groans, and my mouth salivates when I think dessert. I automatically look over the dessert offerings on a menu before considering entree fare; and without dessert, I'll forage after dinner for chips, nuts, pretzels, animal crackers dipped in cream cheese or frosting, or any kind of candy. I don't mind exercising, but I simply cannot control my insatiable appetite.

 The Sister Woman, on the other hand, is petite and controls her natural yen for sweets with an iron will. During an after-meal visit to the wondrous Jacques Torres Chocolatier down under the Manhattan Bridge Overpass, the Sister Woman dizzied herself smelling the aroma of chocolate permeating the shop, but would not sample or purchase any of the decadent confections. Yours truly sampled at will among the offerings and ordered seemingly one of everything in the resplendent cases. I marveled at her will power and told her so, but she put me off with an explanation that her history of abuse with sweets was so profound that it once controlled her life and her runaway weight. "It's like alcoholism, Uncle Jim. It's an obsession with eating that you can't control except through abstinence. Like an alcoholic, once you abstain, your life returns to balance; but you simply cannot drink another drop of alcohol, or you'll be off the wagon again. It's the same with overeaters of sweets. I'm allowed to smell but not taste them! One bite, and I would be binging again." I was overcome with her plight and respect for her self-control; but of course, the real crux is whether Sarah's success with her demons can, in any way, inoculate me. God knows what an angel she has been in my life and what an inspiration she is to me. Oh, why must our stores have those aisles of candy approaching their checkout counters?

The Camp Director

If ever I've learned conclusively that social status and financial worth are not the ultimate mark of accomplishment, I learned it with my friend Kevin Gerrety. Kevin initiated his annual summer camping trip with firstborn Annie and her best friend Marnie, along with Marnie's father. The camp out was, in fact, a cabin rental at Adventures Unlimited on the Blackwater River in Northwest Florida. Each summer, Kevin rented successively larger cabins for Annie and then his son Paul, as well as their expanding invitees, plus a sprinkling of business associates, friends, neighbors, parents, and relatives. When I signed on for my ten-year stint, after my own son Paul had participated for a few years, Kevin was a decade along and renting a two-story cabin named Forest Glen, with two sets of bunk beds in a private room; four single wall beds in a Great Room adjoining a kitchen and simple bathroom on the second story; and six or seven sets of bunk beds along opposing walls with a center aisle and end toilet on the first floor. Meals were prepared outside on a brick fireplace covered with an iron grill and eaten on log benches around a large fire-pit. The second-story Great Room held three eight-foot tables end-to-end, surrounded by thirty or so molded plastic chairs, which served for dining and drinking or, most importantly, for the penny-poker tournaments that raged on all night long.

Attendees assembled at the Gerretys' house outside Gulf Breeze on Friday morning and caravanned to Adventures Unlimited outside Milton. Friday afternoon and all of Saturday were committed to a float down the pristine, sand-bottom Blackwater River on a slow-moving current through a verdant forest of cypress and pine overhanging the banks of the spring-fed river. We were transported from camp to some distant launching point in an old converted school bus owned by Adventures Unlimited. Prior to the ride, each camper selected at least two inner tubes from a large stockade storing them, one for himself and one for his beer. No bottles were allowed on the river; and eventually, no women were allowed on the camp-out in the greater interest of civility. An informational sheet/invite was sent out during the spring to previous and potential campers with dates, prices, and guidelines. For example:

Greeting: Hark, camper, our fondest regards. Lend thy ear and eye to this informative memorandum, for now is your time to shine, scumbag! It's time again for you to find and polish your worthless character.

What: Annual Gerrety Camping Trip

When: Friday until Sunday morning

Where: Meet at Gerrety's house Friday morning @ 9:30 a.m. to caravan drive to Adventures Unlimited, Milton, FL (Forest Glen Cabin, otherwise known as "The Waldorf")

Tuition/Cost: $110.00 USD per human—call a Gerrety (Kevin, Paul, Mark) to reserve your bunk.

Look What You Get:
1. 2 nights in a foul-smelling cabin with A/C, a bunk, a shitter, and a worthless stove.
2. 2 river tubing trips with gut-wrenching lunches.
3. Tons of bad-ass grub: world-famous Smith's casing weiners, Mama T's meatballs, shrimp, seafood, appetizers, and junk food to fill your gullet.
4. Classic, world-renowned T-shirts designed by legendary Jim "Mr. B" Bentley and Jacque Paul Bentley.
5. Comradery with deranged others of your kind.
6. A roaring campfire (a la George) in picturesque surroundings with tree frogs and starlit nights.
7. Liars poker with fellow liars, you lying sack of monkey shit.

Ladies: Sorry, but this will be a guys-only trip. We love you dearly, but when we guys see all you beautiful, voluptuous women in bikinis and we've had too much to drink, we act like crazed wildebeests. We just can't control ourselves. We'll see ya at the beach on Thursday or Sunday.

Things to Bring:
1. Yourself (in good/high spirits).
2. Sleeping gear, pajamas, Teddy bear.
3. An extensive supply of frothy, alcoholic beverages to keep from getting parched.
4. Personal hygiene kit, you ugly slob, including a toilet brush to clean your teeth or scum-filled mug or both.
5. Poker money/change.
6. Clippers for your nose hair, mustache, or the sagebrush on your ugly ass!
7. Sunscreen; remember last year when you burnt your stupid skull and looked like a mummy the next day?
8. Change of underwear; odds suggest that you will crap your pants at some point over the weekend.
9. Sleeping bag; sorry, no wifeys or girlyfriends to share it with (and keep your own hands to yourself, mate!).
10. Your crying towel (for showering and consolation after losing all your money playing poker).
11. Deodorant or aerosol spray for your foul aroma!

Things Not to Bring:
1. Rotgut beer; campers caught drinking rotgut beer will be honey-glazed and staked to an ant hill!
2. Transparent Speedos, spandex thongs.
3. Formalwear; a tuxedo, smoking jacket, women's lingerie, or a wedding dress. A suit of armor is acceptable and appropriate.
4. Spam casserole.

Light Flashes in the Tunnel

5. Firearms or TNT.
6. Rainbow-colored fanny pack.
7. Your bucktoothed, cross-eyed, transvestite brother. Hey, we all love him, but that sumbitch still owes me fifty bucks from that last poker game.
8. Yourself with any afflictions or diseases; such as elephantiasis, dysentery, scurvy, mad cow disease, Asian bird flu, scabies, Klinefelter's syndrome, or dandruff. Anyone with the latter will be thrown into the river with an anvil tied to their nuts!
9. Your parole officer.
10. Your Barbie dolls and Care Bears.

Binding Rules:
1. No whining.
2. No rotgut beer.
3. No leopard skin Speedos (except the camp director).
4. No visible cheating at poker.
5. No BoBo Janeros.
6. Every man for himself.

Final Note: If you are undecided about whether you ought to come camping with us, it's OK. Just stay home that weekend, help your mom bake cupcakes, watch *Brady Bunch* reruns, and prance around the house in a dress, you flaming pansy! We'll send you a post card, if you're lucky.

Come one, come all and leave your wretched past behind you!

In spite of the suggested prices, Kevin never turned down a camper that couldn't come up with the cash. A "Camper of the Year" was selected, mainly for morale contributions, and a humorous trophy awarded to him. Kevin, his brother, brothers-in-law, and eventually, his son Paul were at the heart of camping trip planning and execution. During my time, Paul Gerrety designed the annual T-shirts awarded to all attendees, replete with caricatures and an annual slogan, as follows:

2001: "Gerrety's Good-Natured Gangbuster's Getaway"

2002: "Gerrety's Deliverance for Derelicts 2002" with small skull and crossbones

2003: "Gerrety's Solidarity Summer Camp for Valiant Vagabonds"

2004: "Gerrety's Summer Camp '04 Wildlife Retreat" in memory of Jim Buker and Frank Taverniti, with Forest Glen Cabin and a camper in an inner tube on the river

2005: "Gerrety's Summer Camp '05" with a giant, hand-drawn skull and crossbones on one version and a pirate holding a tankard of beer on the second version

2006: "I'm a Happy Camper; Northwest Florida's Finest 2006" with a frontiersman in coonskin cap

2007: "Gerrety's Training Camp '07" with a knight on horseback slaying a dragon and a mug of beer on the left sleeve

2008: "20th Annual Camping Convention for the Deranged 2008" with a naked Neanderthal

2009: "Doggone Campin'; Good Times, Good Friends 2009; I Came, I Drank, I Don't Remember" with a hound dog in sunglasses holding a beer and four aces while floating in an inner tube on the river. Its logo, designed by Kevin's brother Mark from Erie, Pennsylvania, for the twenty-first consecutive annual campout, is reproduced below as representative of the many.

Of course, the beer-drinking and braggadocio were way beyond reasonable limits, and there were no judges to curb the outrageous claims for the penny-poker hands; but the goodwill generated and the therapy received for this camaraderie in the wild was beyond measure. We floated from sandbar to sandbar in a lazy current, toasting each other's dreams and believing in our immortality, all at the hands of one man who believes that there is more to be had from life than fame and fortune. Long live my friend, the camp director, Kevin River Rat Gerrety!

Jim Sharer Bentley

The American Heartland

Driving from east to west across the farm belt and Great Plains country of the Midwest United States is a scenic adventure. You experience America the Beautiful, with spacious skies and amber waves of grain; yawning expanses of majestic grasses bending wave upon wave in the wind; family farms with verdant hedgerows of trees interspersed with stones separating acres of croplands with corn, wheat, oats, and soybeans from livestock pastures with cattle, sheep, and horses flooding over the horizon, each centered by an island of buildings with barns, sheds, silos, and a farmhouse. Each farmhouse invariably has a fringe of trees bracing a fence surrounding the family's lawn and vegetable garden. A mile-long drive connects the house to the highway on which you travel. It is a picturesque setting that belies its exhaustive and worrisome life, and if you're fortunate enough to meet the latest generation of family living there, it's a hospitable experience. You might be viewed suspiciously at first in case you're a peddler, a politician, or a revenuer; but if you're just plain folks with good intentions, then you'll be greeted and treated with the generosity of that long, wide drive to the heart.

The Dirt Devils of Windy Ridge

It sounds like a second-class, melodramatic desert flick, but it's really just the power of the wind to spin dust and sand into small, rotating spirals. I witnessed this phenomenon atop Windy Ridge at Mt. St. Helens National Volcanic Monument. As Art Yaremchuk and I sauntered along the crest trail overlooking Spirit Lake, the almond-colored ash and pumice prevalent in the landscape would rise unexpectedly into colorful whirlwinds, dancing all around us. Like miniature tornadoes, they leaned this way and then that way, like spastic fingers crossing a page, sometimes jumping up off the ground altogether, only to return and race ahead of us or into us for a stinging sandblast!

XV. KEEPING YOUR ADDICTIONS AND DOCTORS IN BALANCE

When the Body Is No Longer a Temple

Well, given the preponderance of potbellies in America, maybe we're more inclined toward the symbol of Buddhism, except that Buddha is also known for peace and tranquility. Many Americans have somehow missed those traits. We are awash in booze, cigarettes, innumerable drugs (both legal and illegal), energy drinks, every possible form of candy and sweets, highly processed foods, and exotic desserts. Even our diet and weight reduction products tout chocolate-covered or-flavored products to reel us in. It's all addictive, and our behavior follows suit. Our national psyche of depression and paranoia seems borne out of our diet and lack of exercise. Fat is fun! Fat is sexy! Fat is life! We need to return to the admonition of our Christian religious teachings that, loosely translated, say (in James I, 2-4), "Thou shalt not put into thy body any but the purest of food and drink. Thou shalt not consume more per day than thy body will burn in calories. Thou shalt exercise regularly."

Get Fat Slowly, Lose It Fast

Given America's cultural fetish with overeating, how can we combat the deluge of commercial stimuli imploring us to eat more food, more often? Our fast food is just that, with a super-size-it option attached to the order. Our usual restaurant portions are humongous, typically enough for two or three meals. Our one-stop grocery enterprises are so heavily and lavishly endowed with food variety, much of it non-nutritious, that our stimulated minds are ever-inclined to buy more than we should reasonably eat. The displays and presentations are mesmerizing and the claims for health often misleading and outrageous. Doctors of overweight patients typically recommend shopping on the perimeter of grocery stores, where fresh meat, fruit, and vegetables are stocked and not on interior aisles, where processed and snack foods, zero-nutrient, and high-calorie bombs reside. It is no wonder that our diet and exercise industries have grown exponentially with our food offerings. Our new national obsession with dieting, eating, and exercising seems to be turning toward getting fat slowly and losing it fast!

Weighing In

One of the archetypical measures of all things representing us is the common scale. It is, of course, merely a device for taking our weight; but it has evolved into a quantum assessment of our health, our appearance, our personality, our motivation, and our will power. Like a professional boxer, we want to look and be our best at the weigh-in, the critical junctures of our life. We can put on weight and tone down between weigh-ins; but for graduation, for job interviews, for office meetings, for speaking engagements, for dates, for weddings, and for reunions, we want to look and feel in our prime. Our scale tells us all this at a glance: "Ten pounds overweight, not feeling so good, looking a little ragged around the edges, slacking off too much, need to back off on the carbs, perk up with a little exercise, sharpen the wits." A gone goose for being just a few pounds overweight! Whatever happened to pleasingly plump, the jolly old man with a ready laugh and a hearty love for life?

Don't Go Down the Cookie Aisle

Old age and good health are a dichotomy survivable only by listening to your doctor. I have, unquestionably, one of the most competent and conscientious primary care physicians imaginable. Dr. Susan Laenger is personable and patient with my naysaying, but thin enough to simulate a stick figure by comparison to my enlarged girth. Of course, I envy her demeanor and knowledge; but mostly, I envy her thin physique. Her specialty is internal medicine, and she is bent and forthright about getting and keeping my health on a positive track. She is quite learned and disposed to share with me the minute particulars of where I'm off-track and how I can right myself. Our quarterly appointments usually open and proceed as follows:

"Mr. Bentley, let me give you a few minutes to explain why your weight has not decreased from our last visit or, for that matter, our last ten visits. I am noting, with pleasure, that you were 228 pounds in June 2009, 239 pounds in February 2011, and 246 pounds in April 2012. Since that time, you have consistently been at or over 260. Your healthy weight, based upon the BMI Wheel calculation, would be in the 170 to 180 range, but I would be happy to see you around 200 pounds or a lot closer to 200 than 262. I appreciate that you're walking regularly, so perhaps we need to re-examine the dietary half of this issue. What are your thoughts on this?"

"I'm at a loss, except to say that I've inherited a huge sweet tooth from my mother."

"Let's talk about that. Exactly what sort of sweets do you like?"

"All desserts. Anything with sugar in it. I never met a carbohydrate I didn't like!"

"Well, we're going to have to moderate that thinking. How about a bi-weekly or weekly dessert as the reward for abstaining in between? Maybe you could substitute honey for brown sugar in your oatmeal?"

"My mother served a dessert at every meal, and there is no substitute for brown sugar!"

"We also need to moderate your alcohol intake and use of cigars."

"Please let's not get hasty here. There's no cause to rush into action."

"No time like the present. I want to see movement toward reducing alcohol intake per week from your current excesses to four, eight-ounce glasses of wine and one rum and Coke, with no more than six-ounces of rum."

"My son, Paul, just sent me a new humidor to keep my cigars fresh—you know, a Father's Day gift."

"Well, forgive me for not being excited about your new humidor. I'm thinking more along the lines of you giving up cigars altogether!"

"You're going to break my spirit. What I need is a fat doctor that drinks and smokes cigars."

"What you need is good advice. I'm trying to save you from yourself. While we're on the subject, we need to limit salt intake and substitute for sugar, wherever possible. Eliminating carbonated beverages from your diet is one way."

"So what is the substitute for Coke in a rum and Coke? How about I cut down on the chips and dip and go to cantaloupe and pineapple for snacks?"

"I hate to be a killjoy, but fruit has natural sugar; so you don't want to overdo on it, either. Fruit is a better snack than chips and crackers; but we really need to focus on eliminating the candy, cookies, cakes, pies, and desserts."

"You're killing me. Life is over for me if I can't have ice cream and cookies!"

"No, life will be over for you if you keep up a steady diet of that stuff! Do not go down the cookie aisle! Shop on the perimeter of the store, where you'll find the fresh fruits, lean meats, and vegetables. Think fresh, home-made salad with carrots, green peppers, lettuce, onions, tomatoes, and a low-cal salad dressing."

"You're forgetting the feta cheese."

"I'll see you in three months and at least three pounds lighter. Right?"

"Yes, Dr. Laenger. I hear you, Dr. Laenger. You're right, Dr. Laenger, but you're driving me to drink!"

Don't Supersize It, Romanticize It

Instead of thinking of food in terms of meals with selected

components to a certain volume at a particular time of day, think of each component of food as a meal to be eaten at no particular time. Look at your fat and think thin. Think of yourself as thin, desirable, and graceful. Eat less at fewer times and exercise more. As you walk, pump those arms and swing that butt. Dine on granola bars and fruit with lots of water. You are the dancer and master of a magnificent life. Pity all who cannot see you as the ultimate champion.

Just Add Water

I don't follow any prescribed diet regimen, but continue to imbibe and nibble on sweets and snacks with abandon. Occasionally, I feel guilty; but it passes quickly. One evening, when my Seattle son-in-law and I found ourselves alone during the dinner hour, he offered to heat me up a box of Indian fare: "Punjab Choley, a traditional Indian recipe of chickpeas, tomatoes, onions, garlic, and ginger in a richly spiced and tangy sauce," he said. Hungry though I always am, the memory of my doctor's admonition and my earlier bouts with Indian spices combined to mute my appetite. I had been snacking all day, and my girth was such that I could live off my body fat for several years without another bite. "No food needed, thank you very much. Just add water!"

Where's the American Spirit of Adventure

Why is it that the American who succumbs to the pressure of walking for exercise will drive several miles to a track to complete a fixed number of laps instead of walking the same distance through a local city neighborhood or countryside? How can we subject ourselves to the dulling sameness of a track over exploring new sections of our hometown environs? Every yard exposes the unique, creative flair of its occupant.

It's the Little Things That Count

We're all—collectively I'm sure—awestruck by the grandiose sights, sounds, and smells of life at hand. Think popular Broadway musicals, launch and recovery operations aboard an aircraft carrier, sunrise or sunset over mountains, pungent aromas from a city bakery, or a rose garden. We're agape on the rim of the Grand Canyon and mesmerized by the sweep from seaboard cliffs and coastal beaches. The panorama of every major landscape vista is almost always incredible to our minds; but locked up, as we often become, in the numbing tedium of our daily routines, we seldom get that view of the fog-enshrouded Golden Gate Bridge or the New York City skyline by night, even if we live in San Francisco or New York. Between the highs and lows of our consciousness is the great middle ground of isolated incidents, unusual offerings, and fascinating micro-theatre that provide our best interaction with the world's pallet around us. Think the toad that you see often in your garden; the colorful wild flowers pushing up amid cigarette butts and plastic refuse at your bus stop; the sight of a gleeful child hugging a puppy; the tickle of a ladybug traversing your arm; the smell of bacon crackling in a skillet or coffee brewing in a percolator; the opportunity to assist a blind person at a crowded, high-traffic street crossing or a homeless person counting out the last of their change on a store counter.

It includes all of those simple courtesies bestowed by a

generous populace: the smiles, door holdings, directions, compliments, and application of good will as a Golden Rule in a crowded world. It's those pay-it-forward moments when the traveler ahead of you on a toll bridge pays your way and you pay for the one behind you, when the proprietor at your favorite coffee shop gives you a free latte and pastry, or when you're able to buy a latte and pastry for active duty military personnel in appreciation of their service.

How about those good souls in traffic that slow to your turn signal so you can cut in; the nice police person who lets you off with a warning; the store that forgives a late charge; the pleasant waitress who chats you up and keeps your cup full; or the neighbor who not only picks up your mail during time you are away, but takes and picks you up from the airport, as well? These micro-interactions with our environment are but a few of the myriad in a daily chain of little things that keep us going, fire our engines, and tame the savage onslaught of bad news and horrific events borne by us all. It's the accumulation of these little positive nudges to our daily lives that make life bearable and lift us out of our perilous boredom. Make sure you're one of the positive players on life's stage, because it truly is the little things that count.

XVI. DISTILLING THE SPIRIT

The Vibrant, Active, Over-Fifty-Five Adult Lifestyle

I have never been afraid of those words separately; but put them together, and they spell "programmed to death." But what is my fear, my repulsion? It's okay to be old or older. We don't have to break from the gate at the speed of light anymore! We don't have to have every minute during the day scheduled anymore! Relax, sleep in, enjoy it. When someone asks you how you're doing, you should be able to respond, "As I please," instead of, "As my community pleases." But, on the other hand, I suppose it's a reasonable ambition for most folks to want to retain their youth without much exertion as long as they can. Hence, a master-planned, over-fifty-five community with a "full-time Lifestyle Director to introduce you to a world of active opportunities—sports, fitness, classes, parties, trips, and a wide array of clubs." I'm of the belief that you create your own opportunities from the fabric of a random plane. In other words, make do with what surrounds you wherever you are. Everything's available but for the asking or creation. The over-fifty-five communities create these opportunities for you, thus depriving you of the real joy in finding or creating them with your friends and neighbors by yourselves.

    I just had to see an over-fifty-five community for myself, so I visited my beloved brother in his gated over-fifty-five commune to experience the good life firsthand. It was good—maybe too good—almost perfect! The pastel, vinyl-sided houses all looked the same. They were single-story, family ranch style; but were well-built, with plenty of quality upgrades like granite counter tops, exquisite cabinetry, fireplaces, and sunrooms. And all the houses were situated on or bordered the man-made ponds dug throughout the community to give the effect of waterfront. Fred's 360-acre development is billed as a campus community to reflect the integrated lifestyle of many older adults in the common pursuit of happiness, with an umbrella administration to keep the beat. The community motto, advertised widely in brochures and on banners, is "Let your light shine." Also in the brochures are resident testimonials like, "We just never stop! We love being on the move." The flavor of it almost seemed as if boredom and depression are not allowed, and health and morale are regulated to a high level. Don't scowl! It works—at least for those who want to distance themselves from child rearing, family ties, the workaday world, commute and traffic frustrations, and mixed business-residential neighborhoods with differing standards of construction and maintenance. You won't find a local garage in this 'hood or a grocer; druggist; restaurant; church; bank; doctor; lawyer; lumberyard; school; library; or police or fire station, for that matter. All these familiar community services are outside the gate. Life as we generally know it is simply not integrated with the over-fifty-five master-planned community. The active part of "vibrant, active, over-fifty-five adult lifestyle" comes from the "unparalleled activities and amenities within the community where you'll exercise your talents, feed your soul, and develop new pursuits and friendships." The lifestyle director is there to orchestrate resident happiness with a formidable array of offerings, starting with relieving them of the tiresome details involved with planning and building their homes, planting, and maintaining their yards. And that contentious neighbor we've all experienced, with the perennially-soiled wife-beater shirt, working in his yard on a collection of junker cars while swilling beer and shouting unseemly obscenities—well, he's not allowed, on several counts, in the community. Neither is the fence that you would build to block him out allowed, nor are RVs or pleasure boats, which must be stored in a rental facility outside the gate in the real community.

The focal point of the faux community is an amenity center with indoor and outdoor heated pools, state-of-the-art fitness equipment, arts and crafts rooms, chorale/dance studios, a combo concert and ballroom, a gourmet kitchen, and locker rooms. And this center hosts every imaginable activity from scrap-booking to cruising. There are tennis, bocce, and pickle ball courts outside, but golf is outside the gate. There is, however, a community van or charter bus service to take residents outside the gate for golf, baseball games, shopping, or any of the other services that we take for granted in a real community. The residents were, indeed, all active and appeared to be having fun with newfound friends; but the absence of children and integrated common services, plus the burdensome rules promoting a common standard, made it all seem sterile to me. Besides, it ain't natural for citizens to ride around city streets in a golf cart. But, as Dennis Miller used to say at the end of his TV shows, "That's just my opinion. I could be wrong!"

Perfect Weather Bliss

    As an adoptive Floridian, I am used to the sweltering heat of a usual summer day where both temperature and humidity readings exceed ninety degrees, and you can almost cut a slice of hot water for coffee out of the air. Now, Shannon matriculated through her Florida childhood and college years at or near home; and then, as is the usual path for Pensacola, she married a Naval Aviator and pursued life with her husband at various duty stations until their return to civilian life, settling in the land of Pat's Pacific Northwest heritage: Woodinville, Washington. Now, there are many notable features about Woodinville, beyond the obvious Chateau St. Michelle Winery and Red Hook Brewery, none more notable than its weather. I never really understood all the hoopla over minuscule ad infinitum discussions that bombarded us daily about weather measurements and predictions until I arrived in the land with routine summer temperatures of fifty to seventy degrees Fahrenheit, partly to mostly sunny skies and *no* humidity. I mean, how much weather coverage or discussion can be endured about temperature, the possibility of rain, or the amount of sunshine? Nevertheless, as I disembarked mid-June from my U.S. Air flight at SeaTac Airport in Seattle, still wet from the usual summer climate in my Florida homeland, it was a pleasure to have to stop long enough in the passenger pick-up area to recover a fleece pull-over from my bag to endure the cooler climes of Washington State. Instead of air conditioning within a sealed room, how sweet it was to simply crack the windows to savor those fifty-degree overnight lows under the warmth of a blanket.

Of course, Pat, a native Washingtonian, thinks it's too hot when the temperature reaches seventy-five degrees Fahrenheit, even though it's overcast; and he's long-since trained his children to respond to the question of perfect weather as fifty-five degrees and foggy. As for me, I'm still acclimated to ninety-ninety, with a brilliant sun!

The Last Train to Clarksville

This is not an ode to the Monkees' famous song of the same name; neither is it a tribute to the Tennessee city off Interstate Highway 24 near the Kentucky border that I pass en route to and from the AT. Rather, this is the Clarksville in Missouri, on the Mississippi River south of Hannibal, between the towns of Elsberry and Louisiana. It's the residence city and workplace of MeMe and Paw-Paw, so it's at least a monthly pilgrimage for us city folks to vacate our pristine subdivision for a ride through the rural heartland on State Highway 79 aside the iron rails of a busy train route. We are mesmerized by the giant patchwork of fields emanating from distant island homesteads. We blink our lights and pump our arms through open windows during the approach of an oncoming train in hopes that its engineer will signal us with a long, mournful whistle. We point our deer grazing at the edge of fields and forest. We wonder at the destination of two-lane country roads crossing fields and disappearing into hedgerows. We read the weathered history of small towns like Elsberry, Eolia, and Annada in their integrated living, play, and working spaces. Unlike our residential subdivision in Lake St. Louis or my brother's over-fifty-five community near Charleston, commercial and residential buildings meld together with playing fields, churches, and schools. Annada is a grain elevator on the rail line. Eolia, where Bud has a spread for raising his beloved thoroughbred Appaloosa horses, is farm country. Clarksville, typical of the Great Plains river towns, was built around Lock and Dam No. 24 and can be viewed in its entirety along 2nd Street, State Highway 79, through town from the outlying Antique Mall to the end of the residential area, including MeMe and Paw-Paw's nineteenth-century home, a refurbishment project in progress; two churches, Catholic and Protestant, that also constitute the town's political extremities; an Apple Barn, home of Eagle Days' displays including live bald eagle presentations and all manner of homemade crafts and food; a small delicatessen-grocery store; a cluster of artist-in-residence studios/workshops; and the inevitable overgrown shells of former and forgotten homes, businesses, and public works buildings. Prominent are the rusting remains of a failed chairlift operation that was initiated to transport sightseers to the top of the town's only hill to enjoy the view and to purchase local arts and crafts.

MeMe and Paw-Paw greet us with unbounded hospitality, and we catch up on their house renovation; tour their River Road Pottery and Woodworking Shop on Front, 1st, Street next to the Mighty Mississippi; and always enjoy one of MeMe's scrumptious meals. The whole experience is charming, as our small, hodgepodge towns are wont to bloom around us. They present life's minutiae and grandiosity without apology; nothing orchestrated, nothing left out! What you see is what and who you are, shades of a Norman Rockwell illustration—profound, blemished, and unadulterated to savor in full measure.

Exhausting Your Options

In the forefront of your life, the panorama of crossroad options seems limitless. The choice of routes, whether mainstream or less travelled, split off from one another in a dizzying array of directions through education to learn further information; travel to mature; apprenticeship to hone skills; personal interests to cultivate character; and romance to enrich the heart, all while attending to the favor of your health, wealth, and happiness. In later years, as options diminish by choice, after tiring from the fulfillment of earlier pursuits, the simplification of having but a few daily goals, comfortably repeated, is enough to satiate the body and mind. Of course, the soul still requires its daily dose of ice cream.

Life Is Also a Spectator Sport

Of course, we want to jump up and run! Just do it! Drink it all in right now with both hands and feet! Life is a competition for the center ring where the spotlight shines brightest, but it is also a view from the shadows. In youth, the impulse is to do it all with splash and verve; but as the faculties close down around you in old age, a placid view from the bench becomes divine. Not that images of the ballerina or matador don't still float through your dreams, but you've replaced that hurried, worried persona surrounded by standing ovation with a quiet, indifferent, happy tone.

Rituals

For us old-timers, daily rituals are the bulwarks of familiarity.

We can have an inspiring array of new agenda items listed mentally for our day, but they are strung together with the pearls of our blind habits—Sean calls them nitnoids. Each familiar habit provides an island of security in a tumultuous sea.

Hygiene

Flossing and brushing teeth after all meals, showering and shaving occasionally, combing hair, washing hands, and dressing are all self-fulfilling rituals. Contrary to Jimmy Buffet's plaintive refrain in his song "Pencil-Thin Mustache," "I'm getting old; I don't wear underwear. I don't go to church and I don't cut my hair," we senior citizens do honor our familiar hygienic rituals, which include taking medicinals and vitamins and making regular visits to our doctors. We even massage our wrinkled limbs with skin lotions to protect the temple of the body as a repository for the soul. With a heightened sense of smell—even as our eyes dim and hearing fails us—we become ignited with perfumes and scented oils, shaving balms and colognes, soaps and shampoos. We may not be pretty to look at, but at least we can smell good.

Giddy

You know, being old does not exempt you from the allures of the opposite sex, no matter how ridiculous the age difference. I'm sure the term "dirty old man" comes from the pathetic, leering overtures of those aged stud muffins trying to relive their romantic youth; but I must be one, because it has happened to me. As a near-seventy-year-old curmudgeon at my son's twenty-ninth birthday party finale at a local lounge, around midnight, way later than I usually stay up, one of the girls who I have known from her early teens began to hug and snuggle me with appreciation for having been a part of her youth. Well, having changed, in my memory, from a gawky, spindly, shy girl with braces to a long-legged, green-eyed, statuesque twenty-something head-turner with magnificent cleavage, I was not, shall we say, immune to her charms or adverse to being her teddy bear for those few luscious moments as she fawned over me. Ah, the wiles and guiles of women! All I could think and say was, "If only I was fifty years younger!" and "You make me feel so young."

Old Age

We can't rise that fast or go that far. It's a bitch! The spirit is willing, even encouraging; but the bones and muscles won't always comply. Those aches and pains us old-timers whine about, if we can get an audience, are real. In my younger years, I never wanted to sit on a bus or in a theater next to some ancient who would, invariably, recite the entire litany of his or her family and health history. I used to pass up park benches during walks that held one or more octogenarians at the ready to bend someone's—anyone's—ear. Worse still was to be in a doctor's office or hospital waiting room where they could wax on without interruption as you nodded vacantly while thumbing through a magazine. Now, as justice has a way of finding her due, I am the one visiting my family history and ails upon those unsuspecting victims who quite innocently ask, "How are you doing?"

Relaxing Is What I Do Best

The feckless part of my brother's fond and accurate assessment of my general deportment and work ethic in retirement does, indeed, reflect my true modus operandi at seventy years of age. Irresponsibility and worthlessness are the signal traits of my retirement mode. In short, nothing is more important to me than smelling the flowers along the way. I cannot be hurried. Indeed, it is a feat for me to take any action outside of relaxing or having fun. Most days, I'm unshaven in sweat clothes and slippers; reading; playing cards; working Sudoku puzzles; and partaking of good food, friends, wine, and cigars. I've got few bills and little property to consume me. I'm not about to get wrought up again over the depressing travails of our economy or my personal inability to regenerate after losing it all. Now it's all about floating like a jellyfish in the currents of life, with no anchors to confine me.

When You Can't Chew the Leather, Change the Cat Box

If you're going to coerce your support group into taking you on as a boarder, then the least you can do is provide some service in the operation of their household. I can't cook, and I'm not trustworthy with a paint brush or repair skills; but I can do dishes, change diapers, mow lawns, feed animals, and babysit with the best of them. I'm just diabolical enough to keep a baby or school-age boy engaged and fascinated by the unknown. I know about bugs, snakes, and waterborne critters; and I can tell a fearsome enough story to bring rapt obedience to the most contentious child. Of course, none of that matters in a New York apartment with a childless couple who have no lawn and few dirty dishes.

"What can I do to help you guys during the day while you're

at work?" I implored.

"The biggest help to me," replied Paul, "would be to dip the nuggets out of the cats' litter box. It's a daily thing with two cats, and they'll pee or poop on the floor if their box is soiled." That's when I finally realized that my life had come full cycle, when I was relegated from my eminent, revered stature to the cleaner of the cat box.

Fading Away

Those of us in the military during the Vietnam era will recall General Douglas MacArthur's famous departure speech at West Point entitled "Duty, Honor, Country," during which he immortalized the line, "Old soldiers never die; they just fade away." The speech was widely circulated throughout military ranks and offered us as fine a mission statement as you will find anywhere. The whole thing rang with poetry and sentiment, as was the general's bent, so the words "fade away" took on an almost ethereal meaning. Still, as old age besets me and my skin withers into mottled wrinkles of scaly flakes that peel incessantly like the former dandruff of a youthful scalp; my now-hairless head is shorn of once-vigorous hair; my toenails become yellowed with the fungus of age; and my muscles atrophy into frail ligaments, I realize that my fading has taken on an organic nature along with the ethereal.

Drooling and Dribbling

Aging can be graceful, even beautiful; but, as we all learn, it ain't always easy. I recall a very funny evening at the Saenger Theater in Pensacola, listening to a stand-up monologue by the late George Carlin wherein he talked about his inordinate capacity for drooling in his sleep, "about a pint a night." Well, at seventy-something myself, I'm right there with him! Not only drooling, but having the last sprinkle of urine drops dribble into my pants after peeing, no matter how hard I shake my wanker. Old age can also be a bitch!

Riding the Ragged Edge

This courage thing is a tough climb when an aging body can't follow the spirit of your dreams and you're resigned to compromising away the pinnacles for the particles. It's both demoralizing and debilitating to see the majestic goals of your life slip-sliding away into the remnants that are but baby steps toward the big dream that is finally out of reach. Utter failure must always, reasonably, be listed as one of life's project scenarios—but who, more reasonably, would consider it except, like death, as a last resort? Some failure is good for rebounding options; but final failure, like quicksand, is an abominable abyss to enter. The righteous mind cannot accept failure; Lord, resurrect us!

The Age of Disgruntlement

When, exactly, do we pass from the naive optimism of believing that all dreams can be accomplished, all things work out in the end, and all setbacks provide a valuable learning lesson? Most of our lives do encompass some fulfilled dreams and fetes for celebrating notable achievements, if only a birthday party; but so, too, are we replete with failed efforts that deplete us, thwarted aspirations that discourage us, and tarnished ideals that disparage cherished beliefs. We stop going into the woods when the splendor of nature is overcome by our mental and physical torments. We lose faith in our fellow humanity under the siege of artificial compliments, hollow promises, failed support, and the self-serving petitions of hucksters peddling True Divinity. "Oh God, please save me from the Christians." We lose faith in charity under a deluge of incalculable organizations representing animal cruelty, education, multiple environmental issues, various degenerative health concerns, active duty/wounded/retired military veterans, disparate domestic and global wildlife, and human populations. As we are thus besieged and massaged and turned away for lack of funds or for being a bad risk, we naturally close up and often become disgruntled. It can happen at any age, but more often as we pass into our declining years. Thus, us oldsters should not be surprised to hear the soft-whispered warning during our travels, "Here comes that crotchety old man again."

Fear

Aging can create a gradual withdrawal from life. The routine accomplishments of youth—supported by the unbounded spirit to live, love, laugh, and be happy—often wane in a debilitating wave of fear. These fears seize even our simplest actions, preventing us from driving, using public transportation, applying for a job, or engaging in public discourse. We withdraw unnaturally from those things that previously defined us; and, in so doing, we can become nonentities. Fear can mutate into the disease of perpetual depression, which must be confronted and banished by soul-driven weapons of exhilaration.

Exhilaration of the Soul

Growing older—really older—offers wide expanses of sameness: the recurring aches of bodily pain from old football injuries, broken bones, hernias, sprains, strains, arthritic joints, and/or the cold weather of loneliness. Without regular physical exercise, engagement of the mind, and the convivial stimulation from family and friends, the aging process accelerates at an inordinately high pace. It's the druthers of boredom, pain, and disengagement that precipitate the will to die. It is a continuing challenge to renew yourself, a quest to realize former glories. Sometimes when you least expect it, your mind—as master of your body—will kick in to sweep away all the boredom and nagging pains of your existence; your spirit surges; and the will to live, explore, learn, love, and prevail dominate for exhilaration of the soul. Once again, you are young and drinking life's golden elixir with both hands, unfettered, with the boundless energy of dream-filled youth.

A Little More Juice

"Try it again; and this time, give her a little more juice," our mechanical friends yell at us from under the open hood of a broken-down car. I've never fully appreciated that phrase until the tentacles of old age began to siphon off my mental and physical energies. You'll be trolling along in a blue funk with no more reason for despondency than a few aching joints and a little memory loss, when—*bang*! You enter upon a verdant meadow alive with shade trees; long grass; wild flowers; coursing brooks; bird calls; and a jolly, round, red Mister Sun smiling upon it all. Or you become engrossed in the close comradery and hearty laughter of a stimulating conversation with family and/or friends. Or a song, a favorite piece of music, lifts your soul and calls you back to earlier life strains. Or a pungent reality, born from long dreamtime, manifests itself into the concrete present. Or any exhilaration, really, which transports you away from your sorrows into sublime happiness, happens. It's just that little bit of juice that tips the balance and puts you over the top.

Blabber-Mouthed Women and Domino Men

Central Park in New York City is, by even the most conservative measure, an amazing 843-acre swathe of green in one of the world's most compressed areas of humanity. It is such a welcome relief to the crush of overpopulation and the choking heat, noise, and fumes of close living and nightmarish traffic. There are ball fields, gardens, lawns, meadows, ponds, miles of trails, innumerable benches, plaques, statues and terraces, a children's zoo, and even a boathouse and a castle. But most fascinating to me was the arena set aside with shaded tables and benches for those wanting to play dominoes, checkers, or chess. I took a look and found the most resplendent range of humanity engrossed in their table games. Parents played their children in checkers, couples of all descriptions mused over chess, but most fascinating were the old men stoically playing dominoes while their wives or girlfriends (in our modern age) sat together on the periphery blathering on like verbal surgeons dissecting and shaping the carcass of stimuli impacting their world. "Plop, plop. Fizz, fizz. Oh, what a relief it is!"

Do Not Disturb: Renaissance in Progress

How's an old man to explain his occasional nodding off during some tiresome monologue of which he has no knowledge or interest? Sleep does not compliment the well-meaning orator, but it must humble her or him some. You are left to grope for an excuse upon awakening—usually with a drool-stained shirt—such as having been up late the night before, focusing on the message, resting your eyes, praying for enlightenment, meditating upon some spiritual verse printed on the back of your eyelids, or having a renaissance about the cure for global warming. All excuses are off and will be discredited if you cannot remember at least a few snatches of the oration. Lacking that, your boorish personality will be dismissed and your future company avoided by the eager talker. If they are sales people or Jehovah's Witnesses, congratulations, you have found liberation and peace from the dark side of the force.

Sacking In

Sleep deprivation affects the body and soul in innumerable ways. For one, the annals of highway accidents are replete with records of drivers nodding off at the wheel from fatigue. Students, church congregants, and other seminar attendees are wont to snooze during drudgerous monologues from lack of sleep. We're all familiar with those situations where we, or some beleaguered acquaintance, have offered that vacuous look during conversation. Proper sleep is an important component of good health at all ages. As a teen, I routinely logged ten to twelve hours of sleep after my exhausting nocturnal social pursuits, i.e., chasing the skirts; and now, as an old-timer, I still need at least eight to nine hours to keep from flagging early. But beyond the obvious need for rest, who among us does not relish lingering in bed of a morn to soak up that last bit of warmth from swaddled sheets and blankets during the quiet, dim light of dreamtime before the break of day?

Fantasy the Best Reality

Watching children at their imaginary games is the precursor to the hope generated by adult dreams. Pretending that a stick is a gun, a wagon, or a tank during juvenile war games is not much different from actual soldiers in a real time war zone facing the constant threat of death during combat who project themselves mentally into a triumphant return home to passionate embraces from their loved ones, to sumptuous dining fare, to realizing their fantasy dream house, and into the prowess of their enemy. After all, monsters are so much more fearsome in the imagination. Dreaming is just the hope for or fear of an eventual reality that may or may not materialize. But in our dreams, we control the destiny that may elude us in reality. The Barbie doll of a three year-old always acts out the expectant behavior of a child from others and always has the material possessions transposed from their adult counterpart. Inasmuch as so many of our dreams go awry or dissipate from lack of resources, the dream itself often becomes our only reality. But in the dream, there are no bounds to the perfection of our achievements or acquisitions. We must dream to truly be alive, and we must realize some part of our dreams to stay alive.

Time Lapses, Not Mind Lapses

The vigorous mind is a cauldron of ideas steaming toward action. We all have our get-rich-quick schemes and our better mousetrap inventions. We all start projects that never see completion for lack of time or interest, but their finale is always cooking on a back burner of our mind. We'll awaken to a project started years earlier with a fresh perspective and gusto that often ends with unimagined cash, fame, or pleasure, all for having just a little time to resurrect a dream. Getting old shouldn't be about giving up your dreams but about resurrecting them, one by one, and acting on their fulfillment while spinning off other dreams and projects along the way.

A Piss in the Wind

Age is not getting old; it's getting older. The point of wisdom is attained when you have forgotten most of your resentments, which only cause you stress and bodily harm. By now, you're casting off the negative vibes in your life as soon as you can piss them away.

The Pillbox Time Clock

It's almost a condition of aging that time and space constrictions evaporate as you become older. In retirement, many elders cast aside their calendars and wristwatches and let the light of day guide their movements. It's such an enlightened state to be unaware of day or time, not to mention the course of scheduled human events. However, this euphoric condition is interrupted by the need to keep doctor's appointments or to maintain a

Light Flashes in the Tunnel

prescribed schedule of taking pills. To meet this requirement, a one or two week compartmented pillbox is used with days of the week inscribed on each pop-up lid. If a supplemental sheet is used for recording daily meds by mouth, Eureka! The calendar reappears! Days can be circled in red and simple notations made for doctor's appointments, bills due, or money withdrawn, automatic deposits, etc. No senior can exist without a pill record to rule his or her life.

The Check Is in the Mail

Remember the gray-uniformed letter carriers of yesteryear, with a leather saddlebag hanging from their shoulders or a pushcart in front of them, walking from house to house, passing mail through slots in the front door or putting it in outside boxes? Their common motto was, "Neither rain nor sleet nor snow nor dark of night shall keep the postman from his appointed rounds." Today, our efficient postal service embraces all forms of modern technology and every manner of delivery. You can still have your mail delivered to a prescribed box curbside at or near your house; you can pick up your mail from a box in your local post office; you can utilize private delivery services like FedEx and UPS; or you can have your mail delivered to a service that sorts, holds, and delivers it as you wish. After Hurricane Ivan divested me of my house and personal property and I departed the succeeding rental property to enter a gypsy life, my mail has since been forwarded to me by the good people at American Home Base mail service, catering mainly to the travel trailer crowd, as I have called them for it. Since I seldom light anywhere for longer than a few months, AHB has been a lifesaving mail answer for my vagabond lifestyle. It has been, as always, a dependable, familiar support frame in a wash of personal chaos. Long live our postal people at their appointed rounds.

The Rules of Self-Engagement for Ancients

My dictionary defines engage as "draw someone in or cause someone to become involved in a conversation or discussion." Of course, when you're an old, solo entity; and your lifelines are adrift beyond your recall, remedial help for loneliness can only be found in your own company. Enjoy it, for there is no better or understanding company than your own soul. That being said, there are a few simple rules for relying on your own, good company:

Rule Number One: Don't talk or gesture to yourself in public. Most folks already believe that old age has diminished us, so don't give them fodder to put you away in a convalescent facility, better described as a soul dungeon. I know that memory recall is assisted by loud repetition and that remembered jokes are funnier if we smile and laugh out loud to ourselves, but not in public. This rule was recently revisited upon me in our local Walmart as I laughed while remembering Skip's retort to a religion purveyor at his door trying to elicit a discussion and share a pamphlet. Finally, after parrying unsuccessfully with the intruder for several minutes and out of patience, Skip asked the aggressive fellow, "Do you like sex on the move? Then get the f--- out of here!" After mouthing the story and laughing heartily, I looked up to find a half dozen or so people staring intently at me. I'm just glad there wasn't anybody there with a net. Talking and laughing alone is totally normal, even dancing and singing to music while gesturing wildly—but not in public. It scares people to think that we're anything but serenely wise.

Rule Number Two: Old people, especially oxygenarians, should keep their mouths closed as much as possible when not talking, singing, eating, or whistling. That skeletal, open-air look, with a lagging tongue and drool runs, is a death stare that scares people watching you. Better to keep the mouth closed and offer a sweet smile to those meeting your eyes.

Rule Number Three (The Inviolate Rule): Never visit the minute details of your life, including photos and sentimental memorabilia, upon casual acquaintances. It's your surest ticket to solitude when those about to encounter you are aware of their numbing fate. Unquestionably, you are or will be recognized as a compulsive talker with almost-photographic recall; but as much as you enjoy sharing the minutiae of your passage through the tunnel, take pity upon the acquaintances and strangers whom you are assailing. Go slow. Give them equal time. Share equal interest in your partner's life story or, surely, you will never see them again if they see you coming first. Save the pithy details and pictures for your support group and others who actually ask you to share them.

Rule Number Four: Don't stare at anything too long. Remember the Male Rule of Cleavage: It is rude to stare at a woman's breasts instead of into her eyes during conversation. A quick look-see is palatable, tolerable, and usually appreciated if her mammaries are sporty. The same goes for staring at anything else, even if you are daydreaming, making a plan, or just nodding off. Don't sit on a park bench and stare fixedly at anything, or passersby will think you're dead. Get up. Move around. Turn your head from side to side. Smile and nod. Offer greetings. Act alive. Although that vacant, skeletal stare is acceptable in *Vogue*, the women's high-fashion magazine where the models are young and supple, it is not among the ancients beyond the runway.

Rule Number Five: Avoid cabin fever. As much comfort as we get from our domiciles, it is imperative to escape them for other activities and locales. Take a walk. Go see a new movie release. Shop in a different store or at least peruse its merchandise. Eat in an unfamiliar restaurant. Visit your local zoo or art gallery. Attend athletic and cultural events. Volunteer your time through church and charity functions. Travel away from your homestead altogether. The salient point here is that change is an important ingredient in living large.

Rule Number Six: Re-engage with others of our species, however slight, to protect your sanity; but when so engaged, see Rule Number Three.

XVII. IT'S CURTAINS WHEN THE FAT MAN CROAKS

Riding the Flat Line into Eternity

Prevailing death humor in hospitals, funeral homes, assisted living facilities, over-fifty-five communities, and the like revolves around familiar expressions such as circling the drain, taking the last lap, hanging on to the milk wagon for dear life, giving up the ghost, buying the farm, or passing on to her or his reward. It's funny to everyone except those watching the rhythmic blip on their heart monitor. Death and taxes have always been the great nemesis of humankind; but death alone is the great equalizer, and very few of us will accept that reward willingly. Old age compensates death by making us so miserable in later years that we begin to look forward to the trip. Still, all things considered, I would rather live forever than trade the blip for a flat line.

A Hug Before Dying

Like all of us inhabiting Mother Earth, I have become acquainted with the pall of death. My path has been littered with grief over catastrophic losses and my impatience and impertinence with fellow travelers in the tunnel during times of stress has left me with a share of detractors and enemies. Of course, the friction from those opposing you creates ire within your soul that smolders on like an eternal flame. That flame must be extinguished before your death. As is so often reported, the bearing of grudges and hostile enmities only serves to diminish your own physical health and mental happiness, not your adversary's. We must confront our perceived opposers in the most positive way we can muster, hopefully with apologies, forgiveness, and a hug before dying.

That's the Long and Short of It

Uncle Frederick Francis, an animal husbandry man and acclaimed horse whisperer, and his namesake, my brother Frederick William, had a Shetland stallion colt lying staked out on a hilltop next to our family farmhouse. My brother was trying to hold the flailing legs, while Uncle Fred was in the process of turning this male pony into a gelding. You can't have two men in the same kitchen. I was holding the stallion's head and covering his eyes with a blanket when Uncle Fred said, "Good God, the razor's broke! Jimmy, run down to Bob's to see if he's got another." Well, Old Bob was a kind of caretaker for the remote farm, an aged veteran pensioner friend of my uncle's who was living free in the ramshackle farmhouse and mostly spending his time as a trapper, curing and selling his skins for extra money. Old Bob was fearsome, and a smile was not to be found on his unshaven, tobacco-stained face. I knocked on his door several times until my uncle yelled at me to just walk in. I cautiously opened the door and entered the stale-smelling, darkened house. It was a shotgun affair with the several rooms opening into each other end-to-end. I crept through a magazine-stacked living room into an unsavory bachelor's kitchen and across a cracked-linoleum dining area floor to Bob's bedroom door. I knocked softly for what seemed an eternity and then opened the door slowly. Bob lay peacefully on an iron-frame cot atop his yellowed bed linens and olive drab army blanket, bathed in sunlight from the window, unshaven as always, hair askew, fully dressed with boots and suspenders, hands folded over his chest, slight smile at the comers of his mouth. I ran out to tell the two Freds to come quick. They released the energetic stallion and descended the hill. After Uncle Fred phoned for an ambulance, I inquired about Bob's health.

"He's dead, and that's the long and short of it."

The Last Gulp of Life

Don't you know that death is a downer?! Who wants to even think about it? Some people have no choice but to parlay with death as they hover in sickness between the worlds. Age and disease slowly close down bodily and mental functions. As independence and mobility are lost, so, too, is the will to live. Yet we all recover our love for life in all its majesty and sweeping grandeur during those sublime moments of happy passion—like during an adventurous walk in a new landscape, during a time of socializing with loved ones, during the pursuit of a cherished hobby or professional occupation, during contemplation or reverie, or during submission of our senses to the magic of the arts. As the will to capture and continue life washes over you in those moments, we can also become frozen, paralyzed with the antithesis of it ebbing away in one final gasp.

Grim Poem on a Tombstone

Cemeteries, like premonitions of death, hold a certain fascination for the living. There is an eternal peace about them. Gravestones share the sorrow of short lives and the finality of all life. Inscriptions often go beyond dates and names into a story line or, even, poetry like the following lines cut into a tombstone at the Highland-Cowles Memorial Cemetery in Ipswich, Massachusetts:

Death is a debt to Nature due.

I've paid my debt and so must you.

Miss Me But Let Me Go

When our infant son Kirk died after only fifty-one days of life, we all mourned in our own way; but I've been drawn back to his grave time and again. For one thing, Holy Cross Cemetery is close to where I worked in Pensacola, so a lunch respite was never as quiet as in a cemetery. You know, there's not much partying, loud talking, or traffic noise in a cemetery. For another thing, it was en route between my church and apartment during the post-Hurricane Ivan year when I returned alone with the hope of regenerating on the Garcon Peninsula. My ex-wife, who is fond of the expression "Deal with it!" is always quick to move on with her life. For example, "This relationship is over. Deal with it!" or "Kirk is dead. His spirit is not in that grave. Deal with it!" I envy her for that trait, but I'm still disposed to collect, catalog, and file mentally all the sentimental debris of my life, to revisit and examine it interminably. It's maddening to people around me! Since I spent the last sleepless night before he was admitted to the children's hospital holding Kirk as he alternately cried and slept, he has never been far from my thoughts.

Susan is spontaneous and has honed her dismissive skills while teaching high school English. She is also an original humorist who wants her own gravestone to read, "I told you I was sick!" On a routine visit to Kirk's grave one Sunday after mass, I found a program on the ground from a burial service the previous day. It contained the following anonymous poem, which struck a chord within me:

> When I come to the end of the road and the
> sun has set for me,
> I want no rites in a gloom-filled room—why cry
> for a soul set free?
> Miss me a little—but not too long, and not with
> your head bowed low.
> Remember the love that we once shared; miss
> me—but let me go.
> For death is a journey that we all must take, and
> each must go alone.
> It's all a part of the Master's plan, a step on the
> road to home.
> When you are lonely and sick, go to the friends
> we know
> And bury your sorrows in doing good deeds,
> Miss me—but let me go.

Final Words

For starters, I don't like the word "final" any more than I like the words "postmortem," "death," or "bereaved." And the color black is not in my rainbow. Thankfully, my stalwart brother and his clan; my former wife and her greater family; a few friends and professional associates; my five children including Kirk Andrew, now deceased (another word I do not like), and, in succession, their spouses, including their ripple families, friends and relatives, and of course, seven beloved grandchildren, have painted in every color of my rainbow except black.

It has been my sublime joy (how about that phrase?) to meddle and participate in the continuing saga of the separate, successive lives introduced to me during my own. Most of you drew the eternal circle around yourselves that included me; and for that, I am expressly grateful. I have lived a most enviable life with the diverse players on the periphery or in my immediate support group. I learned much from you; and any success you ascribe to me as your fellow human was, in greatest measure, reflective of that which you shared directly or by example. If the unborn can become inspired, then you have moved me to write of your gifts in these occasional flashes that illuminated my life. Thank you!

Parting Advice

1. **Practice the two Universal Truths.** Extend your love to the Lord thy God and to thy neighbor as thyself.

2. **Give and let give.** It is definitely more blessed to give than to receive. The feel-good benefits far outweigh the time and resource sacrifices made in giving. Every child who has operated a neighborhood lemonade stand knows this.

3. **Don't rollerblade on a freeway during rush hour.** This is

the updated version of "Don't roller skate on a buffalo herd." Simply said, it means, "Don't take on more than your psyche can bear!" or, "Don't commit to more favors, little jobs, or work details than you can accomplish with ease and pleasure." Above all, don't cut into personal time.

4. **Take personal time for yourself every day.** It's important to your psyche, to completing yourself.

5. **Enjoy your own company.** You are the best person you know, so take some time to explore your natural interests and talents.

6. **Fertilize your support garden.** Always nourish the half-dozen or so faithful family and friends who add luster to your being.

7. **Read something redeeming.** Business reports and conclusions change daily with the stock market and have no lasting personal value. Neither does reading your local newspaper, unless it's the *New York Times, San Francisco Chronicle, Wall Street Journal,* etc.

8. **Beware of rituals that swallow the grandiose.** We're all familiar with the saying, "You can't see the forest for the trees," but its corollary is more appropriate for not letting the familiar drown you in a sea of minutia.

9. **Don't fry bacon in the nude.** This means that personal safety is always a focus. You can't hike long distances without hydrating regularly. In fact, old-timers shouldn't even garden in warmer climates without proper hydration and sun protection. Never take undue chances without proper preparation and/or training. Safety must be adjusted for age. The adventure of walking across a railroad trestle in your twenties would not be prudent in your seventies if you're deaf and can't run. If you've

got Montezuma's Revenge, don't stray too far from a toilet.

10. **Woe to the messenger of illicit gossip.**

11. **Explore!** Become Winnie the Pooh and have an adventure in your Hundred-Acre Wood. Satisfy your curiosity about what's around the next corner, be it on foot or by planes, trains, and automobiles.

12. **Beware of white carpeting.** If you want children and pets, do not install white carpeting.

The Time to Call It Quits

When is enough, enough? Where do you draw the line in the sand? Life, after all, with or without you, continues on ad nauseam. We enter the ring for a few rounds of whatever—our family life, our hobbies, our school days, our careers, our military service, our explorations, and our daily projects. And, usually, regarding the effort we're expending on a particular goal, "It ain't over 'til it's over." We move away; we graduate; we are discharged—hopefully honorably; we run out of time; we lose interest; or we lack resources. We are alone or crowded together, often sharing common goals, as passengers in the tunnel, exploding off each other and our environment, accumulating almost minute-to-minute memories or experiencing, instead, great yawning abysses of time with no stimulation. Thus, the flashes of unforgettable fodder, or the interludes of irretrievable nothingness, unfold in our lifetime panorama. Always, the memory box overflows with the salving and the painful. Periodically, during times of calm or stress, we open the box to examine its contents and to savor lost glories or console unforgettable tragedies. These memory flashes occur by intent, as in the drifting and dreaming of old age, or by

Light Flashes in the Tunnel

accident at any time, as when a person or situation pushes the memory button of an earlier time. They are the personal Light Flashes that constitute the fabric of our lives. We all have many more flashes than are possible to recall in small spans, much less to gather into an authoritative whole.

As I sit here, coffee in hand, nine years after son Paul and Aunt Teresa threw down the gauntlet and goaded me into these scribblings on lined yellow pads with a succession of ballpoint pens, my mind still reverberates with the ghosts of many unwritten flashes, distinguished only by their prospective titles: *A Shameless Display of Mendacity, Ogling the Honeys, Patrolling the Perimeter, Psychotic Frailty, Egg on My Face, Gee Willikers, Love on the Fly, It's Always Darkest Before Dawn, Too Much of a Good Thing*—to name but a few. Then there's my shame at forgetting to pay just tribute to Uncle Frederick Francis and Gramps, whose farm my brother Fred and I worked in our boyhood, with resplendent memories—like the hot, dusty days during haying when we loaded the 50-to-80-pound bales onto a flatbed wagon behind a tractor in the field, then transported them to a nearby barn where we futilely attempted to back that loaded wagon up a circular grade into the barn, same as the big dogs (we usually had to be relieved at the wheel), to deliver and unload them into two high, opposing lofts. At sundown in the empty field, with all hands dehydrated and parched from the day's intake of field dust, Uncle Fred would invariably drag out his stash of milk cans laden with bottles on ice and joyfully exclaim, "Now, let's crack out a bottle of beer!"

But getting back to the initial questions that I neatly dodged, "When is enough, enough? Where do you draw the line in the sand for a lifetime experience or just a temporary patch?" As you know by now, I could have made this book my lifework—more like my life's pleasure. I could go on forever, but couldn't we all, in the lull of what we love. As we live our lives in minute-to-minute flashes, we stop when concluding the individual task at hand or completing the breadth of a dream. At some point in any effort we become satisfied with our input and decide to bail out. Or we lose interest. We can change direction from exposure to new ideas and then become incapable of pursuing old ones. Often, the rewards don't justify the means, so we turn from our current path and wring off old goals. We run out of steam. We've run our string. We call it quits.

My challenge to you is to pick up my string, to, "Get off that tired, old ass and pen a few lines for posterity." It <u>will</u> be a positive memory, and your support group <u>will</u> appreciate it. But regarding my own considerable efforts toward this book, as my sainted mother used to say, "It's time for me to call it quits." Profound thanks for your indulgence. Pax vobiscum. JSB

XVIII. APPENDIX

APPENDIX OF PRINCIPAL CHARACTERS AS THEY APPEAR IN THE "LIGHT FLASHES..."

Full Name	Nickname(s)	Relationship to Author
Jim Sharer Bentley	Windy, Pelican King, Jungle Jimbo	Himself
Paul William Bentley	Brother Bentley (BB), Apostle Paul, Pumpkin, Waggle Man	5th child
Teresa Rose Banfell	Aunt T, Queen Bee, Little Missy	Ex-sister-in-law, married to Uncle Skip, mother of Robin, Amber Vance, and Chryssie Banfell
Joshua Sharer Bentley	Boomer, Mister Moopers, Scooter Bean	Grandchild by Robin/Sean
Eleanor White Brady (deceased)	Aunt Buddy	Ex-wife's aunt

Robin Machelle Bentley	Bena, Ma Bear	Daughter-in-law with son Sean
Sean Christopher Bentley	Hawk, Fly-by-Night	Oldest child
Madison Rose Bentley	Rosebud, Maddie Moo-Moo, Wee Waddie Woo-Woo, Stinky-Clinky	Grandchild by Robin/Sean
Lisa Anne Diaz	Pee-Pie	2nd child
F. David Diaz	Dave, Gear Head	Son-in-law with daughter Lisa
Madeline Alexis Diaz	Keepsie	Grandchild by Lisa/David
William Bentley Diaz	Bubba Bullfrog	Grandchild by Lisa/David
Shannon Elizabeth Edmonds	Blondie	3rd child
Patrick Edmonds	Pat, Veggie Might	Son-in-law with daughter Shannon
Erin Noel Edmonds	Tootie	Grandchild by Shannon/Pat
Jack Matthew Edmonds	Black Jack	Grandchild by Shannon/Pat
Brigette Bentley	Raz-A-Ma-Taz	Daughter-in-law with son Paul
Sophia Rose Bentley	Cada	Grandchild by Brigette/Paul

Frederick William Bentley	Stinky, Uncle Fred, Freddums	Brother
Martha Alice Bentley (deceased)	Perversity	Sister
Dave Brown	Green Bow	AT hiking companion
Reverend Clark (deceased)	-----	Presbyterian minister during early teen years, Newport, RI
Gina and Kelly	-----	A gay couple of Robin's acquaintance
Frederick Francis Bentley (deceased)	Uncle Fred	Father's brother, Lapeer, MI
Miss Edna Murphy (deceased)	-----	4th grade teacher, Second Ward School, Lapeer, MI
Henry Roy Bentley (deceased)	Gramps	Grandfather, Lapeer, MI
John McBride (deceased)	-----	Best childhood friend, Lapeer, MI
Jeanette Grace Bentley (deceased)	Aunt Jean, Gee-Gee	Father's and Uncle Fred's sister, Lapeer, MI
Mike and Vince Flynn	-----	Best childhood friends, Coronado, CA
Mike Cottrell	-----	Best friend and classmate, St. George's School, Newport, RI

Jim Sharer Bentley

Frank (Jr. Officer, US Army)	-----	Roommate in the Hotel Victoria, Cholon, Vietnam
Suko Higuchi	-----	Pre-school friend and neighbor, 1941, Pearl City, Hawaii
Susan Brown	-----	Cafeteria Mgr., C.A. Weis Elem. School-worked together in the Escambia School District feeding operation
Chrystelle White Nickelsen	MeMa	Ex-wife's mother
Erin Garrison	MeMe Garrison	Robin Bentley's and Rosemary Crowder's mother
Trina	-----	Dessert Chef, Fish House Restaurant—fan of her notable desserts (especially Key Lime Pie)
Joey Puzy	-----	GB High School/UNF College classmate and friend of Paul's
Kathleen/Jon Kagan	-----	Next-door neighbors, Soundside Drive, pre-Hurricane Ivan
Jack Lowe	-----	Other next-door neighbor, Soundside Drive, pre-Hurricane Ivan
Susan White Bentley	Su-Su	Ex-wife, mother of our 5 children

Kenny White	-----	Ex-wife's brother, retired from Gulf Power Company, Pensacola, FL
Paul Renaud	The Ole Man	Military vet, AT thru-hiker, employed by the Hiker Hostel near Woody Gap, GA
-----	The Dumbbells	Husband-wife AT thru-hikers, Walasi-Yi Hostel, Neels Gap, GA
-----	Faith Walker	AT hiker encountered on the trail, Georgia
Andy Bond	Preacher Dude	Encountered at Deep Gap Shelter along the AT, Georgia
-----	Almost There	AT hiker encountered in Georgia
Rosemary Crowder	Aunt Ro-Rose	Robin's sister
Mary Louise Sharer Bentley (deceased)	Mary Lou	Mother
Skip Banfell	Uncle Skip, Mullet Master	Ex-brother-in-law, married to Aunt T, stepfather of Robin/Amber Vance, father of Chryssie
Amber Vance	Ambo, Elmer	Ex-niece by Aunt T/Uncle Skip, Sister of Robin/Chryssie
Sarah Bentley	The Sister Woman	Niece by ex-sister-in-law/brother Fred

Teresa Gerrety	Tidy T	Long-time friend with husband (Kevin), business partner in "Fit for Women" with Aunt T
Kevin Gerrety	River Rat, Camp Director	Long-time friend with wife (Teresa) and their children, Annie, Paul, and Alicia
Paul Gerrety	Surfer Dude	Long-time friend of son, Paul Bentley, co-director with father (Kevin) of annual summer campout
Art Yaremchuk	-----	Daughter Shannon's father-in-law
Susan Laenger, MD	-----	Primary care physician, Tiger Point Family Care, Sacred Heart Health System, Santa Rosa County, FL
Bud Garrison	Paw-Paw	Robin's and Sean's father-in-law, married to Erin
"Old Bob"	The Caretaker	Aged veteran pensioner friend of Uncle Fred who lived in the Bentley farmhouse, Lapeer, MI
Kirk Andrew Bentley (deceased)	-----	4th child

FAMILY STRUCTURE-Nearest Relatives

Parents	Children (oldest first)	Spouses	Grandchildren
Jim and ex-Susan White	Sean Christopher	Robin Machelle	Joshua Sharer Bentley
			Madison Rose Bentley
	Lisa Anne	David Diaz	Madeline Alexis Diaz
			William Bentley Diaz
	Shannon Elizabeth	Patrick Edmonds	Erin Noel Edmonds
			Jack Matthew Edmonds
	Kirk Andrew (deceased)	-----	-----
	Paul William	Brigette	Sophia Rose Bentley
Jim's Siblings	**Children**		
Frederick William	Jennifer Marie Cordeaux, John William Bentley, Sarah Katherine Bentley, Tyler Roy Bentley		

Jim Sharer Bentley

Jim's Parents			
Mom	Mary Louise Sharer Bentley		
Dad	James Calvin Bentley		
Jim's Grandparents	**Father's Side**	**Mother's Side**	
Grandmother	Alice Matilda Bentley	Mary (Hill) Sharer	
Grandfather	Henry Roy Bentley	William Jasper Sharer	
Ex-wife	**Parents**	**Siblings**	
Susan	Kenneth Aloysius White, Danny Chrystelle Nichols	Kenneth A. White, Jr	
		Pamela Ann	
		Theresa Rose	
		Mary Lynn	

www.ingramcontent.com/pod-product-compliance
Lightning Source LLC
Chambersburg PA
CBHW071559080526
44588CB00010B/956